Crunch Lit

21ST CENTURY GENRE FICTION SERIES

The *21st Century Genre Fiction* series provides exciting and accessible introductions to new genres in twenty-first-century fiction from Crunch Lit to Steampunk to Scandinavian Crime Fiction. Exploring the history and uses of each genre to date each title in the series will analyse key examples of innovations and developments in the field since the year 2000. The series will consider the function of genre in both reflecting and shaping sociopolitical and economic developments of the twenty-first century.

Forthcoming titles in the series

Apocalyptic Fiction by Andrew Tate
Scandinavian Crime Fiction by Jakob Stougaard-Nielsen

Crunch Lit

Katy Shaw

Bloomsbury Academic
An imprint of Bloomsbury Publishing Plc

B L O O M S B U R Y
LONDON • NEW DELHI • NEW YORK • SYDNEY

Bloomsbury Academic
An imprint of Bloomsbury Publishing Plc

50 Bedford Square	1385 Broadway
London	New York
WC1B 3DP	NY 10018
UK	USA

www.bloomsbury.com

BLOOMSBURY and the Diana logo are trademarks of Bloomsbury Publishing Plc

First published 2015

© Katy Shaw, 2015

Katy Shaw has asserted her right under the Copyright, Designs and Patents Act, 1988, to be identified as Author of this work.

All rights reserved. No part of this publication may be reproduced or transmitted in any form or by any means, electronic or mechanical, including photocopying, recording, or any information storage or retrieval system, without prior permission in writing from the publishers.

No responsibility for loss caused to any individual or organization acting on or refraining from action as a result of the material in this publication can be accepted by Bloomsbury or the author.

British Library Cataloguing-in-Publication Data
A catalogue record for this book is available from the British Library.

ISBN: HB: 978-1-4725-0630-6
PB: 978-1-4725-1006-8
ePDF: 978-1-4725-1330-4
ePub: 978-1-4725-1212-3

Library of Congress Cataloging-in-Publication Data
A catalog record for this book is available from the Library of Congress.

Series: 21st Century Genre Fiction

Typeset by Newgen Knowledge Works (P) Ltd., Chennai, India

For Catherine Joy Bell-Atkin

CONTENTS

Acknowledgements viii
Preface ix

Introduction 1
1 The final countdown 21
2 9-8-7: The credit crunch 47
3 'Capital' cities 69
4 Masters of the universe 89
5 Recessionistas 115
6 Financial performance 139
Conclusion: The future of finance 163

Notes 169
Index 187

ACKNOWLEDGEMENTS

This book has been a real adventure. Starting out as someone who thought they had a decent grasp of economics, I quickly realized that I was a good example of the wider problem of financial illiteracy that had come to characterize the relationship between the general public and the financial sector by 2007. I am indebted to the people and organizations who collectively inducted me into a complicated and, at times, confusing world of facts and figures. Many individuals at major international banks and hedge funds I spoke to did not want to be named, but I remain grateful to their efforts to contextualize events in our off-the-record discussions since 2008. Particular thanks go to the ex-employees of Northern Rock for their insights into being part of a bank that was the first to fall.

The professional advice of colleagues who commented on various iterations of this work was very much valued. Particular gratitude is extended to Mike Sanders, Deborah Philips, Lynne Crook, Kate Aughterson and Vedrana Velickovic for academic dialogue. Thanks also to the University of Brighton for a sabbatical award. David Avital at Bloomsbury has been unswerving in his support for this book, and the series as a whole. Elsewhere, Rachel Revell, Victoria Clements, Helen Runalls, Sarah-Jane Roberts and Corry Shaw have collectively heard far too much about credit culture to ever go near a store card again, and for that, and their kind counsel, I am forever grateful. As always, special thanks go to Joy, Mike and Kristian.

Sections of Chapter 3 were published as 'Capital' City: London, Contemporary British Fiction and the Credit Crunch', *The Literary London Journal*, 11 (1) (Spring 2014).

A version of Chapter 6 was published as 'Feminist Finance: Recessionistas, Debt and the Credit Crunch', in *CLR: Culture, Language and Representation*, xii (1697–7750) (2014): 113–25.

The author is grateful to the journal publishers, and for the publishers of the fictions cited by this study, for their kind permission to reproduce sections of the works here.

PREFACE

2007 was a difficult and challenging year for Northern Rock
(NORTHERN ROCK ANNUAL REPORT, 2007–8)

Friday, 14 September 2007 seemed like any other day in the northeast of England. At the Newcastle branch of Northern Rock, the landmark bank on the city's high street, a large queue was forming ahead of opening time. 'The Rock' had its headquarters in Newcastle, was a familiar feature in northeast towns, and had recently spread across the UK, thanks to a growing profile as a national lender. Official sponsor of Newcastle United Football Club, a significant donor to community schemes and one of the biggest employers in the northeast, Northern Rock played a major role in the area and was a source of great pride for its people.

From 1990 to 1994, Northern Rock developed from a building society into a commercial bank and began to offer mortgage loans in the south of England, a perceived 'safe site' for property values. During this period, it grew threefold in size, increased its profits fourfold and halved its management expense ratios.[1]

By 2005, 'The Rock' had an annualized growth rate of 20 per cent, was a national market leader on residential mortgages, 'buy to let' and unsecured personal loans, and regularly featured in newspapers and television reports as one of the strongest performing organizations in British finance. Moving the northeast of England from mining to money in only fifty years, Northern Rock was lauded as a saviour of the post-industrial region. Fuelled by the optimism and growth of the new millennium, the company seemed unstoppable.

However, in 2007 the collapse of the US subprime market meant that Northern Rock was quickly and adversely affected by events overseas. The subsequent liquidity crisis in wholesale money markets hit 'The Rock' hardest because more than 75 per cent of the bank's funding originated from this single source. When interbank lending ceased altogether as a response to the growing global economic crisis that became known as the 'credit crunch', the bank was unable to secure the basic funding it required to operate. 'The Rock' applied for, and received, emergency financial support from the Bank of England, a decision it planned to announce in a carefully worded press conference on Monday, 17 September 2007. But on 13 September 2007, the BBC broadcast an exclusive report exposing the problems facing Northern Rock. The report suggested that Northern Rock customer deposits were no longer secure, and this implication caused a catastrophic response.

From first light the following day, hundreds of savers nervously positioned themselves in a queue that began at the Newcastle branch of Northern Rock but stretched as far as the eye could see. The scene was replicated in branches of the bank across the UK, while the company website crashed and its phone lines jammed. This 'run on the Rock' – the first run on the retail deposits of a UK bank since the nineteenth century – shocked the world. In the space of twenty-four hours, Northern Rock – a regional institution and a national success story – became a byword for economic meltdown and loss of faith in the banking sector. Once a proud supporter of community heritage and a symbol of financial prowess, the brand is now forever associated with the images broadcast that evening on television news, showing customers queuing around the clock to withdraw their savings from a bank that they no longer trusted. By 2008, the bank had been nationalized and, by 2012, it was bought out and rebranded by rival bank 'Virgin Money'.

From business models dependent on reckless lending and characterized by a hunger for growth, to a lack of regulation and ineffectual governance, Northern Rock constitutes a micro-study of the impact of financialization in the pre-crunch period. The story of Northern Rock is significant, not only for illuminating lessons about events that led up to its collapse, but because it exposed the precariously close relationship between individual savers and global economic systems that had developed across the late twentieth and early twenty-first centuries. Before 2007, the banking system was a form of fiction, a myth which was widely believed. The story generally went like this: the bank, a physical place that was known and trusted, took customers' money, kept it safe, lent it to other equally safe lenders, who then paid it back with interest, enabling customers to gain reward for their savings, and the bank to lend to more customers. This fictional system was based on a long-gone relationship, one that the public were happy to believe and, along with the banks, were guilty of perpetuating.

In reality, financial systems were a world away from this fairy tale narrative of responsibility, ethical mutuality and safety. When a large number of customers chose to withdraw their money at the same time – as in the case of Northern Rock – the bank collapsed, unable to honour either the funds entrusted to it by customers, or sustain common beliefs about how the banking system worked. The 2007–8 credit crunch blew popular narratives about banking apart, proving them to be literally incredible. It showed the general public that the stories about finance in which that they had invested their trust were false. In response to a need for new understandings of banking, the economic crisis and its aftermath, in the months and years that followed literature set about establishing alternative narratives and representations of these era-defining events.

Introduction

Finance is central to the operation of contemporary society, and in twenty-first-century economies, the money markets matter more than ever. Money is one of the most familiar and intimate aspects of daily living and has been central to human progress across the ages. Concerns about money – having it, not having it, spending it and saving it – continue to permeate contemporary society. Yet money is, as DiGaetani suggests, 'a slippery and complex subject',[1] a concept that is 'hard to define because its definition depends entirely on the context of its analysis'.[2] Money is so complicated because it operates as a symbol, a representation of both a concept and an ideology. The source of value in money lies elsewhere, it is always spectral and, as a result – as Marx argues – money can often hide the systems of which it is a part. In reality, only 30 per cent of money in circulation takes the form of notes and currency: the rest operates in the virtual and constantly moving realm of the contemporary financial sector. A sanitized symbol of familiarity and control, money masks financial practices, mobilizes mystifying terminology and disguises the power networks that characterize its movement. Money is also fetishized by societies and cultures concerned with reproducing its power as a status symbol for the wealthy, and a 'symbol of trust' for the public.[3]

Operating with the apparent aims of efficiency and cohesion, the financial sector has long been an extended benefactor of this public trust. Historically, customers have regarded their bank as another member of the family, maintained loyal relationships with these businesses and promoted them to new generations. However, over the course of the twentieth century, the core identity of the 'family' bank was gradually diluted as a result of wider processes of globalization. Since the 1970s, the size and importance of the financial sector relative to the overall economy of individual countries grew exponentially. This process – often referred to as 'financialization' – has been subject to renewed interest in the wake of the 2007–8 financial crisis. Krippner describes financialization as a 'pattern of accumulation in which profit-making occurs increasingly through financial channels rather than through trade and commodity production'.[1] Fuelled by the growth of the 'FIRE' (Finance, Insurance and Real Estate) industries, financialization occurred as a result of a shift away from industrial capitalism across the twentieth century. This move impacted on both macro and micro economies by changing how financial markets were structured and by enabling the rapid growth of the financial sector. In the United States, for example, the financial sector comprised 2.8 per cent of GDP in 1950; by 2012, that figure had risen to 7.8 per cent.[5]

Developing from wider trends in liberalization and neoliberalism, financialization 'involves the replacement of industrial or production capitalism by a more predatory form of financial capitalism [. . .] which has not only transformed the way the markets work, but carries with it important political, cultural and economic consequences'.[6] However, as Epstein argues, financialization can also refer 'to the increasing influence of financial markets, financial motives, financial institutions and financial elites in the creation of the economy and its governing institutions, both at the national and international level'.[7] Suggestive of the increasing dominance of financial systems over society, Epstein's definition points to both the ascendancy of the financial sector and the penetration of finance into everyday life in the contemporary period. This process has not only created a dependency on the financial industries, but has also changed the ethics, values and outlook of the wider society. Transforming everything into an 'asset' and all exchanges into competitive encounters, alongside globalization and neoliberalism financialization marked a new stage for capitalism in the twenty-first century and came to define the first decade of this era. Elevating the significance of the financial sector, financialization created increasing inequality among classes, races and genders, as well as profoundly altering the relationship between individuals and financial institutions.

Over the course of the twentieth century, movements away from older banking practices into the rapid exchanges and increased accessibility of contemporary economics conspired to create conditions in which financial knowledge became separated from public knowledge, and was positioned as a specialist and opaque area. This dangerous development meant that, at the start of the twenty-first century, very few individuals had a working knowledge of new technological innovations in the complex financial markets, the rates of the credit card companies to which they owed purchase and mortgage debts, or even the operations of the trusted high street banks that held their savings. Yet, due to the disproportionate influence of the 'FIRE' segment of the economy, by 2007 even fewer could say that their lives and fates were not bound up with the operation of these financial systems in some way.

Prior to the credit crunch, the financial sector led the public to believe that individuals had more control over, and understanding of, their money than ever before. From Internet and telephone banking, to mobile phone payments and the rise of the credit card, money appeared hyper-visible. By 2007, everyday finance such as mortgages and consumer debt had become deeply embedded into everyday life; consumers readily spent money that they did not physically own in the form of credit. This fiction masked the truth that money was neither tangible nor safe. Dubbed 'Moneygeddon',[8] a financial apocalypse became a common way to describe the financial crash of 2007–8. This crash shattered a popular belief in money, creating doubt about its representational value and security, and made money – the very thing we think we know most intimately – uncanny. As Andy Haldane reflects, the 2007–8 financial crisis marked the beginning of a 'collapse' in a long-standing 'trust' in the financial sector.[9] Fragmenting the symbolic illusion that money stood for something safe and valuable, the credit crunch exposed the fiction of money, causing the narrative of the financial system to fall apart. When paper money became aligned with virtual forms of currency whose worth was not materially anchored, the true instability of money and the systems through which it operated were exposed, and our popular narratives about finance failed as fictions.

Finance has always proved a popular topic for fiction, culture and the arts. Literature, in particular, has responded to changes in economic circumstance by representing the tensions and challenges of its age in narrative form. As literary critic Elaine Showalter asserts, 'Money has played such a large part in so many great novels that it is hard to imagine fiction without it.'[10] Exploring the manifold ways in which the economic has functioned to shape the literary, writers have historically been concerned with examining the material relations of the economy and its impact on literary representation. Literature has been used by writers across the centuries to critically examine money and its effect on individuals and societies. As a narrative device, money can enable and destroy individuals, economies and nations and, as such, a financial crash quickly became a significant trope of popular fiction.

The pervasiveness of the topic of financial speculation in novelistic renderings of the nineteenth century has been noted by literary critics. In his survey of nineteenth-century fiction, McLaughlin maps the rise of the novel in Britain and points out that Victorian society engaged in its most intense philosophical debates about political economy at the time that the novel was at the peak of its popularity.[11] He concludes that 'economic issues have never been far from British fiction'.[12] Producing 'some of the most engaging fictions of the century',[13] Victorian authors mobilized money to tell tales of fiscal irresponsibility and financial temptations, employing plot structure and figurative language to transform instability into a structural metaphor for a financial crisis. Since both money and literature are representations, literature seems well suited to staging the contradictions of the pursuit of capital gain that creates financial crises. Nineteenth-century fictions in particular link social mobility to solvency through characters who are rich, ruined or obsessed with finance.

Shaped by cultures of speculation, financial risk and changes in economic practice, the nineteenth-century novel was formally and historically inflected by the financial contexts of its period. Mobilizing cyclical financial crises as a plot device, novelists absorbed the financial anxieties of their period and proposed solutions to a pervading cultural and social preoccupation, often by transferring economic concerns onto a domestic stage. Offering satires of credit systems or moralizing warnings against avarice and greed, fictional writings from this period harnessed financial instability as a powerful source of narrative drama. Examining the fetish of finance, the crisis of financial tragedy became the basis of many of the great narratives of the nineteenth century. Through the adaptation and creation of specific motifs and themes, tropes and extended metaphors, recurring characters and figures, Victorian authors transformed economic crises into viable and compelling plots for novels. In *The Way We Live Now* (1857) Trollope follows the panic of the 1873 stock market crash and the subsequent six-year depression, while in *New Grub Street* (1891) George Gissing represents aspiring, but eventually bankrupt, writers. George Eliot also frequently wrote about money and offered critical perspectives on the centrality of finance to the lives of people at every level of nineteenth-century society. The money-obsessed protagonist of her novel *Silas Marner* (1861) realizes true value only when he has been stripped of his fortune and must face poverty. Debt and wealth also famously characterize the writings of Charles Dickens. Across Dickens's canon, financial crises and monetary mismanagement drive plot development. In the opening of *Nicholas Nickleby* (1839), a corrupt delivery company is exposed, while the Chuzzlewit company operates fraudulently, and in *Little Dorrit* (1857) financial mispractice is understood as a form of moral infection that is rife in nineteenth-century society. The sympathetic realism of novels such as *Bleak House* (1853) brings the misappropriation and generation of money under the literary microscope, profiling characters whose lives are forever altered by the manipulation and ambition of those in pursuit of power and status.

The failure of financial institutions constitutes another primary concern of many nineteenth-century novels. William Makepeace Thackeray's *The Newcomes* (1854) centres on the world of financial family, the Newcomes. As major shareholders in what was then known as the Anglo-Indian Bundelcund Banking Company (and is now more commonly known as the BBC) the operations of the family and the banks are described by the novel as a complicated, enormous, outrageous swindle. After ensuring their own financial security, the family directors and bank managers abandon the company, leaving the bank to fail and the customers to deal with financial ruin. George Gissing's *The Whirlpool* (1897) also begins with the failure of the Britannia Loan, Assurance, Investment and Banking Company. The company director eventually commits suicide, but many of the novel's other financial villains escape unpunished at the novel's conclusion.

The pursuit of earning money in the Victorian period was only overshadowed by the fear of losing that hard-earned capital. Associated with the success of realism and a concern with humble subjects, financial fiction of the nineteenth century often centred on the subject of financial failure and the shame of bankruptcy. Weiss argues that 'bankruptcy is the most spectacular form of economic failure in Victorian society. It is sudden, catastrophic and final – an acute crisis as opposed, for example, to insolvency, which tends to be a chronic and tedious condition'.[14] The spectre of debt haunts the literature of every age, but the development of the realist mode during the Victorian period foregrounded the horror of a financial crash and sudden ensuing poverty for the nineteenth-century reader.

Mapping the present onto eternal truths about our past and future, crises in capitalism became a form of mania to which whole populations and governments subscribed, and therefore offered prime material for socially engaged novelists of the time. Crises make the money economy tangible, real and visible, while economic ruin and social destabilization prove a great equalizer, affecting every sphere of life from the economic to the political, social and domestic. Representing financial crises through the life stories of individuals and communities, the novel proved an effective form through which to forge a sustained literary engagement with credit and consumption, cultures of investment, financial motifs and moral economies. From internal politics, boardroom debates and successes, to rags to riches, moral dilemmas and money as solution, a financial collapse offered significant satirical and dramatic capacity as well as verisimilitude for these novels.

This established relationship between the literary and the economic means that the cyclical event of the financial crash has not only been 'expressed, formulated and reassessed in literature', but also 'transfigured there'.[15] As Marsh reflects:

> Contemporary literature has been a powerful site for unravelling the assumptions that are contained within the rhetoric of money's fictitiousness. The novel's particular attention to the construction of fictitiousness has offered it a range of strategies for revealing, countering and qualifying the disabling mystification sustained by the apparent ability of money to be everywhere and nowhere, everything and nothing.[16]

While it is clear that 'creative writers select, distort, exaggerate'[17] the exact circumstances and type of these crises, the paradox of financial fictions is that 'fictional works may tell truths about economic realities, while apparently factual works on economic realities may be infiltrated by fiction, so that they offer covert myths and fantasies, or disguised dramas with heroes and villains'.[18] During the twentieth century, speculation became normalized and institutionalized in the financial sector as well as in literary representation. Turbocharged by technological advances and new transnational networks, it formed a key component of the new cultures of financialization that spread across the globe. Literature responded by developing the financial crash into a recognized trope of the latter half of the twentieth century and, following the 2007–8 financial crisis, represented new concerns regarding the rise of financialization and the concurrent growth of a new genre of contemporary writing.

The phrase 'Crunch Lit' was first used by critic Sathnam Sanghera in a review of one of the many financial confession narratives that emerged following the global economic crisis.[19] Claiming dramatic responsibility for events during 2007–8, financial confessional writings – including *Cityboy: Beer and Loathing in the Square Mile* (2008), *How I Caused the Credit Crunch: An Insider's Story of the Financial Meltdown* (2009) and *Diary of a Very Bad Year: Confessions of an Anonymous Hedge Fund Manager* (2010) – offer reflective accounts of life inside the financial markets in the heady years preceding the credit crunch. Flooding the publishing market following 2008, these semi-autobiographical texts documenting illegal and unethical dealings are authored by ex-financiers apparently motivated by a sense of 'guilt', as well as a need to reveal and share the inside operations of banking in the dramatic years leading up to the crunch. Responding to a readership eager for experiences of the crisis, and as part of a wider growth in confessional cultural forms in contemporary publishing in the new millennium, financial confessional narratives are concerned with explaining behaviour, justifying actions and repositioning prominent individuals as moral agents in the wake of the crisis. Foregrounding the moral bankruptcy of the financial sector before 2007, these texts tackle the hubris of bankers' experiences of the credit crunch, and often document a transformation occurring in their banker protagonist, usually in the form of an ethical awakening, but not always. In narrative fiction, as in real life, the moralistic is presented as subjective, and even in the wake of the credit crunch, not all characters subscribe to the need for a new moral compass going forward.

Following this wave of financial confessional narratives, the years after the credit crunch produced an explosion of new writings that sought to represent the credit crisis in fictional form. Writer and literary reviewer Alex Preston initially called these new fictions 'State of the Nation novels'.[20] However, as the volume and range of literary responses to the credit crunch grew, the term

'Crunch Lit' began to be more widely employed to describe a new genre of fiction representing events immediately before, during and after 2007–8. The term 'Crunch Lit' is used by this study to describe a body of writings that collectively function to represent the 2007–8 financial crisis. This new literature includes fictional works, as well as writings for stage, television and films. These new writings engage in critical dialogue with competing representations of the credit crunch, as part of a broader cultural response to, and understanding of, the financial crash. Drawing upon and developing shared themes and concerns across fiction, stage, television and big-screen writings, Crunch Lit collectively evidences an emerging critical and evaluative awareness of the causes of, events during and the consequences of the financial crash of 2007–8.

In Sebastian Faulks's Crunch Lit novel *A Week in December*, a character claims that, in the twenty-first century, writing remains 'the key to understanding. The key to reality.'[21] A consideration of how and why new writings have attempted to demystify understandings of the credit crunch forms the key concern of this study. Moving from an examination of the informing influence of financial fictions set in the three decades leading to the crash, to fictional representations of the unfolding drama inside financial organizations during 2007, and finally to the effects of these events on individuals, communities and literary production, it aims to offer an intervention in an evolving and dynamic new genre. Exploring ways of representing a global financial crash in the new millennium, Crunch Lit draws on an established tradition of financial fictions – from Chaucer to Dickens, Conrad, Zola and Trollope – to interrogate the challenge of representing a crisis that is subject to continued consternation. This study aims to establish the genre of Crunch Lit to explore how the global credit crunch inspired a new wave of fiction, as well as a range of original works of drama, comedy, television and film. Interrogating the socioeconomics of the post-millennial, from the dissolution of credit culture, to the 'unknown unknowns' that destroyed popular narratives about banking and finance, Crunch Lit is offered as a significant source of alternative representations of changes in socioeconomic and political control, as well as the continued relevance of culture and the arts in the new millennium.

These works both individually and collectively suggest the powerful critical role played by culture and the arts in acknowledging the pervasive effect of financialization in a post-crunch context. Presenting cultural representations as an alternative to dominant financialized narratives on events, Crunch Lit grapples with the fallout from the financial crisis and dissects the wreckage left in its wake. Using the 2007–8 crash as a jumping off point to examine wider issues pertinent to twenty-first-century society, these fictions offer new possibilities, perspectives on and, critical engagements with this period.

As a publishing phenomenon and the subject of mainstream press attention as well as literary criticism, Crunch Lit offers a particular form of writing, content and technique, aimed at shaping understandings and promoting a new awareness of the relationship between finance and society during the first decade of the new millennium. This is perhaps because, as Niall Ferguson reflects, 'no serious attempt at a state-of-the-nation novel can hope to avoid the subject'[22] of the credit crunch after 2008. Authors often write about what worries them, but also about 'what puzzles them', and as a result, the 'peculiar nexus where money, narrative or story [. . .] intersect, often with explosive force'[23] became a popular subject for twenty-first-century fiction. In 2010, *The Independent* newspaper even proposed the post-crunch period as an apposite point at which to 'inaugurate a whole genre dedicated to fiscal calamity'.[24]

The meaning of 'genre' has been the subject of continued controversy. The word originates from the French language where it means a 'class' or 'kind', and relates to matter and form in the shape of a specific content or a recognizable structure or framework. Genre speaks to a shared need to organize and classify experiences in order to make sense of them. As forms of textual organization, the problems of taxonomy, of the sorting of texts into genres, is crystallized in the reality of genre classification. Kaminsky and Mahan argue that the 'word genre simply means order [. . .] All things are ordered by human beings so that they can be dealt with'.[25] The material manifestations of genre can be found in book shops, filing systems and library catalogues as extensions of a need to make order while, commercially, the practice of 'genreflecting' has come to characterize bookstore displays, cover designs and website customer recommendations.[26]

In literary studies, 'genre' has also been used to describe the setting of a text, the symbols, images, motifs and topography it features, as well as stylistic conventions, tone and mode of address. The genre of a text can then refer not only to the framework and the set of clues surrounding the text, but also to the content of the text itself. Derrida reminds us that 'a text cannot belong to no genre, it cannot be without [. . .] a genre. Every text participates in one or several genres, there is no genre-less text'.[27] Yet, as Stam points out, 'a number of perennial doubts plague genre theory. Are genres really "out there" in the world, or are they merely the constructions of analysts? Is there a finite taxonomy of genres or are they in principle infinite?'[28] Whether classifications or signifiers of a hierarchical taxonomy, the phrases 'genre', 'sub-genre' and 'super genre' all point to the fact that 'genre itself is an abstract conception rather than something that exists empirically in the world'.[29]

Genre establishes and perpetuates a set of knowledges about formal features, thematic structures, rhetorical functions and settings. It presents rules, patterns, forms, styles, as well as instructions to readers that supervise the work of reading. As a framework within which a text is produced and interpreted, genre requires a semiotic shared code between author and reader, establishing 'horizons of expectation' for readers and 'models of writing' for authors.[30] Genres are not simply features of texts, but mediating frameworks between texts, makers and interpreters. Genres are distinctive, yet they share conventions within themselves, encouraging audiences to expect certain things to feature or occur in a given work. This expectation is acquired through the process of experiencing a range of examples within a genre, and establishing a knowledge of genre-specific content. As Alastair Fowler suggests, 'readers learn genres gradually, usually through unconscious familiarization'.[31] Genre signifiers also make it easier for authors to reach their target readership, whose sense of prediction, expectation and anticipation is based on a prior understanding of the features of the genre being consumed.

This generic knowledge is a key part of cultural capital. Since genre 'indicates the formulaic and the conventional',[32] it can often be subject to simplistic readings that gloss-over the skill and consideration necessary to frame a narrative within a set of pre-established conventions and features. In the twenty-first century there exists a hierarchy of value between 'literary' and 'generic' texts. Genre texts are often regarded as inferior fictions, excluded from the realm of 'serious' literature as a result of their commercial appeal and connections to popular culture. As a template of assumptions or a formula for rules of engagement with a text, the term 'generic' often evokes negative connotations that overlook the advanced level of awareness, skill and engagement with a range of texts that is necessary to engage in a successful generic reading.

Genre then 'consists of a coded set of formulas and conventions which indicate a culturally accepted way of organising material into distinct patterns',[33] and only through experience and immersion can audiences become adept at decoding generic conventions. Offering a structuring role to both authors and audiences, genre operates as a spectral contract, one that emerges through shared recognitions of compliance, deviation or innovation within a framework of expression. As 'a set of expectations',[34] a lens through which an audience can consume texts, genre functions to provide a frame of reference, making form – the conventions of the genre – more visible, while also aiding the sense-making function of narrative. Telling a story within a recognizable world, genre offers both a sense of belonging and a means of understanding, mobilizing layers of background knowledge about other texts.

Historically, genres have been identified as fixed forms. As a pathway into the conventions of content – including themes and settings, form, structure and style – the genre of a text speaks primarily of a commonality of features and a unity of approach. In practice, the forms and functions of genre are dynamic, shifting and evolving. As Buckingham argues, genres are 'in a constant process of negotiation and change'.[35] Generic boundaries do not involve 'rigid rules of inclusion or exclusion' since 'genres [. . .] are not discrete systems consisting of a fixed number of listable items'.[36] Stam suggests that genres can develop through four main pathways: extension (via breadth or narrowness); normativism (through preconceived ideas about readership); monolithic definition (that can only belong to one genre); or biologism (an evolution through a preset path).[37] Derrida agrees that genres are not 'fixed, new genres emerge and operate at the edges and margins of existing genres as open ended frameworks that are subject to constant development and growth'.[38]

The evolutionary quality of genre means that it can also function as 'the driving force of change in the literary field'.[39]

Some genres are revived or go through phases of popularity, while others are resurrected in response to changing social, political and economic conditions. Thwaites et al. argue that this relationship is reciprocal, not only that 'a genre develops according to social conditions' but also that 'transformations in genre and texts can influence and reinforce social conditions'.[40] In contrast to the anti-generic tendencies of Romanticism and Modernism, movements that tended to focus on art as an individual piece of work, contemporary society has drawn upon the elevation of popular culture to establish genre as 'redefined and democratized' for the contemporary period.[41] Connecting literary structures, genre has become 'the meeting place between general poetics and event-based literary history'.[42] The number of genres has increased and continues to expand, matching the diversity of the age. The internal dynamics of genre are formed by contextual situations but, in turn, go on to shape responses to and understandings of the period. Genre then 'embodies the type of recurring situation that evokes it and [. . .] provides a strategic response to that situation'.[43] In the twenty-first century, genre has continued to not only represent, but also engage with, current social concerns and contexts.

John Swales notes that 'a discourse community's nomenclature for genres is an important source of insight' into contemporary contexts.[44] Post-2008, a new genre emerged in response to the events and aftermath of the new millennial global financial crisis. Crunch Lit fictions are concerned with the tensions, conflicts and fallouts related to an economic reversal of fortunes for capitalism in the new millennium. Fictionalizing the financial crisis, these texts offer contemporary readers social studies of finance, not just stories about economic misfortune. Although the 2007–8 financial crisis was a global phenomenon, the Far and Middle East emerged from events with relatively less damage to their economic stability, while the United States and Europe bore the brunt of the financial fallout. As a result, Crunch Lit situates its narratives in recognizable Western financial sites to underscore the authenticity and trauma of a crisis played out in previous centres of strength and economic and political prowess. Focusing on financial capitals, these works foreground understandings of, and reactions to, a financial trauma that was felt most profoundly in the West.

The task of literature to 'introduce the sometimes arcane world of finance to the intelligent, non-banking reader'[45] is by no means an easy one. Financial contexts often involve 'big questions without simple answers'[46] and many internal contradictions and tensions. Yet, as Žižek argues, the way the credit crunch will be remembered 'depends on how it will be symbolized, on what ideological interpretation or story will impose itself and determine the general perception of the crisis'.[47] Crunch Lit is part of a corpus of post-2008 representations that attempt to make interventions in the telling of this story. Stretching the crisis away from facts and figures onto a broader pictorial canvas that illustrates individual impacts, experiences and consequences, these new writings speak to a public desire for new narratives about this period.

The credit crunch caused profound trauma and doubt regarding the capacity of narrative to frame events in contemporary society. Like literature about 9/11, writings addressing the credit crunch offer reflections on a recent history that is still in formation in the popular consciousness. These fictions are in orbit around the historical facts of the crunch; attempting to understand how literature can and should represent such events, while at the same time offering interventions in discourses, beliefs and values still in-becoming at the time of writing. A concern with the language of finance – from SIVs (special investment vehicles) and CDOs (collateralized debt obligations), to derivatives and hedges – means that Crunch Lit is also an enabling genre, one that encourages readers to grasp the principles, if not the intricate details, of how these new financial mechanisms operate and the role that they played in creating a new context for financial markets. The genre mobilizes a range of motifs from the contemporary financial world – including money, banks, trading screens, corporate brands and modern art – that function to underscore the impact of and tensions between finance and society in the new millennium.

The shadow of the credit crunch casts a structural shade over these fictions. Since narrative developments hinge around an anticipated or already declared crisis, the task for Crunch Lit authors is to mobilize stylistic conventions in order to manipulate the structural possibilities offered by the financial crisis. Imposing structure on boom and bust narratives, the dramatic irony of knowing what is coming transforms both the structure of Crunch Lit writings and the relationship between the audience and the text. The tone of

Crunch Lit is often educational, reflective yet revelatory, offering alternative, fictionalized perspectives on what are now recognizable recent historical events. Yet, unlike the financial confessional narratives that emerged immediately after the crash, Crunch Lit rejects the singular 'I' in favour of plural, dialogic accounts of the financial crisis. This mode plays a significant part in a wider retelling of the financial crisis as not the responsibility of any one individual or organization, but rather a composite creation and experience of a variety of groups. Suggesting that no single story can contain an event such as the credit crunch, Crunch Lit offers a plurality of fictional viewpoints on the financial crisis and, in doing so, creates starting points from which new critical discussions can take place.

The 2007–8 credit crunch is a story with which contemporary society is becoming increasingly familiar. At the heart of the story lies desire, a desire to have more and make more: from domestic consumers to bankers, governments to financiers. In the wake of the crisis, many questions remained unanswered and many events unrepresented. Stepping in to fill this void, cultural responses to the 2007–8 financial crisis highlight the capacity of culture to make sense of a period formerly defined by doubt, confusion and fear. In the wake of the 2007 financial crash, individuals turned to the news media, governments and economists to make sense of the crunch and for guidance on ways forward from it. In the immediate aftermath, some critics asked how the story of the financial crisis could be told at a time when society appeared to have lost faith in previous narratives about money and finance. Naomi Klein reflects that, following a crisis, a state of shock sets in and 'we lose our narrative, we lose our story, we become disorientated'.[48] Frederic Jameson also highlights the increasing difficulty of 'mapping causality' under globalization. He argues that the 'narratives we once used to explain our lives, where we fit and what we can achieve no longer seem reliable or particularly useful in explaining the massive complexity of the global system and its subtle and not-so-subtle impacts on all our localized lives.'[49] Historicizing the credit crunch, Crunch Lit focuses on the global financial crisis, its continued topicality and potential effects on society for years to come.

Translating social, political and economic anxieties into cultural forms that examine struggles over the meaning of money, economic power and cultural representations of finance, financiers and financialization, Crunch Lit provides a reaction to real contexts still fresh in the popular memory of readers. Considering the role of culture in illuminating not only understandings of what happened, but ways forward from it, these fictions refuse simple distinctions, asking questions of the reader as well as of events before, during and after the 2007–8 crash. As John Lanchester argues:

> One way to reassert a degree of control is to try to understand what's happened. It gives us back a sense of agency [. . .] Since the aftermath of the crisis is going to dominate the economics and politics of our societies for at least a decade to come. It's important that we try to understand it, and begin to think about what's next.[50]

Encouraging readers to reflect on contemporary society and the role of finance in the modern world, Crunch Lit offers the crisis as an opportunity to rethink the relationship between the state and the markets, and between individuals and finance in the twenty-first century. The representations of the crunch offered by these new writings do not seek to refute explanations or understandings offered by competing political, social or economic analyses from governments, banks or sociologists. Instead, they draw upon competing narratives to offer alternative representations of events. As responses produced during an age of austerity, what shapes these representations is a need to understand the crunch and, as such, they form a significant part of a wider process of telling new stories about our experiences with capitalism in the new millennium. These narratives represent an emergent awareness of both the crunch and the need for alternative approaches to our relationship with finance in the future. From national politics and policies, to individual negotiations with gender and identity, Crunch Lit considers the extra-economic effects of money as well as its centrality to the events of the crunch itself.

This study of representations of the 2007–8 financial crisis in writings across fiction, stage and screen, adds to the many existing media representations of events during and after this period. Placing literary representations in dialogue with competing representations in the media, it aims to mobilize the potential of such writings and the new perspectives on the period they offer, to move beyond existing accounts into a multi-vocal collaborative consideration, one informed by and aware of, the contributions of a multiplicity of perspectives. It therefore seeks not only to examine new writings, but also to juxtapose the representations they offer with counter-representations and heterodox sometimes contradictory ways of understanding the events in question. The significance of these competing representations as they engage in a wider battle to represent the credit crunch – a brush between the aesthetics of form, literature and culture and the actuality of economics, crisis and experience – is central to the following discussion.

This book begins by considering the informing influence of the decades preceding the credit crunch and the influential role of the ideologies and technologies of this period in forming the cultures of finance in operation before 2007. Financial fictions set in the two decades preceding the 2007–8 financial crisis challenge dominant post-crunch narratives that the crisis was impossible to predict. Charting a history of deregulation, individualism, technologization and an increasingly intimate relationship between Wall Street and Main Street, these fictions suggest that the seeds of the millennial credit crunch can be found in the new systems and behaviours of finance in the years leading up to 2007–8.

Examining a range of financial fictions set across 1980–2006, Chapter 1 explores how and why these novels chart the growth of practices that sowed the seeds of the post-millennial credit crunch. From rising discourses of deregulation and individualism, to the temporal economics of fast finance and emerging tensions between domestic and global economies, the chapter argues that pre-crunch financial fictions chart an important literary history of a period that, in the wake of the global economic downturn, demands cultural re-examination.

Chapter 2 explores a new wave of fiction inspired by the credit crunch of 2007–8. Addressing the dominant narrative that the events of the credit crunch were too complicated for ordinary people to understand, Crunch Lit re-presents the unfolding drama inside finance to illuminate the cultures of credit and role of fictitious capital in the crisis. Confronting dominant political and media master-narratives with a range of alternative micro-narratives, Crunch Lit challenges the unrepresentability and confusing status of finance as a contemporary subject. Offering a selection of representative texts from this new genre in print at the time of publication, the chapter interrogates author John Lanchester's initial claim that 'the credit crunch can't work in fiction'[51] to consider how, why and to what effect Lanchester and other authors went on to represent the first global economic crisis of the new millennium in writing. Actively engaging with media representations and political rhetoric, the chapter focuses on the ways in which Crunch Lit fictions reframe the financial crisis using individual stories to tell wider narratives about the fate of Western societies and economics in the early years of the twenty-first century.

Chapter 3 explores how and why Crunch Lit represents two-world cities, capitals jointly populated by those who run, and those who service city space. Confounding claims that the city no longer enjoys agency or significance in a twenty-first century system of globally networked capitalism, Crunch Lit highlights the representational significance of city space in making visible the impact of financialization on business, domestic and virtual environments. Offering insider views on the city – of ordinary houses now multi-million-pound homes, and shifts in residents from frugal respectable citizens to decadent financiers, oligarchs and footballers – these fictions foreground the breakdown of communities and emotional connections that occur as a result of the financial crisis. Interrogating financial architecture and minority invisibility, the chapter examines how Crunch Lit generates new definitions of a 'capital' city and offers city space as a lens through which to read the twenty-first-century world.

Variously dubbed the 'Man-cession' or the 'He-Cession' by media commentators, accusations that an excessively 'masculine economy' contributed to the 2007–8 credit crunch grew in the weeks and months following the economic downturn. Chapter 4 considers why, in the post-crunch period, economic focus fell on banks and banking systems, while social and political focus fell firmly on bankers, and male bankers in particular, as being responsible for the financial crash. The chapter interrogates the various languages and fashions of financial culture to question alternative representations of male bankers offered in Crunch Lit fictions, contradicting competing narratives that sought to frame the financial crisis as a crisis of masculinity.

Chapter 5 also considers gendered responses to the credit crunch in the character of the 'Recessionista'. Analysing representations of debt, employment, entrepreneurialism and the possibilities for personal transformation brought about by the global economic downturn, the Recessionista reframes the narrative of the credit crunch from one of loss to one of opportunity for some women. Following the crisis, the female protagonists of Crunch Lit eschew cocktails and heels in favour of financial practicality. 'Shopaholic' heroines facing a harsh new reality are forced into a position where they must take stock of their lives and start again from the midst of financial ruin, divorce or a major career change. Internalizing and reifying the attitudes of society during and after the credit crunch, the Recessionista brings a gendered perceptive on financial crisis, as well as a taste of reality to an outdated Chick Lit genre faced with extinction. Foregrounding the impact of the credit crunch on women as an opportunity for positive transformation, Crunch Lit rejects dominant narratives of victimhood and silence to re-voice and represent female characters who find fulfilment and liberation as a result of changed post-crunch conditions and contexts.

Chapter 6 examines how writings for stage and screen have forged new understandings of the credit crunch. In the wake of the financial crisis, critics were quick to ask 'what [. . .] is the best "narrative of the meltdown"?'[52] In the weeks and months following 2008, cultural representations entered into a competitive exchange to tackle the subject of the credit crunch across musical theatre, stand-up comedies, television and films. As Crosthwaite argues, novels, films and television dramas can 'play a major role' in challenging 'the prevailing rhetorical constructions of risk and crisis in the contemporary moment'.[53] Critiquing the impact of risk and crisis on twenty-first-century life, new writings for screen and stage that represent the events of 2007–8 offer significant critical space for consideration of the lived reality of financialization in the contemporary period.

Exploring representations of the crunch in fiction, on the stage and screen, this study considers the ways in which culture has created new narratives to make sense of the financial crisis and its aftermath. In each chapter, a necessarily selective range of texts is mobilized in support of the arguments made and analyses offered. These analyses are not intended to offer comprehensive accounts of all Crunch Lit texts currently in publication – rather, the texts used by the various chapters are representative exemplars of this new genre. The bibliography at the end of the book offers a more comprehensive overview of additional texts, and new writings continue to proliferate.

The study argues that Crunch Lit constitutes not only a significant evolution of the trope of financial crisis in the literary, but also an important critical forum which helps to consider the impact of financialization on contemporary society. Charting far-reaching, damaging consequences and associated tensions, Crunch Lit examines the impact of the excessively financialized state of contemporary society before, during and after the financial crisis. Attempting to understand the ways in which the credit crunch has been represented, mediated and problematized by a variety of forms from novels to plays, movies to television dramas, the following chapters examine, for the first time, the role of literary culture in considering both 'the character of finance capital and its narrative manifestations'[54] in the new millennium.

1

The final countdown

The seeds of the 'credit crunch' were sown [...] in the US and UK in the late 1970s and early 1980s.

JOHN D. BONE[1]

Sociologist John D. Bone argues that the seeds of the 2007–8 credit crunch were sown in a turn to neoliberalism, and a concomitant reordering of the economy and society, that began in the UK and the United States during the late 1970s and continued throughout the 1980s.[2] Bone suggests that 'the (re)financialization of the economy, the deregulation of markets, together with the cultivation of a culture of rampant individualism and acquisition, pervading the markets and wider society [during the 1980s] have coalesced to sow the seeds of reckless profit seeking that have led to the current crisis.'[3] The close ideological affiliations of the UK and the United States across the decades preceding the 2007–8 credit crunch are a key concern of financial fictions set in this period. Considering contextual discourses of deregulation and individualism, the impact of new communication technologies on time and money, and increasing interconnections between Wall Street and Main Street, financial fictions based in the years before 2007 examine relationships between money and the individual, the virtual and the social, the local and the global.

Countering dominant post-crunch narratives that the 2007–8 financial crisis could not have been predicted, financial fictions representing the decades immediately before the credit crunch chart the growing dominance of the financial sector and its values over twentieth and early twenty-first-century society. Interrogating representations of this 'period's speculative hysteria' in both the UK and United States, they confront the dual challenge of representing the seemingly unrepresentable world of finance and making it a viable and sustaining subject of contemporary fiction.[4] From the spreading of financial practices and values into popular culture, to the temporal economics of fast finance and emerging tensions between domestic and global economies, pre-crunch financial fictions chart an important literary history of a period that, in the wake of the 2007–8 economic downturn, demands a thorough cultural reexamination.

Deregulation and individualism

During the 1980s, global stock markets went electronic and increasing numbers of financial businesses merged with foreign competitors and began to trade across time zones. In the UK, Prime Minister Margaret Thatcher announced the 'Big Bang' reforms as part of the deregulation of the financial district of London known as the 'City'. Launched in 1986, the 'Big Bang' reforms were so called due to the predicted increase in economic activity and competition anticipated as a result of a series of changes designed to enable the 'City' to compete in a market increasingly dominated by foreign banking. These developments brought globalization to the markets and cemented the status of the financial industries as a transnational phenomenon.

After the Big Bang, the financial district of the 'City' in London became more open and democratic, but it also became a lot harder to regulate. Whimster proposes that, before deregulation, a closed and elite group of financiers culturally socialized and self-policed the financial industries and prevented malpractice.[5] Thereafter, the increasing application of new technologies to the financial markets meant that money could move faster than ever with fewer controls and that individual transactions and accountabilities were harder to trace. The impact of deregulation also began to extend to the cultures and practices of finance. The adoption of entrepreneurial practices and individualist approaches to accumulate wealth and exploit the Conservative philosophy of the British government under Margaret Thatcher produced a generation of newly rich members of the City. Deregulation was accompanied by a turn to foreign wholesale money markets for greater funding, and also a rise in the amount of money allocated to bankers' bonuses. What began as an incentive scheme, quickly grew vastly out of proportion with the annual salaries of the population at large, and became a notorious symbol for the banking profession.

During the 1980s in the United States, President Reagan mirrored the deregulation ideology of UK prime minister Margaret Thatcher. Following a time in which inflation became the main economic concern, he campaigned for smaller government, deregulation and free market policies, believing that an upswing in the economy would have a knock-on effect for society and public confidence. Like the UK government, Reagan thought that the key to national prosperity lay in the removal of controls over corporate business. An advocate of supply-side economics, he argued for lower taxation to encourage employment and reduce market instability.

Fuelled by faith in the financial sector, Reagan's term in office became defined by policies that centred on tax cuts in order to fuel consumer spending and increase earnings. As a result, the 1980s in the United States were marked by a rise in the power and independence of the financial sector, and the promotion of the power of the individual, rather than the state. With the top marginal tax rate for individuals reduced from 70 per cent in 1980 to less than 35 per cent in 1990, the conditions for individual prosperity in America were greater than ever. However, it was an explosion of growth in the US stock markets that really fuelled of the Reagan era. Between 1981 and 1989, real GDP per capita increased by nearly 23 per cent and, in the same time span, the value of the stock market more than tripled.[6] Tax incentives for workers to invest their savings in stocks created a bull market that generated more wealth creation than any previous boom in history. While these good times were not matched for those away from Wall Street, Reagan's time in office marked the 'financialization' of the American economy, as trading overtook industrial manufacture as the country's major economic force.

The transformative influence of deregulation on financial practice and the development of new cultures of finance on both sides of the Atlantic is the central concern of some of the most iconic novels representing this period. Set in the UK and the United States during the 1980s, Martin Amis's *Money* (1984) offers an infamous study of emerging discourses of deregulation and cultures of finance in its protagonist John Self, whose transatlantic adventures suggest that ideologies of individualism and deregulation were equally prevalent in the UK and America during the 1980s.[7] Self is 'one of the top commercial directors' (51), the 'new kind, the kind who has money' earned from entrepreneurial skills in the thriving international media markets. Having made his fortune from producing advertisements for products and brands, Self opens the novel on a mission to secure funding for his first feature film. Antisocial and misogynistic, Self has become the poster-boy for the individualism and conspicuous consumption that define this era. Like Thatcher, he does not believe in society but instead operates via a network of individualist relationships. As a rampant producer and consumer, Self embodies the deregulated capitalist excesses of his period.

Despite an obsession with accumulation, money is not the end goal for John Self. Rather, Self becomes obsessed by the control money affords him. For Self, 'money is freedom' (270) because 'without money you're one day old and one inch tall [. . .] if you haven't got any money. They could do things to you. But if you have got the money, they can't be fucked' (383). Literally clothed or exposed by his access to finance, Self builds his identity around his relationship with money. He openly declares his 'dream in life – is to make lots of money. I would cheerfully go into the alchemy business, if it existed' (92). References to the 'conjuring up' of money frequent Amis's novel, drawing attention to a strange disconnection, a lack of understanding of how money is produced and circulated, as well as the relationship between governance and financialization in the late twentieth century.

Anthony Giddens notes that in Marx's early writings money is termed the 'universal whore' because it is a 'medium of exchange which negates the contents of goods or services by substituting them for an impersonal standard'.[8] In Amis's *Money*, the more capital Self acquires the less pleasure he experiences, culminating in the commodification of relationships, emotions and, finally, the value of his own life. Self is perpetually haunted by an inability to control the fidelity of his personal and professional partners and tries to maintain their faith through finance. Addicted to sex and drugs as an expression of his own deregulated excess, Self is convinced that there 'is only one Earthling who really cares about me [. . .] All the others—it's just the money. Money is the only thing we have in common' (116).

Openly identifying his bonds as financial, rather than emotional or physical, Self only nurtures relationships that are centred on finance and exchange. Observing that 'pornography and money enjoy a close concordat' (69), he confesses that while making love to his girlfriend Selina 'we often talk about money. I like it. I like that dirty talk' (151). Turned on by his own ability to accumulate money and exercise power, Self enjoys control via the acquisition of wealth, reducing his social relationships to mere forms of financial exchange. When Selina begs to be reunited with him, it is only because she is 'pennyless' (68) and misses money, not Self. Yet this transparent dimension of money carries an innate appeal. Self reflects that 'you know where you are with economic necessity. When I make all this money I'm going to make, my position will be even stronger. Then I can kick Selina out and get someone even better' (24). Regarding personal exchanges as another form of competitive trade or opportunity for advancement, Self reminds contemporary readers that in this 1980s world, money 'is always in the picture somewhere' (315), underpinning personal relationships, decisions and ambitions.

In the binary contrast it creates between *Good Money* and *Bad Money*, Amis's novel makes an early intervention in debates about real and virtual finance, credit and debt, that became decisive factors in the 2007–8 credit crunch. Doubling not only the meaning of money, but also the author/character and hero/antihero, Amis uses fiction to explore shifts from old forms of industrial capital to new financial practices. The freedom for finance produced by the deregulation reforms and releases on currency controls of the 1980s are offered as an important factor in both the wider liberalization of financial cultures, but also the influence of new financial values in popular culture at large. Fuelled by the promise of the many possibilities money brings, Self is driven by the topic of the novel's title and is used by Amis to offer a critique of the period's growing transatlantic financial relations.[9] By the 1980s, in the words of John Self, 'you just cannot hide out from money anymore' (153). Whether in the skies over the Atlantic, on the streets of London or on the set of LA advertisements, money is in control of this period, deregulating relationships between people and places, wealth, power, culture and class, and pushes Amis's protagonist ever-closer to a literal 'Self-destruction'.

Financial fictions set in 1980s America represent the impact of deregulation on the other side of the Atlantic, profiling male characters who enjoy limitless abandon, pleasure-orientated personal indulgence and uneasy morality. Released one week before the Wall Street Crash in 1987, *Bonfire of the Vanities* is the quintessential novel of 1980s American finance.[10] The protagonist, Sherman McCoy leads a narrative that is a product of the specific political and economic conditions characterizing the 1980s in America. Sherman – a 'sure man' – begins the novel filled with the excessive confidence and self-belief of his newly deregulated era. In control of the 'lever that moves the world' and labelled a 'Master of the Universe' – even though 'he has never so much as whispered this phrase. He was no fool. Yet he couldn't get it out of his head' (67) – Sherman describes his fellow financiers as resembling:

> A set of lurid, rapacious plastic dolls that his otherwise perfect daughter liked to play with. They looked like Norse gods, who lifted weights, and they had names like Dracon, Ahor, Mangelred and Blutong [. . .] On Wall Street he and a few others – how many? – three hundred, four hundred, five hundred? – had become precisely that [. . .] Masters of the Universe. There was [. . .] no limit whatsoever! (11)

As toys of capitalism, these demi-gods are presented as a superhuman select group whose control extends beyond that of the ordinary. Connecting the power of finance to an established narrative of myth and strength, Sherman underscores his identity as one of the new deregulated masters of his period.

The home of these masters of the universe lies in the 'gloomy groin of Wall Street' (58). Sherman describes the bond trading room of company Pierce and Pierce's as:

> An impressive space, with a ferocious glare, writhing silhouettes and the roar [. . .] The writhing silhouettes were the arms and torsos of young men, few of them older than forty. They had their suit jackets off. They were moving about in an agitated manner and sweating early in the morning and shouting, which

created the roar. It was the sound of well-educated young white men baying for money on the bond market. (58–9)

The reward for commanding this competitive universe is financial. The speed at which young men amass vast fortunes in this space is subject to implicit criticism in the opening chapters of the novel. Sherman reports that 'If you weren't making $250,000 a year within five years, then you were either grossly stupid or grossly lazy' (61). However, this pay cheque carries with it another price tag, the cost of total commitment to the job at the expense of a personal life. The expectation in this 'new Wall Street' (74) is that you are 'willing to devote 100 percent to the job, or you got out' (63).

A lack of understanding regarding the role and responsibility of financial traders is articulated by Sherman's daughter. In her direct question to Sherman – 'what do you do?' – the little girl confronts a wider self-perpetuating mystery surrounding the operation of financial systems during the 1980s. Sherman's explanation regarding his role as a bond dealer attempts to describe bonds as 'a way of loaning people money [. . .] but every time you hand somebody a slice of the cake a tiny little bit comes off, like a little crumb, and you can keep that [. . .] If you pass around enough slices of cake, then pretty soon you have enough crumbs to make a gigantic cake' (248–9). The analogy of a cake functions to make innocent the highly complicated and morally murky aspects of Sherman's occupation, but does effectively emphasize the economies of scale involved in the bonds industry.

The title of Wolfe's novel variously refers to the many vanities of Sherman – pride, status, wealth, control and power – which are gradually eroded through his interaction with the rest of society as the plot unfolds. As a 'King of the Jungle' (75) and 'A Leader of the People' (143) Sherman takes an explicitly 'masculine pride in the notion that he could handle all sides of life' (400). However, this claim is tested when he is accused of a hit-and-run accident in the Bronx and is forced to face up to the fact that his Master of the Universe status is not impervious to legal or moral judgement. Financing a legal defence leaves Sherman professionally and financially destitute, a downfall the narrative describes in explicitly monetary terms. As a feeder of capital, Sherman ends the novel fatally 'haemorrhaging money' (395), 'bleeding to death' (603) as his lifeblood – money – ebbs away. The trauma of this loss is emphasized by Wolfe's journalistic style, with exclamation marks and italics underscoring moments of tension and release throughout the novel. The epilogue takes the form of a newspaper-style report on the outcome of the court case which reveals Sherman's final judgement as a 'Wall Street murderer' and 'Capitalist killer' (198).

The novel makes clear that, far from being an anomaly in financial culture, Sherman and his 'masters of the universe' are 'practising the capitalism of the future' (163). *Bonfire of the Vanities* charts a significant shift in popular perceptions of capital, moving away from notions of 'something you own [. . .] factories and machines and buildings and land and things you can sell and stocks and money and banks and corporations' (162) and towards a credit culture connected to the virtual and future, projected time. Through his iconic caricature of a time and place, Wolfe's novel aligns the free market political and economic contexts of the 1980s individualism advocated by the social, economic and political policies of both Thatcher and Reagan. Beginning to develop the discourses that would go on to produce the conditions of twenty-first-century credit culture, the novel now appears 'prophetic' of the decades that followed (xxvii).[11] Focusing on greed and competition, the text traces the emergence of financial values and practices that would go on to influence the cultures of deregulation and individualism that went on to contribute to the 2007–8 credit crunch.

Propelled by policies of deregulation, ideologies of individualism and the growth of credit culture, cultures of finance grew to play an increasingly influential role in transatlantic popular culture during the 1980s and 1990s. In *American Psycho* (1991), Ellis presents a protagonist who, defined and enabled by these contextual developments, takes 1980s cultures of finance to disturbingly logical conclusions.[12] Patrick Bateman works as a specialist in mergers and acquisitions at the fictional Wall Street investment firm Pierce & Pierce, the same company that employs Sherman McCoy in *The Bonfire of the Vanities*. Bateman is the ultimate consumer and expects the best of everything. No restaurant bill is large enough, no steak rare enough, and no price tag high enough to satisfy Bateman's rampant consumer compulsion. His American Express platinum card marks his unlimited access to excess, and he gradually becomes obsessed with using the card as a symbol of status and wealth. The growth of the credit card played an important part in a wider process of normalizing cultures of credit during this period.

Between 1980 and 1990, the number of credit cards in the United States more than doubled, while spending on credit cards increased five-fold, with the average household credit card balance rising from $518 to nearly $2,700. The credit card companies began to use credit scores and other financial data to develop differentiated pricing and credit strategies, and also earned additional income from the imposition of penalty fees for late payment. Bateman wields his card with pride because its Platinum status denotes not only his wealth and influence, but also his spending power and perceived control over credit.

Linking the impersonal world of institutional markets and the intimate world of personal finance, Bateman actualizes many of the practices already active in the language and cultures of Wolfe's Wall Street. Takeovers, killings and the metaphorical 'eating' of competitors are taken to their logical conclusion in *American Psycho*. Bateman openly declares himself as 'a corporate raider [...] I orchestrate hostile takeovers' (155). The epigraphs of *American Psycho* offer early warnings of the dangers of transposing aggressive financial cultures into day-to-day life. Taken from a song by 1980s band Talking Heads, the first warns that 'as things fell apart/ Nobody paid much attention', while the second reminds readers, 'in civilisation there have to be some restraints. If we followed every impulse, we'd be killing one another'. As a soldier in a wider 'army of professionals from Wall Street in tuxedos' (55) and propelled by a 'repulsive amount of dough' (39), Bateman's external appearance is one of 'pure prep perfection' (46). Much like the financial culture of the period, Bateman is superficial and cold, his outward appearance operating as a mask to hide his own inner moral decay.

Opening with images of New York graffiti and its warnings resonant with Dante's vision of hell – 'ABANDON ALL HOPE YE WHO ENTER HERE' in 'blood red lettering' (3) – the context of 1980s Wall Street functions as a backdrop to Bateman's symbolic enacting of the values and practices of contemporary financial culture, and presents 1980s Wall Street as a modern day hell on earth. Increasingly aware that others regard him as 'the opposite of civilisation' (199), Bateman becomes unable to excuse his increasingly erratic behaviour as 'rock and roll' and struggles to 'maintain a credible public persona' (285). Asked how he would like be addressed, Bateman chooses 'CEO/King' (326). Eventually 'totally immobilized by the monster of reality' (292), the context of the 'terrible times' (332) in which he operates are not offered as salvation for his actions. The final words of the novel emphasize that 'THIS IS NOT AN EXIT' (384) – there is no escape for Bateman or from the culture and practices that he enacts. The nihilism, capitalism and individualism of this deregulated period reign unchallenged at the close of the novel. Concerned with appearance and fashion rather than the legal or moral implication of his actions, Bateman is presented as a dark product of his times. Offering his protagonist as the logical end point of deregulated capitalism, a literalization of the brutality of this ideology, the barbarism in operation throughout Ellis's novel actualizes the policies of its period. Using murder as a metaphor for the dog-eat-dog individualism and competitive violence underpinning 1980s cultures of finance, Ellis's heartless and pretentious Bateman satirizes tensions within the economic policies of the period.

D. J. Taylor proposes that 'most of our "great writers" [. . .] are simply not capable of defining the 1980s'.[13] Yet, *Money*, *Bonfire of the Vanities* and *American Psycho* have all been described as the quintessential novels of their time as a direct result of their interrogation of the complicated relationship between economics, society, politics and the increasingly global dimensions of capitalism during this decade. Capturing the 1980s beyond its shoulder pads and trendy new wine bars, these novels are suggestive of why, how and to what effect money acquired a new meaning and sense of purpose during the 'sexygreedy decade'.[14] Reconstructing culture along firmly economic lines, they illuminate the manifold ways in which trends of deregulation went on to enjoy an informative influence over new financial developments and practices on both sides of the Atlantic in the years leading up to 2007.

As the product of newly deregulated practices, 1980s financial culture drew upon ambition in business, and freedom in practice, to produce a hedonistic lifestyle among a generation of male financiers on both sides of the Atlantic. What began as an economic and ideological strategy of Thatcherite and Reaganite economics soon became a cultural and social trend that propounded the benefits of individualism, laissez faire approaches to financial practice and the value of money as a form of power and control, while deregulation produced a culture that celebrated accumulation and a lack of self-awareness that quickly spread beyond the trading floors and into wider society. Liberating the powers of the financial sector and circulating values of competition and marketization via the emerging power of transatlantic popular culture, deregulation underscored the increasingly intimate relationship between the worlds of the financial, political and social across the 1980s.

Time is money

Confidence in the redemptive forces of deregulation, the power of the financial sector and contextual advances in communication technology combined to produce a renewed appreciation for the relationship between time and money during the 1990s. Low inflation, rising numbers of jobs and a stock market turbo-charged by new technological innovations placed the financial markets in an ever-stronger position. As an increasingly virtual and global operation, the world of late twentieth-century finance gradually became detached from the reality of day-to-day life and dislocated from the physical spaces of the City and Wall Street as money began to inhabit a virtual sphere. Moving from the physical matter of currency and financial centres to the virtual space of technology, the years 1990–2000 became characterized as the decade of 'fast finance'.

Like the 1920s boom period in the United States, the 1990s were defined by a healthy stock market. From February 1995 to June 1999 American interest rates were raised only once, maintaining a buoyant environment in which financial industries could flourish. Despite being bookended by two short recessions, the 1990s built upon the Reaganomics of the 1980s to produce another ten years of economic optimism and the GDP of the United States increased year on year. Under President Bill Clinton (1993–2000) the economy took advantage of the fall of the Soviet Union and the new opportunities for trade that arose, while new communication and computer tools enabled higher speed international exchanges. Internationally, the end of the Cold War, the collapse of the Soviet Union and the physical fall of the Berlin Wall defined the beginning of the 1990s. These developments were widely celebrated by the West as a victory and, in the wake of the death of a viable alternative, capitalism abounded across the globe. In his 1989 essay 'The End of History', Francis Fukuyama claims that the fall of communism marked the victory of economic and political liberalism at the end of the twentieth century. His argument suggests that in a globalized world only liberal capitalist democracy can hope survive, and all future struggle will be economic, rather than ideological, in nature. Fuelled by historical developments, capitalism continued its march of dominance following the fall of communism. As Crunch Lit author John Lanchester reflects, 'the end of the Cold War was important in terms of letting the financial sector indulge in a victory party that started in 1989 and never stopped'.[15]

DeLillo's *Cosmopolis* (2003) is set in April 2000, significant since this month marked the peak of US stock markets.[16] Following a decade of deregulation, growth and optimism, the novel is concerned with the effects of increasing connectivity between the monetary and the temporal in the new millennium. Framed by the optimism and confidence of its period, the novel examines power, technology, violence, the role of crowd culture, counter-culture, cultural change and the role of time in a post-millennial period. The difference between a world economy and a global economy is that of time. Castells argues that 'during the 1990s the convergence of global deregulation of finance and the availability of new information technologies and new management techniques transformed the capital markets. For the first time in history, a unified global capital market, working in real time [. . .] emerged.'[17] DeLillo's novel considers the way in which a global economy, enabled in late twentieth century by the rise of information and communication technologies and deregulation and liberalization by governments of financial institutions, can operate in real time and on a planetary scale.

DeLillo engages his protagonist Eric Packer on a mission to travel across New York to get a haircut. As the novel develops, this deceptively simple journey gradually becomes a representative odyssey that critically comments on the future of finance and the contemporary city. Throughout the text, finance as a temporal form impacts on narrative structure, offering insights into the effects on the markets of those who seek to pervert the temporal order by withholding or leaking information. A sense of static motion, of a 'narrative gridlock' with bottlenecks and jams caused by communication flow comes to characterize a text in which protagonists are subject to constant delay from New York traffic.

Like his literary predecessor Patrick Bateman, Packer considers himself to be a new generation 'master of the universe' but is ultimately unsatisfied by money alone. Setting screen images against real-time narrative events encountered simultaneously, the delay between Packer's experience of reality – via trading monitors, limousine CCTV lenses, and the many screens that inform his daily life – draws attention to the simulacrum of finance that defines his world. Wanting more of everything, he becomes obsessed with knowing, seeing and experiencing extreme situations. This culminates in Packer putting himself in physical danger at the hands of anti-capitalist protestors and his would-be assassin in order to achieve a heightened sense of reality. The only way Packer believes he can experience reality is via the prospect of his impending demise. As a result, he attempts to refute the fate of time by encountering this prematurely. In a world where technology mediates experience and even the exchange of value has become virtual, Packer longs for an experience of the 'real' as an alternative to his controlled and largely silent world. Encased in a limousine or office, and exposed to the unreality of the financial world, he responds to the energy and vitality of the protestors and their explosions not by hiding, but by rushing to participate.

In an article that considers the role of finance in *Cosmopolis*, Jerry A. Varsava argues that 'it is not hard to see Eric Packer as an incarnation of evil, a diabolical sociopath and crypto-fascist who plays out his fantasies of domination and personal hegemony in the arena of global finance'.[18] Yet Packer is more than simply a villain for the fast finance generation. Driven by 'thinking past what is new' (152) and always needing 'to be one civilization ahead of this one' (152), Packer moves beyond the present and embraces a futurity of virtual markets and global time. Recognizing that 'power works best when there's no memory attached' (184), he is 'a man ahead of his time'.[19] Basking in the 'glow of cyber-capital. So radiant and seductive' (78), Packer embraces the new virtual time of contemporary finance in the belief that behind all modern money, the central

> idea is time. Living in the future. Look at those numbers running. Money makes time. It used to be the other way round. Clock time accelerated the rise of capitalism. People stopped thinking about eternity. They began to concentrate on hours, measurable hours, man-hours, using labor more efficiently [. . .] Its cyber-capital that creates the future. What is the measurement called, a nanosecond? (79)

Signalling a shift in the relationship between time and money, the role of time in the global spread of capitalism is foregrounded by Packer as central to understanding the past, present and future of finance.

The relentless pace, movement and anxiety of Packer, the markets and the city are constructed in the language of the novel. Everything is about speed and travel – or the lack thereof – and Packer regards anything outside the closed circuits of technology-driven banking as an 'archaic business' (6). The narrative makes clear that the 1990s and 2000s are a good time for money, a point at which faith in the power of the markets is at a high. The cause of tension in this novel is time: the thundering pace of virtual capitalist time as set against the ebb and flow of older banking methods and alternative economic systems. Disruptions to the flow of time occur during moments when information is withheld or released, causing time to speed up or slow down and the markets to respond accordingly. The rapid movement of financial time is marked by the continual pressure of 'currencies to track and research reports to examine' (7) since the 'currency markets never close [...] All the major exchanges [operate] seven days a week' (29). As Packer watches the visual display run through the exchange rates and market points, he is mesmerized by

> money moving [...] numbers gliding horizontally and bar charts pumping up and down. He knew there was something no one had detected, a pattern latent in nature itself, a leap of pictorial language that went beyond the standard models of technical analysis and out-predicted even the arcane charting of his own followers in the field. There had to be a way to explain the Yen. (63)

Packer's desire to explain the seemingly inexplicable, to master knowledge and weave a narrative from the visual representation of money is offered as the ultimate demonstration of power and influence. He recalls a time in which 'forecasting was pure power' but stresses that he is now searching for 'something purer, for techniques of charting that predicted movements of money itself' (76). Examining not only the drive for acquisition of wealth, but the absence of ethics and the dominating culture of power and control over knowledge, his statement outlines the shift in markets and market time in the years preceding the new millennium. Packer's overview illustrates how quickly technology has developed and affected the markets, and the impact this has on the scramble to control or get 'ahead' of market time.

In the early twenty-first century, cyber-capital moves capital into the virtual, just as nanoseconds continue to break time down into ever smaller units in order to accelerate its movement and momentum. In *Cosmopolis*, even 'time is a corporate asset [. . .] It belongs to the freemarket system' but 'the present is harder to find. It is being sucked out of the world to make way for the future of uncontrolled markets and huge investment potential' (79). As a result, Packer reflects that any twenty-first-century financial manager needs 'stamina to do this job. The single-mindedness [. . .] The relentless will. Because I keep hearing about our legend. We're all young and smart and were raised by wolves. But the phenomenon of reputation is a delicate thing. A person rises on the word and falls on a syllable' (12). Mobilizing the language of his fictional predecessors, Packer represents the movement of the markets as faster than ever in the twenty-first century. Increasingly 'borrowing enormous sums' and 'speculating into the void' (21), he perpetuates the myth of his own legend, but falls victim to a fatal combination of excessive confidence and speculation on the Yen that verges on an 'assault on the borders of perception' (21). Technology is not fast enough for Packer, but ultimately it proves too fast and is beyond his power to control.

Beginning the novel as a confident practitioner in 'the art of money-making' (77) but ending it by sacrificing his wife's $735 million inheritance on the markets, Packer attempts to kill both the time and space of 'old money'. However, with 'bank failures [. . .] spreading' Packer, like many other 'strategists could not explain the speed and depth of the fall' (115) and is forced to realize that while his limousine may be bulletproof, he is not. As Packer's Chief of Theory Vija Kiniski informs him, in the new millennium 'money has taken a turn. All wealth has become wealth for its own sake. There's no other kind of enormous wealth. Money has lost its narrative quality the way painting did once upon a time. Money is talking to itself' (77). Even Packer's mistress admits, 'I don't know what money is anymore' (29).

While Packer is intent on speeding time ever faster, his would-be assassin, ex-employee Benno Levin (or Richard Sheets), wants time to slow, in order to reflect earlier, more personal and less commercial values. An ex-currency speculator who worked for Packer under his birth name Richard Sheets (a name which tellingly means 'nothing' [192] to Packer), Levin represents an older relationship with money, one grounded in contact and physical exchange. He takes pride in the fact that he still has a 'bank that I visit systematically to look at the last literal dollars remaining in my account. I do this for the ongoing psychology of it, to know I have money in an institution. And because cash machines have a charisma that still speaks to me' (60). Situated in a firm routine, a sense of ownership, value and worth, Levin's physical banking practices deliberately avoid the automation and impersonal exchanges that characterize millennial finance. In comparison to Packer's high speed, virtual, break-neck large-scale dealings, Levin's small sums, slow processes and physical spaces of finance appear archaic. Enacting the claim that the 'logical extension of business is murder' (113), Levin's attack on Packer at once services the investor's hunger for a 'real' encounter but also responds to Levin's need for a voice, revenge, and for his identity and values to be recognized.

The protestors that surround Packer's limousine exercise a similar desire to be heard and communicate an alternative approach to finance and financial time in the twenty-first century. In their desire to delay the future, they actualize the 'assault on the investment bank' (99) implicit to their ideology. Committed to correcting 'the acceleration of time' caused by new financial technologies, their actions are suggestive of Vija's assertion that the contemporary is 'dealing with a system that's out of control [. . .] We create our own frenzy, our own mass convulsions' (85). Bastardizing the opening lines to *The Communist Manifesto* ('A SPECTER IS HAUNTING THE WORLD – THE SPECTER OF CAPITALISM,' 96), the protestors highlight the many threats facing Packer, the loss of meaning in capitalism, a spiritual void and an emotional lack of connection to wider society.

By the new millennium the globe was not only more 'interconnected but also more interdependent'.[20] This interdependence produced not just vulnerability but also resistance, and these effects are made visible across the narrative of *Cosmopolis*. Highlighting divides created by the growth of financialization, the novel presents the violent revolution proposed by the protestors as a spectacle, an event that promises the physical overthrowing of the state by means of organized opposition. However, the protestors are ultimately unable to operate outside of the system they rail against.

In *Cosmopolis*, all protest is futile, since there is no alternative to the global march of financialization. In this depressing political outlook, the novel offers readers a new perspective on the civil unrest that literally surrounds Packer's limo-throne and invades his financial world. Packer attempts to overcome the limits of time and space, but is ultimately unable to manage the high speed financial flows of an increasingly complex global financial network. Although Packer ends the novel shot and apparently dying, he lives on in the representations of money and debates about the future of finance and financial time offered by the novel's conclusion.

As a mediation on the impact of technology on financial cultures and practices, *Cosmopolis* suggests that Packer is not in control, of money or himself, and cannot have total knowledge of the markets. A desire for a financial master narrative, for ultimate knowledge and control over time, drives Packer into a tail spin of Faustian levels. Unable to submit to laissez faire capitalism, Packer will not stand well back and watch capitalism work, but instead becomes increasingly agitated by his lack of influence over the disastrously rapid decline of the Yen. In a novel where money is ever present, and in which readers are relentlessly reminded of its ability to permeate time and space, the logical product of accelerated time is a financial market that is everywhere at all times, and this proves beyond even Packer's ability to control. Mesmerized by the virtual images of money that populate his technology-driven world, Packer offers readers important foresights about the relationship between money and time at the start of the new millennium. Blake Morrison argues that 'DeLillo has always been good at telling us where we're heading. What he describes here is an enslavement to money markets, scrolling screens and virtual realities. The heaviness of the message squeezes the life out his novel. But we ignore him at our peril.'[21] Far from being interchangeable, in *Cosmopolis* time and money are part of an inextricable equation in which present and future values engage with one another in constant, responsive relations.

From the 1980s onwards, developments in the financial sector including deregulation, technologization and media connectivity, changed not only the conditions in which money could operate, but also the relationship between time, technology and finance in a global context. Examining these evolutions as influential factors in the financialization of the markets during the late twentieth century, financial fictions set in the period from 1980 to 2000 illuminate the significance of these decades in establishing the conditions and cultures that went on to inform financial events of the new millennium. Underwritten by the 'idea you can engineer away risk using clever maths', the technologies of finance engineered during the 1990s were anchored by 'perfect mathematical structures', but eventually 'drifted too far away from reality' and began to operate at a speed that no one could control.[22] Accelerated by technology, flows of money became virtual, rapid and difficult to follow, control or regulate. Examining the increased role of technology and time in the world of finance across the late twentieth century, *Cosmopolis* explores the ways in which fast-finance facilitated a new relationship between time and money in the new millennium.

From Wall Street to Main Street

Across the twentieth century the American economy grew at a steady rate, until it reached a ten-year period during the 1990s that was judged by the US Bureau of Economic Research to be the longest economic expansion in history. However, from the year 2000 onwards the country witnessed the worst economic spell of its modern times. In the United States, the early years of the new millennium were blighted by a recession resulting from the burst of the 'dot-com bubble'. This was closely followed by the events of 9/11 that produced stock market falls, led to the war in Iraq and increased government spending on security at home and abroad.

The new millennial economic downturn in the United States created a renewed focus on the value of the domestic, the family home as set against international conflicts and financial challenges. During this period, the increasingly interrelated relationship between the local and the global, between Wall Street and Main Street, was made evident by the impact of a downturn in national finances on the lived reality of everyday citizens.

Financial fictions set in America during the first years of the new millennium are concerned with the impact of global systems and disputes on domestic US communities. Interrogating the implications of local conflicts within national contexts, these novels tell the tale of the increasingly problematic relationship between the American family and the American nation in the twenty-first century. Foregrounding a lack of communication and transparency at all levels in society, from marriages to corporations and international relations, authors use family plots to tell wider stories about the relationship between global finance and individual freedoms. Spotlighting credit, corruption and competition, they not only document declining moral standards and professional ethics, but position these issues as a significant legacy from the deregulation discourses of the 1980s and the technologization of 1990s. Charting the increasing implication of ordinary people in cultures of credit and debt and the infiltration and normalization of loans and mortgages into everyday life, these financial fictions shine new light on the state of the financial sector in the years preceding the crunch. Suggesting a growing connectivity among local, national and international conflicts, they chart the development of an evergrowing web of credit and corruption that culminates in the events of 2007–8.

Sabin Willett's *Present Value* (2004) tells the story of mid-Forties, executive couple, Fritz and Linda Brubaker, who enjoy high-powered careers in business and law respectively.[23] Their children attend private school and they reside between a mansion in the Boston suburbs and a holiday cottage in Nantucket. The family begin the novel as the epitome of American success in the new millennium. However, when Fritz is accused of insider trading, and Linda's law firm suspends her, fearing that their image will be damaged by association with Fritz, their children begin to rebel, their home is repossessed and the family unit begins to fall apart. Following the fate of Fritz Brubaker as he engages in illegal economic activities and their consequences, the novel is punctuated with flashbacks to Fritz's undergraduate Economics 101 classes in which his lecturer debates the question 'what is value?' (119).

Appearing at key points in the present-tense narrative, and offering brief moments of respite from, and reflection on, the financial traumas of the plot itself, these Economics lectures explore the fluidity and relativity of key economic concepts such as supply and demand, surety and mistrust, in an attempt to understand how, why and with what effect 'value should be determined' (105). The final 'Farewell lecture' asks whether a system of personal values can operate simultaneously with a system of economic values in which 'everything's for sale [. . .] even the bets on the future' (372).

Posing a timely pre-crunch question, 'is economics just?' (376), the lecture concludes that 'real values. Love. Constancy. Faith', which do not have 'value an economist would understand' are things 'we prize [...] above all else. We value them above all else' (376–7). In a post-millennial society in which 'everything is relative [...] there are no absolutes' (373), value is offered as a subjective concept, one profoundly relative to context and time.

Set in the first years of the new millennium, the novel charts the challenges posed to the US economy not only by a major terrorist attack, but also from increasingly unethical practices in the financial sector. A satire of post-9/11 America, the narrative uses *Playtime* – a fictional toy manufacturer with insider trading problems and dishonest profit projections – as an Enron-type disaster waiting to happen. Exploring financial manipulations during the months and year before the credit crunch, the novel offers a critique of social and political institutions that failed to intervene in a widespread culture of silence that cloaked the activities of the financial industry in the lead up to the 2007–8 crash.

When Fritz is discovered, he is individually demonized, while the wider corporate corruption of which he is a small part warrants a less intimate examination. The moral indignation and requests for reflection expressed by his economics lecturer suggest that there are no real villains in this world, beyond the shared capitalist system in which the characters operate. Linking suburban aspiration and corporate greed, the novel reveals that it is only when Fritz is forced to the brink that he can see the way forward from the damaging practices and values that led to this crisis point. Sabine's satirical approach to the underlying tensions of pre-crunch America – business, housing, credit and conspicuous consumption – offers the family as an effective metaphor for the nation at large. Mobilizing family plots to illustrate the interconnections between broader economic practices and the lives of ordinary citizens, the novel links morality, the economy and the hopes of small-town America to the abstract actions of businessmen and traders in the capital to suggest a profoundly interrelated, and vulnerable, set of pre-crunch social, political and economic networks in the United States.

Union Atlantic (2009) is also concerned with the local and national tensions faced by early millennial America.[24] Given the central role of subprime mortgages in the 2007–8 credit crunch, it is apt that Adam Haslett's novel centres on the fate of two houses – one built using the new money of city banker Doug Fanning, the other an inherited family home of retired history teacher Charlotte Graves. The ensuing domestic dispute between these two neighbours functions as a metaphor for wider state-of-the-nation problems in the lead up to the 2007–8 credit crunch. As the narrative develops, a local dispute in small-town America becomes symptomatic of pre-crunch credit cultures that conspired to produce a context in which money was plentiful and property was perceived as a fail-safe investment. The narrative recalls that:

> After the tech bust in 2000, the Federal Reserve had cut interest rates, making mortgages cheap, and thus opening the door for all that frightened capital to run for safety into houses. The attacks on 9/11 had only sped the trend. These new mortgages were being fed into the banks like cars into a chop shop, stripped for parts by Union Atlantic and the other big players, and then securitized and sold on to the pension funds and the foreign central banks. Thus were the monthly payments of the young couples in California and Arizona and Florida transformed by the alchemy of finance into a haven for domestic liquidity and the Chinese surplus, a surplus earned by stocking the box stores at which those same couples shopped. With all that money floating around, the price of real estate could only rise. Before Doug ever opened the front door, the value of his new property has risen thirty percent. (18)

Placing Doug's build in an assured context of price-high, mortgage-heavy, credit-friendly America, the novel situates a local, domestic conflict in a wider context of global trends towards positive finance in which everything is rising, strong and without danger of crisis. The logo of Union Atlantic – the 'outline of a cresting wave' (43) – functions as a symbol of this optimism, the company's approach to surfing a credit bonanza and their monopolization of the subprime mortgage explosion of the new millennium.

The impact of national and international issues on the life of ordinary Americans during this period is observed by Doug as he dines in the town where he grew up:

> Doug saw a guy at a table by the window, early twenties, dressed in expensively faded jeans and a sweater pre-patched at the

elbows. He was leafing through a magazine, the white wires of his earphones trailing down into his pocket, a laptop open beside him. He saw these people everywhere now, these aging children who had done nothing, borne no responsibility, who in their bootless, liberal refinement would judge him and all he'd done as the enemy of the good and the just, their high-minded opinions just decoration for a different pattern of consumption: the past marketed as the future to comfort the lost. And who financed it? Who loaned them the money for these lives they couldn't quite afford with their credit cards and their student loans? Who else but the banks? (74)

Considering the local impact of global developments, Doug highlights the personal wealth, standard of living and political approach produced by a credit-ready society. Financed by the banks into education, cultures and experiences otherwise beyond them, the individuals Doug observes in this small town are implicitly connected to much wider international market forces, and consequently equally at their mercy.

For Doug, money is a by-product of his command of systems and control over other people. He reflects that his happiness lies not in 'the likely size of his bonus or the further expansion of his informal dominion. The execution was what gratified him. The focus and precision and directedness of his will [. . .] the resistance of the physical world reduced to the vanishing point. He felt then like the living wonder of the most advanced machine, as if he'd been freed of all organic hindrance to glide on the plain of pure efficiency. A place of relief, even peace' (48). Doug's personal quest eventually centres not on money, but on 'dominance. That's the childish pleasure you people can't get enough of. You get your fix dressed up in a suit, but it's no different than a drug' (210). Doug is employed to oversee expansion at Union Atlantic, taking advantage of the pre-2007 market conditions to exploit plentiful credit and high market demand for housing.

Doug's military background is of clear and immediate appeal to the company, and he is encouraged to attack the financial markets like a military campaign. Previously, Doug 'had run air defence on the most advanced ship in the navy and he'd seen action in the Persian Gulf' (53). At Union Atlantic, Fanning strategically directs an assault on the sector and considers his staff as a mere extension of his own money-making abilities. Doug instils in his teams an aggressive approach to trading:

> On his advice, the bank had brazenly commenced acquisitions that were strictly speaking illegal but that Doug foresaw would be approved by the time the deals were finalised, in part because of Union Atlantic's own lobbying, but also because their competitors, as soon as they caught on, would follow suit, adding their own legislative pressure to scrap the old protections. Leading the pack. (45)

Drawing implicit connections between greed and personal financial power, banking is presented as a form of warfare, as Doug's skills from the army are effortless and disastrously put to work on the 'special financial operations' of Union Atlantic. As both military man and banker, Doug is a predator, and the novel makes clear political links between manipulation of the markets and private involvement in the second Iraq war that ends the novel. An obsession with leading groups into battle reaches a pinnacle when Doug's head of operations in Hong Kong gambles too far. He reflects that Doug had always told them that money 'was there for the taking [. . .] you always said the losers were the people afraid of risk' (166), but then the Hong Kong wing of Union Atlantic loses enough money to cause alarm bells that sound as far as America and initiate a fraud investigation into Doug's operations.

The character of Doug is used to represent both the moral and economic bankruptcy at the heart of not only Union Atlantic, but also modern America and its domestic and foreign policy. In an interview with William Skidelsky, Haslett observes that 'lots of readers may think of Doug as an evil character but I don't. I wanted to investigate what might be thought of as the confinement of a certain kind of masculinity. It's not my role to judge that.' As he wrote the character, Haslett recalls that 'one of the things I discovered [. . .] about [Doug] is that the emotion that vivified him was anger. And I could see that anger was the emotion vivifying both militarism and high finance, which are the two things that have been dominating American life for the past decade.'[25] A veteran of the first Gulf War, Doug is also the estranged son of an alcoholic single mother. Significantly, he chooses to build his new home in the same town she used to work as a cleaner. Returning to challenge the class boundaries that defined his childhood and rewrite his relationship with both time and space, Doug builds his dream house as a landmark to his achievements, new status and his own American Dream.

Doug is firstly a victim of the capitalist economies that motivate his actions and secondly of his Union Atlantic bosses. Like Fritz Brubaker in *Present Value*, Doug is used by his superiors as a scapegoat and abandoned to a baying media which is hungry for banker punishment. Exposed, Doug is forced to flee the United States and return to Kuwait City as a security agent for a private business seeking to profit from the next Gulf War. This new role involves protecting not a government or a democracy, but individuals and business documents related to the creation of new private infrastructures in newly 'liberated' countries. Offering a critique of not only his character, but of a national approach to contemporary economic contexts, the novel presents Doug as both villain and victim.

In Graves versus Fanning, Haslett offers readers a battle between the moral economies of domestic, small-town America pitched against the impersonal, corporate economies of twenty-first-century finance. No business is too big to fail, but Union Atlantic can and does brush up against the historical forces of American values and notions of liberty when the needs of the economy and the desires of the individual are set in opposition. As studies of the problems in financial cultures and systems during the post-9/11 era, both *Present Value* and *Union Atlantic* present a single protagonist in a financial institution as a domino in a much wider, fragile system in the lead up to the credit crunch. Offering a timely critical review of the relationships between global economics and individual citizens in the new millennium, both novels are suggestive of how, why and with what effect American's Main Street became intimately connected to Wall Street during the pre-crunch period.

Examining tensions between doing the right thing and doing the most profitable thing, domestic economy fictions of the new millennium present the element of choice in behaving for the common good. Interrogating the guidance offered during times of challenges and the consequences of choices taken during moments of hysteria or pressure, these texts centre on actions, inactions or character flaws to offer warnings against the financial behaviours and practices that culminated in the 2007–8 credit crunch. Representing the moral dimension of cultures of credit and technology-driven trading, they mobilize the domestic family and local community as symbols of wider social demographics to question the market economy and impact of corporate practice on the domestic streets of contemporary America.

Narrating the individual and economic consequences of a lack of regulation and accountability in financial practices, *Union Atlantic* and *Present Value* critically examine the extent to which finance has grown to encroach on small-town American life in the pre-crunch period. In narratives that are structured around a series of falls – via not just the personal narrative of the individual, but also the moral and economic downfall of a nation – these novels function as a current affairs review of events leading up to the economic downturn. Interrogating the impact of bad mortgages, dishonest financial statements and excessive confidence in the markets and those who controlled them, domestic economy tales suggest that, in the early millennium, Main Street cannot escape from the impact of actions taken on Wall Street.

In the wake of the credit crunch and the hindsight it affords, it can be argued that the financial reforms and developments of the 1980s did not just unleash a temporary 'Big Bang', but actually shaped the conditions of finance that went on to inform the events of 2007–8. Describing the wider 'Ghekoisation' of society that saw its origins in the 1980s, sociologist John D. Bone concurs that fiction played an important role in representing the role of the pre-crunch years in giving birth to cultures of individualism, deregulation and neoliberalism that contributed to the financial crash.[26] As such, pre-crunch financial fictions reveal their protagonists not as monsters of another era, but as very timely reminders of the paths that led to the current crisis.

Highlighting the social and local impact of virtual and global financial transactions, these novels interrogate the corrupt ethics and greed for power building across financial industries during the preceding decades that effectively sowed the seeds of the 2007–8 credit crunch. Critiquing not only the corruption of an individual but of a credit-dependent culture sprouting from Wall Street that is ethically out of kilter with the values that built Main Street society, domestic financial narratives predict the individual costs of a global crisis. Examining the money-without-morals culture of a pre-2007 world, the ultimate revelation of these novels is that their protagonists – whether Self or Sherman, Bateman or Packer, Fritz or Doug – are not a 'simple part of the "pre-history" of the post-millennial period' but are vital to 'the analysis of a symptomatic malaise central to the contemporary moment: a key to those disturbing times in which we continue to live'.[27] For each man, an obsession with money becomes part of a wider struggle for power. In their unswerving pursuit of money-as-power, these protagonists face self-destruction and are eventually consumed by the power of finance.

From the shaping influence of 1980s cultures of deregulation and individualism, to the impact of new communication technologies on time and money at the turn of the century, and the increasing interconnections between Wall Street and Main Street in the early years of the new millennium, pre-crunch financial fictions offer new understanding of, and ways of reading, the period that sowed the seeds of the 2007–8 credit crunch. These texts are not simply symptomatic of their times but remain relevant as a result of the emergent culture of financialization that they identify during the 1980s, developed in the 1990s and became dominant in a global arena during the early years of the twenty-first century. It is now vital to appreciate these texts as more than retro-nostalgia, since the representations of finance and financial cultures they offer shed new light on the financial events of the present, encouraging an acknowledgment of the informing influence of the years before the credit crunch, and contesting claims made in its aftermath that no one could have seen it coming. These novels form an important part of a canon of financial fictions from the pre-crunch period that sow the seeds of, and chart the final countdown to, the 2007–8 crunch. As a direct result of their examination of 'the cultural impact of finance capital'[28] on society across the pre-crunch period, these fictions speak as much to the financial context of the twenty-first-century world, as much as they do their own decades.

2

9–8–7: The credit crunch

Finance has become increasingly abstract and self-referential, the complexity of its operations virtually impossible for those on the outside to envisage.

PAUL CROSTHWAITE[1]

The breakdown of a clear understanding of how contemporary finance operated during the years before 2007–8 meant that, when the world of money fell off a fiscal cliff, the causes of, and events during, the financial crisis seemed impenetrable and impossible to comprehend. However, as Pym and Kochan argue, many of the 'roots of the crisis go some way back into the mists of time'.[2] The decades preceding the 2007–8 credit crunch were characterized by the 'liberalization of markets, deregulation of the economy and especially the financial sector, privatization of state assets, low taxes and the lowest possible amount of state spending'.[3] While these measures produced a short-term economic boom, they laid the foundations for a longer-term economic time bomb.

Some of the causes of the 2007–8 crunch were attributable to these circumstances of historical context, others were associated with the proliferation of a series of toxic cultures and practices across the global economic sector during the early twenty-first century. In January 2011, the US Financial Crisis Inquiry Commission reported its findings from a report on the causes of the credit crunch. It concluded that:

> The crisis was avoidable and was caused by: widespread failures in financial regulation, including the Federal Reserve's failure

to stem the tide of toxic mortgages; dramatic breakdowns in corporate governance including too many financial firms acting recklessly and taking on too much risk; an explosive mix of excessive borrowing and risk by households and Wall Street that put the financial system on a collision course with crisis; key policy makers ill prepared for the crisis, lacking a full understanding of the financial system they oversaw; and systemic breaches in accountability and ethics at all levels.[4]

The years following the financial crisis gave birth to a range of Crunch Lit writings that sought to 'subvert some of the prevailing orthodoxies in contemporary financial disclosure',[5] and represent the causes behind and events during 2007–8 in order to demystify, mediate and illuminate popular understandings. Representing 'toxic mortgages', 'excessive borrowing', 'risk' and credit culture, Crunch Lit writings offer new fictionalized case studies of the financial crisis, its causes and events. Rejecting the obtuse terminology and opaque practices of finance, new writings representing the causes and events of the credit crash encourage readers to consider the factors that contributed to the freezing of the financial markets. Confounding media claims that the nature of contemporary finance and the events of credit crunch are too difficult to understand, these writings reimagine the crisis as a narrative event experienced *media res* by characters at the heart of financial industries. Representing a wider breakdown of control and meaning, the true tragedy in these texts is that readers are already aware of the crisis that is about to unfold. As a result, Crunch Lit authors mobilize dramatic irony to transform their fictions into moral tales of a crisis in credit-culture and the ultimate failure of the financial practices developed and promoted in the preceding decades.

A crisis of credit

In fictions that represent the 2007–8 financial crash, the rise of credit and mortgage debts during the pre-crunch years form a central narrative concern. In Lanchester's Crunch Lit novel *Capital*, the conditions of the pre-crunch economy inspire immigrant nanny Matya to marvel at 'the currents of money [. . .] it was everywhere [. . .] in the cars, the clothes, the shops, the talk, the very air. People got it and spent it and thought about it and talked about it all the time. It was brash and horrible and vulgar, but also exciting and energetic and shameless and new' (337).[6] The credit culture that Matya describes had become widespread and normalized across the West by the year the crunch hit in 2007. Despite the fact that UK Prime Minister Gordon Brown had promised an end to the 'boom and bust' economics that defined the Thatcher era, from 1997 to 2007, total private sector debt in the UK leapt from 133.5 per cent to 227.4 per cent of GDP.[7] When New Labour was first elected, total debt held by individuals in the UK was £570.0 billion. By the time the crunch hit in 2007 it had risen to £1,511.7 billion. As Turner points out, this was 'a leap of 165.2 per cent. That was equivalent to an average annualized increase of 10.0 per cent'.[8] The UK had wholly embraced debt-culture, possessing half of Europe's credit card debt[9] by 2007, with the average British household owing 160 per cent of its annual income.[10] Cheap credit also made it easy for US consumers to spend beyond their means, amassing large quantities of personal debt in addition to mortgages, and accessing further credit readily.

The development of this credit culture was celebrated as a key part of the new financial confidence of the late twentieth and early twenty-first century on both sides of the Atlantic. Western consumers with their credit cards and credit-happy lifestyles played an important role in the credit crunch. The normalization of credit and debt encouraged borrowers 'to gorge on cheap credit, like geese being stuffed to create foie gras'.[11] Gradually, a shadow banking system developed, one that was not directly involved in and regulated differently from banking, that specialized in cheap credit through home loans, credit cards, insurance, private equity, hedge funds and securitization. The globe was 'awash with money in the early years of the 21st century'[12] and for investors the best potentials were to be found in the new mortgages offered to high risk lenders, since these offered the biggest premiums and returns.

The development of a credit culture was further accelerated by the formation of new markets for the purchase of credit for houses and mortgage debts. In both the United States and UK, owning your own home remains an important factor in an individual's status, identity and success. In the UK, the election of New Labour in 1997 came with new targets for pushing up homeownership but the subprime crisis really began in the United States. Subprime was part of a longer term push in America centred on homeownership for those on low incomes. During the 1970s, Jimmy Carter aimed to create mortgages for ethnic minorities, while the 1990s saw Clinton's aim that half of all mortgages should be allocated to low income household. Congress gave priority to low income home owners and in 1992 'passed laws requiring that government-backed mortgage providers Fannie Mae and Freddie Mac develop more sub-prime lending [. . .] By 2008, the two giants had amassed more than half of all the nation's home loans'.[13]

Credit for houses was generally divided into two types: conforming mortgages – people who seemed safe debtors, and were therefore offered lower rates of interest – and non-conforming mortgages – people who could not afford a mortgage, had poor credit ratings or were underserved by the traditional mortgage market. In his post-crunch financial confession narrative *Confessions of a Subprime Lender* (2008) Richard Bitner identifies five types of borrowers: the slow to pay, the under-qualified, those with limited credit history, the person who experiences a negative life event (such as death or illness), the unlucky (redundancy) and those on the edge of the prime/subprime boundary, but pushed into the subprime category deliberately by a mortgage broker intent on selling a riskier, higher rate mortgage that will achieve a higher commission in the short term and get a better return for investors in the long term.[14] The mortgage market wanted to encourage more risky debtors precisely because they were less creditworthy and therefore far more lucrative in terms of rates of return on investment.

Those on the edge of the economic lines were targeted hardest. So-called 'ninja' loans – given to those with 'no income, job, or assets' – were awarded not because the lenders believed that customers' personal circumstances would change, but because the lenders planned to sell on this risk almost immediately, repackaging and passing on the loans to someone else. As Atwood reflects, 'some large financial institutions peddled mortgages to people who could not possibly pay the monthly rates and then put this snake-oil debt into cardboard boxes with impressive labels on them and sold them to institutions and hedge funds that thought they were worth something.'[15] Risk was imagined, initiated and instigated as someone else's problem. In the pre-crunch period, data was not available on how subprime mortgages performed. This lack of default statistics meant that many buyers took out insurance on these subprime debts in case their high-risk, high-return debtors defaulted. Instead of being addressed and quantified, the risk was securitized and sold on to free up funding that could be invested in more debt obligations.

A proliferation of subprime mortgages increased market demand for housing as new buyers flooded the market. This created an asset price bubble for houses whose values were already unreal, overvalued and based on an inflated market underpinned by risky credit. A potent combination of consumer debt and rising house prices meant that people were under the illusion that they were wealthier than they were. In relative terms, houses were only ever valuable in relation to the market price of other houses, which were themselves overinflated. In the UK, a shortage of properties and a proliferation of 'buy to let' mortgages taken out by capital rich investors pushed house prices up further. In 1998, 58,500 buy to let mortgages were granted compared to a million in 2007 (this equated to 10.3% of all mortgages outstanding).[16] As 'Capital-rich landlords were scooping up houses, fuelling a virtuous cycle of rising prices, falling supply and inevitably a plentiful supply of tenants, from those forced by a rising market to rent' this impacted upon the personal debt levels of individuals.[17] Governments passed off these rising debt figures as representative of rising home ownership and, since committing to home ownership was something governments encouraged, the credit figures were allowed to grow.

This confidence was based on the assumption that house prices were unlikely to fall. From 1990 to 2007, average house prices in the United States and UK rose nearly 200 per cent.[18] Resulting faith in the security of the housing market meant that by 2008, 120 per cent mortgages of up to six times the borrower's salary were regularly being offered with little proof of income. Yet, amidst this fever, optimism and impression of security, the 'technical experts seemed to have ignored or forgotten previous house price slumps'.[19] Alan Greenspan, Chairman of the Federal Reserve Board, and other key financial directors and government ministers in the United States and UK effectively allowed speculative bubbles to develop, so when the UK land registry announced that house prices had dropped 8 per cent in the year to September 2008, panic began to spread.[20]

The pre-crunch mortgage boom is described by the protagonist of Elton's novel *Meltdown* (2009) as a 'monumental balls-up, turns out they were giving mortgages away like loyalty points and now they're fucked' (21).[21] Faulks's *A Week in December* also reflects that, before the crunch, 'American mortgage companies had dangerously oversold mortgages to poor people ("sub-primers") who would be unable to make the monthly repayments if anything – anything – went wrong.' As a result, 'People were losing their jobs, defaulting on their payments; interest rates and monthly repayments were set to rise' (13).[22] As flows of finance began to freeze, so did the housing developments that had grown in the contemporary city.

Abandoned sites, lingering in stasis, foreclosed houses were quickly adopted by squatters who utilized the infrastructures of half-finished homes to take advantage of indefinitely stalled multi-million-pound projects. Examining Hackney as a representative example of a much wider phenomenon, *Meltdown* investigates 'Webb Street. A semi-derelict and entirely abandoned property development that had run out of cash. At one end of the street some of the properties have been nearly renovated. These desirable billets had been squatted by smart savvy class-war warriors with dreadlocks and posh accents who changed locks and sorted out the lecy' (37). Populated by multi-million-pound town houses and streets of residential developments funded by over-leveraged finance, the London landscape of Crunch Lit novels are littered with the architectural victims of a credit freeze. Novelist of another Crunch Lit text, Justin Cartwright, argues that the 'task for the novelist who wants to capture the essence of the real estate bubble, and to apportion the blame for its bursting more fairly, is to wade into the swamp of ordinary middle-class life and dig up those roots, in order to trace their hidden connections with the commanding heights of high finance.'[23] Connecting abstract financial machinations to the bricks and mortar of people's homes, Crunch Lit foregrounds the reality of the credit crunch on individuals at the very end of the chains of credit that structure global financial networks to suggest the impact on day-to-day life of decisions made by the global financial sector in the new millennium.

Risk culture

Crunch Lit fictions represent the development of risk culture and the impact of new financial practices in the years preceding the crunch to examine the role they played in causing the financial markets to freeze during 2007-8. These novels suggest that the roots of the financial crisis lay in the deregulation of the financial markets from the 1980s onwards. At the turn of the millennium, deregulation was taken to a new developmental stage by the 1999 abolition of the Glass-Steagall Act. This rule had ensured that commercial banks – those that take deposits from customers – were prevented from entering into riskier forms of banking, such as hedge funds. The suspension of the act meant that banks could start borrowing money from the wholesale markets, as well as from their customers' deposits. As a result, many banks took this new income stream and began to gamble in an attempt to make more money. The process of leverage – using borrowed money to invest, make more money, paying your initial debt and reinvesting your excess – formed the basis of this growth in risk culture. Financiers increasingly gambled with money sourced from loans, as well as from clients' savings deposits to exploit the rising markets and cheat the low interest rates. Old models of safe, predictable banking – in which banks simply lent out the deposits left with them by savers – were now combined with new strategies of leverage (borrowing money to make more money) to borrow short, lend long and leverage further risk in the pursuit of greater returns. In 2001, the Bank of England estimated that British banks were lending the same amount they were taking in deposits but, by the first half of 2008, the surplus of lending over deposits had reached £700 million.[24]

Securitization furthered this risk through the apparent 'management' of credit. The packaging up of mortgages and other assorted loans and debts into securities that could be sold on effectively freed more money for reinvestment and was popular with investors looking to fully leverage their resources. Known in the industry as 'tranching', securities were categorized into various levels of default-threat, priced according to their risk, with the highest risk securities achieving the highest prices, and then sold on. Tranches of debt containing various degrees of risk were packaged as 'asset backed securities', the asset in question often being the house the lender would eventually own if the mortgage debtor defaulted on their credit agreement. These 'CDO's were bought, sold and passed on so quickly that they rarely appeared on bank balance sheets, or were often left on the margins as cryptic 'SIVs'. Few knew what SIVs were, and fewer asked. In reality, SIVs were ghost risks – unidentified on paper and often undetected, they grew from the margins and spread invisible risk across the banking system. Along with 'CDS's (credit default swaps), these new practices injected an 'intriguing cocktail of financial elements' into the markets that increased risk, and therefore profit.[25] The process of securitization through derivatives became an international game of 'pass the parcel', but no one knew how much risk was in each parcel, or when the music was going to stop.

Other People's Money (2011) tells the story of an established Anglo-Jewish British banking family that fall victim to the new financial practices of subprime mortgages and CDO trading in the years preceding the crunch.[26] Setting a small business against a big corporation,[27] the novel explores the decline of traditional banking practices in the face of the energy, avarice and greed of contemporary trading techniques. Representing an older generation of bankers defined by their relationship with customers and refusal to run their business through speculation, the novel draws on an epigraph from John Maynard Keynes in 1936 to suggest that 'when the capital development of a country becomes a by-product of the activities of a casino, the job is likely to be ill done'.[28]

In a novel that sets traditional banking practices against a new risk-friendly culture of contemporary finance, the reality of these trades is represented by a situation in which investors end up with useless CDOs made up of 'chunks of mortgages on an alligator farm in a swamp, two thousand worthless homes in Mississippi, a shopping mall in a town which has been flattened by a hurricane and a lake-side clapboard holiday development in Antigua which is currently underwater, so that, when the waters recede, the holiday homes will be pulp' (15). The actions of traders are presented in clear terms that outline an implicit moral as well as financial responsibility for their actions. The narrative notes that traders have 'sliced and diced derivatives and recklessly lent money' (71) to the extent to that it is impossible to 'know which bits of these assets we own. Nobody does' (71). Exposing people who 'have misappropriated some hundred millions of other people's money [. . .] and have placed pensions and investments in jeopardy' (210), the novel is highly critical of derivatives trading and risk culture as significant contributing factors in the credit crunch.

Structurally, the novel builds on a growing dread of the approaching credit crunch that signals the death of the family business and the decline of both a financial system and an intergenerational way of life. Although financier protagonist Julian is weak and confused, as the son of the dying chairman of the bank he does not understand the new financial instruments available to him. Charting a period in which the 'City fell in love with the idea of frictionless wealth' (175), *Other People's Money* suggests how and why old banks and banking practices were driven into the ground by new traders 'too dazzled by the profits others had apparently made' (15) using these new financial practices. Interrogating the popular financial shorthand 'OPM', the novel examines the speculative fantasy that finance had become by 2007.

Ultimately, the text proposes that risk can never be totally removed from the financial sector, but that the lack of social concern for the impact of financial decisions and the belief that finance can operate above the law were fatal errors. Although they deal in trusts, the financiers of this novel suffer from a fundamental lack of trust in anything but themselves. Making subtle connections between the greed of Britain's colonial era and its simple (and scarily efficient) transfer into the financial markets of the contemporary via risk-friendly derivatives and CDOs, the novel positions an established bank in the City of London against big, international investment banks to highlight the consequences of changes in financial practices during the pre-crunch period.

Faulks's *A Week in December* (2009) opens with an equally damning representation of cultures of risk and the widespread refusal to acknowledge warning signs that the markets could not sustain levels of leverage and derivatives trading before the crash. Quoting Chuck Price, the chief executive of CitiGroup in an interview with *The Financial Times* on 9 July 2007 ('As long as the music is playing, you've got to get up and dance [. . .] We're all still dancing') the novel's epigraph explicitly connects the narrative with the pre-crunch situation of early 2007. In Faulks's novel, the financial world stands in a 'kind of suspended animation [. . .] the writing was smeared in letters ten feet high across the wall, but still people were trying to ignore it. The party was still on; the hard core, drunk on risk, unable to believe the gold rush might never end, would not go home' (151). For some of his characters, even the concept of derivatives is difficult to understand. Upon hearing that 'the Samuels had bundled up and sold on other people's debts',

Sophie realizes she 'couldn't understand who the buyers for such things were – why would you *buy* debt?' (8).

However, the novel's more profound concerns regard leverage schemes and derivatives trading that relate to the entrenched position of large banks and financial institutions. Financier protagonist John Veals charts the changes at 'Allied Royal Bank', an organization that had slowly

> developed an aggressive investment banking arm which had generated most of its profits over the last two decades. Largely through its business in derivatives (many relating to commodities it had traded for real in empire days) the management had been able to deliver an average of twenty per cent a year to the shareholders [. . .] These insurance policies against a bank failing to meet its debt obligations were always cheap, because the chance of default was so slight; but to insure against a Royal Allied debt failure over the standard five-year period of the insurance, or 'credit default swap', was just a whisper more expensive than it was for any comparable bank (33).

Acknowledging the 'aggressive' development of a 'banking arm' responsible for making most of the bank's money over the past twenty years, the overview offered by Veals is laced with dramatic irony in the apparently unimaginable notion of 'a bank failing to meet its debt obligations'.

Later in the novel, at Veals's dinner party, guest Roger Malpasse becomes drunk and openly criticizes Veals's bank and other institutions that engage in derivatives trading. Citing the swapping of debts and futures as a form of financial malpractice, Malpasse describes derivatives as 'a fraud as old as markets themselves. The only difference is that it's being done on a titanic scale. At the invitation of the politicians. Behind the backs of the regulators and with the dumb connivance of the auditors. And with the fatal misunderstanding of the ratings agencies' (16). In a novel that offers two major threats to civilization – the economic and political extremism – it is the former that is presented as the most urgent challenge. While jihadist Hassan does not execute his plan, financier Veals ends the novel returning to the office on a day off and closing his deal. The unknown risk-status of the debt parcels he trades is presented as core to understanding the international freezing of credit circuits that followed.

Dee's *The Privileges* (2010) offers an American perspective on institutionalized risk practices and increasingly irresponsible trades in the lead up to the crunch.[29] In his review of the novel, Jonathan Franzen calls it a 'case study of America mega-wealth [. . .] a balancing of sympathy and critical distance'.[30] This balance is crucial to the novel's representation of twenty-first-century financial practice and its exploration of the limitations of wealth and privilege. The Moreys – so-called because they always seem to want 'more' of everything – are represented as a family engaged in a perpetual quest for money, status and privilege. More than simply an evolution of the protagonist in *Bonfire of the Vanities* (1987), the Moreys are used to explore the pressures of pre-crunch American family life.

Cynthia and Adam are 'a charmed couple' (33) and become 'privileged' via Adam's job in finance. Indeed, Adam's hedge fund becomes 'so successful people begged him to take them on as investors' and perceive him as 'shamanistic [. . .] people earnestly believed that he was performing a kind of magic' (267). However, as his success grows, Adam begins to take ever greater risks with his financial trades. 'It was rare', the novel notes, 'for him to write anything down; he kept accounts in his head' (218). Adam's version of accounting is eventually revealed to be deeply flawed, involving the 'selling of [. . .] stock, spread out through about thirty small accounts with dummy names [. . .] each account transferred its profits to different offshore banks, all of which are then sent the money, in slow increments, to the Royal National Bank of Anguilla, where oversight policies were business friendly' (158). Eventually, his motivation ceases to be the making of money and mutates into a sustained pursuit of power. He reflects that 'it wasn't just about the money, in any case. More than the money [. . .] It was about exercising that ability to repurpose information those around him were too timid or short-sighted to know what to do with [. . .] that was its engine and its reward' (158). Adam feels 'invincible, like a martyr, like a holy warrior' (227) even while under investigation from financial authorities. The novel examines this sense of dominance and duty to finance in the pre-crunch privileged classes, featuring characters whose lives operate inside the financial sphere at the time of the credit crunch and following their fate as the impact of the crash affects their lives. The Moreys gradually come to represent a wider society and approach to this particular historical moment, a wealthy clan who realize that the goals they have spent decades chasing, and the risks they have taken, amount to little.

Risk-friendly financial cultures, combined with excessive confidence and self-belief in the ability to control the markets are offered by Crunch Lit as a potential cause of the credit crunch. A refusal to learn from mistakes, a predisposition to engage in increasingly riskier trades and practices and an aversion to looking backwards are key traits in characters that carry on gambling even when the odds are stacked against them. Encouraging readers to acknowledge the widespread institutionalization of risk practice in the pre-crunch period, Crunch Lit foregrounds a need to understand the changed conditions and cultures of millennial finance in order to comprehend how and why credit systems froze in 2007–8.

The increasing power of the financial industry and the normalization of credit and risk culture meant that by 2007 the global money markets were being played like a twenty-four hour casino, as 'all across the economically liberal world, the banks treated financial irresponsibility as a valuable commodity, almost as a natural resource, to be lovingly groomed and cultivated'.[31] The great tragedy is that although this is 'one of the things that was crystal clear in hindsight', at the time, 'people just didn't realise'.[32] For a Western society 'lulled by easy money' and readily available credit seemingly advertised everywhere and given to everyone no matter what their financial circumstances, the temptation to question the eventuality of all this spending and funding was never too great to confront.[33] Until they could assess their debt risks, banks simply had no idea if they had enough assets to carry on trading and realized that they had to assume that all owned debts were toxic in some way when, in August 2007, the music – finally – stopped.

9–8–7

Representing events as they unfolded across 2007–8, Crunch Lit offers fictionalized insider-accounts of defining moments during the financial crisis. The 9 August 2007 has been likened to a heart attack, 'a wakeup call for the human race'.[34] Managing Director of Northern Rock Adam Applegarth described it in hindsight as 'the day the world changed'.[35] On this day, French bank BNP Paribas issued a warning that triggered a rise in the cost of credit. The investment bank told investors that they could not move money from two of its funds because it was unable to value the assets in them, owing to a 'complete evaporation of liquidity' in the market. On the same day, the European Central Bank and the US Federal Reserve injected $90 billion into increasingly nervous financial markets. This was followed in September by a rise in the London Interbank Offered Rate (LIBOR) – the rate at which banks lend to each other – to the highest point since December 1998, further stifling lending. These were clear signals that banks were either concerned that they needed to keep hold of their cash or were worried whether the banks they were lending to would pay them back. The 'crunch' itself refers to the final refusal of banks to lend money to each other, as the financial borrowing system suddenly seized on an international scale.

In reaction to these changed conditions, banks started to 'deleverage', cutting their losses and bailing out of all high-risk investments. The previous asset inflation caused by runaway house prices combined with delinquencies (as borrowers missed repayments on debts) led to foreclosures as banks were forced to repossess their capital assets and mortgage-based investments were quickly regarded as toxic assets. Banks also cut lending to individuals and businesses and mortgages became very difficult to attain as foreclosures began on defaulting mortgages. In response to Iceland's decision to freeze its national assets, the British government even resorted to using anti-terrorist legislation to prevent any remaining Icelandic money from leaving the UK. This breakdown of credit supplies – the 'Reykavikisation of the world economy'[36] – taught the young twenty-first century 'how fast, and how completely, things can go wrong for a society if its banks go bad'.[37]

Solvency, the ability of the banks to pay back their debts at any given point, was challenging. Many of their asset-backed securities, such as mortgages, could not be turned into cash quickly since house prices had fallen and no one was buying in a saturated market or offering mortgages to buyers. Governments were therefore forced to pump fresh funds into economies to ensure that their banks remained solvent. Quantitative easing mobilized tax payers money to assist the financial world, oiling the wheels of market liquidity in an attempt to get banks lending to each other again. Governments also reduced interest rates to make borrowing cheaper and offered to guarantee banks' borrowing on the money markets. The UK government alone pumped £50 billion into its economy and guaranteed £250 billion of banks borrowing, while a 'special liquidity scheme' saw the Bank of England release an additional £200 billion of funding onto the money markets in an attempt to unfreeze interbank lending. The UK government also rushed through new rules to re-regulate finance, including the suspension of cash bonuses (though bankers could still take shares), government preference shares which paid dividends before the shareholders received their payouts and the introduction of a government representative on the bank's board.

In the UK and United States – the same countries that had previously pushed hardest for deregulation and privatization – financial institutions were eventually saved by state intervention. In an attempt to stabilize its own banks, the British government effectively renationalized not only the beleaguered Northern Rock, but also Bradford and Bingley, while HBOS was forced to merge with Lloyds TSB in October 2008. In the United States, Bear Sterns was bailed out by the national government in September 2008, the same month in which Fannie and Freddie were effectively nationalized. AIG, a giant of the insurance world, was also bailed out since the company was heavily implicated in CDS and insurance for defaulted debts. But in 2008, the widespread belief that such financial organizations were 'TBTF' ('too big to fail') was proved incorrect. On 15 September 2008, Lehman Brothers filed for Chapter 11 bankruptcy protection, following a significant loss of clients, dramatic drops in stock value, and the devaluation of its assets by credit-rating agencies. It was the largest bankruptcy filing in American history and, the following day, British bank Barclays announced its agreement to purchase, subject to regulatory approval, Lehman's North American investment-banking and trading divisions along with its New York headquarters building. In allowing Lehman Brothers to fail in September 2008, the US government made an example of the business as a model for unsafe financial practice in the lead up to the crunch. A 2009 Bank of England study showed that state bailouts of the financial system has cost £14 trillion in the United States, Britain and the Euro-zone, nearly a quarter of all global output.[38] The Bank of

England estimated that altogether UK banks would have to write off US$2.8 trillion by the end of the crisis – nearly double its annual GDP.[39] The US bailout alone is estimated to stand at $7.76 trillion. To put this number in context, it is an amount 'bigger than the cost of the Marshall Plan, the Louisiana Purchase, the 1980s savings and loans crisis, the Korean war, the New Deal, the invasions of Iraq, the Vietnam war and the total cost of NASA including the moon landings, all added together'.[40]

Crunch Lit fictions represent these chaotic events using fictionalized, insider protagonists operating at the heart of the financial industries as witnesses to the weeks during which international circuits of credit froze. Tackling not just the events of the credit crunch but its aftermath for the traders and bank workers involved, *This Bleeding City* (2010) offers an intensely voyeuristic perspective on this period of panic.[41] Written by Alex Preston, a financier in the position of 'Global Head of Trading in The Carlyle Group's Leveraged Finance Division' at the time of the crunch, the novel considers the role of the individual in the crisis and the failure of the sector to recognize the alarm bells that sounded beforehand. One of the first fictionalized accounts of the financial crisis to be written by an 'insider', *This Bleeding City* exposes the reality of banking life for young graduates like Preston who ultimately found that they could not achieve happiness through their manipulation of the markets.

Protagonist Charlie is initially delighted to be recruited into the sector, but gradually becomes conditioned into the dubious practices of this new era of finance and begins to take ever greater risks in his trades. Deaf to the warnings of analysts and fuelled by the confidence and self-belief of his profession, Charlie recalls enduring 'long meetings as economists mouthed dismal words about the coming depreciation of the dollar and the end of the bull market and how cycles must turn and I let their words bleed down the walls' (81). Ignoring the alarm bells they sound, Charlie reasons that it 'was much easier to go along with market sentiment and embrace optimism, much easier to believe that the great powers of the Fed and the Bank of England and the giant investment banks were steering us unwaveringly towards a future of comfortable luxury' (113). Ultimately, Charlie and his fellow financiers do not just embrace the optimism of the period but become blinded by it, choosing to place the unwavering confidence of the sector above the caution and historical cycles outlined by his economist advisors. At the end of his narrative, Preston's fictional antihero Charlie reflects that 'Something like this, it makes you realise [. . .] makes you realise so much' (203). 'Scared' that the financial 'world is about to end [. . .] And no one is listening' (134), Charlie realizes that 'the panic was everywhere', and notes billboards that read 'Market Carnage' and 'City Bloodbath' (187).

Drawing on real-life events to mobilize dramatic irony and highlight the impact of financialization on employment, Crunch Lit charts the unfolding events of 2007–8 through individual experiences of loss and trauma. *Other People's Money* reflects on 'the day that capitalism almost went down in September 2008' (245), while Elton's *Meltdown* reports that 'everything was happening suddenly in the second half of 2008. Banks were folding. Governments collapsing' (320). 'Almost overnight' the novel's 'once-mighty Royal Lancashire Bank' is transformed 'from gilt-edged venerable financial fortress to tottering basket case' in a chain of events that 'had shocked the nation' (358). By the Autumn of 2008, *Meltdown* recalls that the financial crisis

> which had engulfed the world so brutally and unexpectedly was deepening by the day and nobody could remember a time when share prices and lending rates had been the number-one story on the morning news for so long. The shocking collapse of a couple of major investment banks had shaken everyone. When well-known firms suddenly fold and you see guys very similar to yourself wandering out into Canary Wharf holding boxes with their staplers, family photos and the remains of last years' Christmas hampers in them, you know that an unfamiliarly chill wind has begun to blow. (304)

These redundancies in the financial sector became a shorthand media symbol for the effects of the credit crunch. Widely circulated images of workers at Lehman Brothers and Bear Sterns in London and New York leaving their offices brandishing cardboard boxes stuffed with personal items became central to criticisms of risk practices that contributed to the crunch.

Marking the end of an explosive growth period in which the normal rules of finance and exchange were not only suspended but side-lined, in favour of risk and speculation, by 2007 cheap credit and readily available finance had turned the economic systemic into a fantasy world of transactions without consequence. Involving readers in the drama of this time as experienced through the eyes of fictional individuals located in *medias res*, Crunch Lit emphasizes the trauma, shock and pace of events during 2007–8. As a form of info-fiction, these novels create empathy with and for the people at the heart of financialized systems, mobilizing now infamous media images and incorporating them into character comments and experiences. Imposing an understandable and relatable narrative and chronology on allegedly abstract and chaotic events, Crunch Lit repositions the story of the credit crunch from one 'too opaque for the averagely well-educated reader to understand' to a coherent chronology of events whose causes, events and impacts are as much social, as they are political and economic.

'Why did no one see it coming?'

During a visit to the London School of Economics in December 2008, the Queen of England asked leading economists, 'why did no one see it [the crunch] coming?'[42] The question that the Queen, novelists, historians and politicians keep asking has a very simple answer: some people did. History tells us that 'financial crises are as old as capitalism'.[43] Everyone who has a credit card knows how debt works: if you are unable to pay the interest on the credit, you fall into arrears and the relationship between creditor and debtor breaks down. Credit is a necessary cog in wider economic systems, a 'fundamental fact of how capital works',[44] but once a system becomes reliant on credit for growth, or the foundations of that credit become compromised, the whole system quickly becomes unstable. As Morris reflects, because 'credit is the air financial markets breathe [. . .] when the air is poisoned, there's no place in hide'.[45] During 2007–8, this was the situation in which many individuals, financial organizations and even countries, found themselves.

The 2007–8 credit crunch might have been the 'first major financial crisis of the global era',[46] but it was by no means the unique or unexpected occurrence proposed by those who failed to see it coming. As economist Bob Swarup reflects, 'the biggest surprise is precisely why this crisis was such a surprise to everyone'.[47] Although Federal Reserve Chairman Alan Greenspan claimed that the crunch was a once in a century event, history proves that events such as the credit crunch actually happen all the time, and frequently more than just once in a century. The history of finance is 'a rollercoaster ride of ups and downs, bubbles and busts, manias and panics, shocks and crashes'[48] that is profoundly cyclical. In *Manias, Panics and Crashes: A History of Financial Crises* (1978), Charles P. Kindleberge suggests a pattern of manias throughout history that constitute an actual phenomenon whereby an opportunity arises, then is exploited as investors over-commit, until it collapses or, as Lanchester puts it: 'it works, until it stops working'.[49] While the credit crunch of 2007–8 was undoubtedly a significant twenty-first-century event, it was also the latest in a long line of crashes and busts that regularly punctuate the historical record. From Tulip Mania in seventeenth-century Holland (where at its peak point one bulb could cost twenty times an average worker's wage) and the 1720 South Sea Bubble (during which London investors sunk money into a company that promised huge returns based on the slave trade in South America until the bubble burst, there was a scramble to sell and most investors lost everything), to the Wall Street Crash of 1929, financial history is marked by regular meltdowns that are often caused by over-speculation.[50]

Between the deregulation of financial systems in the 1980s and the credit crunch of 2007–8, there were nine major financial collapses across the world and numerous large-scale stock exchange collapses.[51] Over the two decades leading up to the crunch, these crashes had collectively increased in scale. On 19 October 1987 (also known as 'Black Monday') the Dow Jones Index fell by 23 per cent, losing nearly a trillion dollars in stocks. Black Monday should have functioned as a warning against the increasingly aggressive selling and technology issues in the automated transaction systems that came to dominate the markets in the late twentieth century. However, the US Federal Reserve prevented reflection by injecting liquidity back into the system via the purchase of government bonds, thereby limiting the lessons of this crisis.[52] From the housing slumps of the 1990s, the South East Asia Crises in 1997 and the Hedge fund Long Term Capital Management issues of 1998 – the history of the twenty years preceding the 2007–8 credit crunch proved that financial crashes were extremely common.

The events of 2007–9, however, marked a new 'super-crisis'. UK growth was unbroken for 16 years leading up to the crunch. The global derivatives market had grown too large, and the Bank for International Settlements in Basel (an organization that produces rules for banks) issued warnings from 2005 onwards that current levels of growth were not sustainable. In 2000, George Soros, a leading US investor, warned about the risk of derivatives and joined a chorus of discontent about technology uncoupling the market from actuals and speeding up transactions to the point where they could not be traced or accounted for. In April 2007, one of the giants of the new subprime market, New Century Financial, filed for bankruptcy and cut half of its workforce, while in July, Federal Reserve chairman Ben Bernanke warned that a US subprime crisis could cost up to $100 billion. These developments signalled a clear alarm that not all was well within this once buoyant, new sector of 'credit culture'.

Although Alan Greenspan famously claimed that the crunch was an 'unforeseen event' – and that 'the unforeseen event is the unforeseen event, by definition'[53] – suggestions can be found in the financial press and, as this study suggests, in financial fiction that the pre-crunch cultures of finance sustaining economic growth were deeply flawed. Along with the novelists in Chapter 1, many leading financial journalists regularly expressed reservations about these new systems of credit and leverage in the months and weeks leading up to the crunch.[54] However, since 'in the business world, the rear-view mirror is always clearer than the windshield', their calls for caution are only now being heeded and reread.[55]

In the wake of the collapse of Northern Rock, Crunch Lit author John Lanchester offered some early warnings about what might happen next: 'If our laws are not extended to control the new kinds of super-powerful, super-complex and potentially super-risky investment vehicles, they will one day cause a financial disaster of global systematic proportions . . . you would be forgiven for thinking that some sort of crash is imminent.'[56] Lancaster's predictions were based on the view that the previous period of sustained growth 'wasn't fair and it wasn't sustainable'.[57] As Lanchester reflects,

'I can't claim to have been on to this story early, but once I had started working on it in the later summer of 2007, it was immediately clear to me that the global banking system was facing a structural crisis. If it was clear to me, why wasn't it as obvious to the people in charge of the economy and to the people whose job it is to advise them?'[58] This cocktail of contributing factors produced the circumstances that generated the biggest economic disaster of the twenty-first century.

Over the space of a few months in 2008, 'credit crunch' became a household phrase, and 'people were hungry for knowledge'.[59] Publishers initially responded to this demand by reissuing economic studies of previous economic crises. In 2009, Penguin reprinted Galbraith's seminal text *The Great Crash 1929* (1954). In his study, Galbraith argues that:

> There is merit in keeping alive the memory of [the 1929 Wall Street Crash]. For it is neither public regulation nor the improving moral tone of corporate promoters, brokers, bankers, and mutual fund managers which prevents these recurrent outbreaks. It is the recollection of how, on some past occasion, illusion replaced reality and people got rimmed.[60]

These warnings against the dangers of unbridled capitalism found new relevance with twenty-first-century readers who were eager not only to identify reasons behind the 2007–8 crash, but also to learn from historic lessons on coping with economic fallout. As Callinicos reflects, from 2008 onwards 'the dominant ideology in the era since the end of the Cold War, and crucially the belief – most famously articulated by Francis Fukuyama when he announced the End of History in 1989 – that liberal capitalism offered the only basis on which humankind could hope to enjoy peace, prosperity and freedom' was now under review.[61] Sales of *Das Kapital* (1867) also rose following 2008, as Marx became fashionable with a generation keen to explore alternatives to capitalist endeavour.[62] Interest in books on Keyensian economics equally grew, and readers turned to Keynes's advice on helping economies recover from crashes.

The potential of fiction to tell new narratives on the credit crunch, to offer representations on its causes, events and aftermath, has been cited by many Crunch Lit authors as a key motivating factor in their decision to take on the topic in fictional form. John Lanchester reflects that when he began writing *Capital* in

> early 2006, I was sure that a crash was coming: I wasn't sure what form it would take, and I certainly didn't know it was going to be as structural, systematic and globally all-encompassing as it has turned out to be. But I wanted the book to begin with the reader knowing something that the characters don't: that this moment in 2007 to 2008 is the peak of a bubble. It's a curious thing to say about a book set in such a recent past, but Capital was intended to be a historical novel. The main thing that has changed between then and now – while everything looks the same – is the inside of people's heads, and that is the most profound kind of change there is.[63]

Highlighting the dramatic irony that defines this genre, Lanchester explains how reader knowledge of the credit crunch as an inescapable experience of the new millennium can function as an advantage for the narrative of his novel. Intervening in a historical event as it happened, *Capital* and other Crunch Lit texts written across this period, examine the psychological, social, political and economic reframing that occurred in response to the crunch as a means of making sense and drawing agency from these complex and highly contested events.

Other People's Money ends with a consideration of the variety of competing narratives that seek to represent historical events. Concluding that 'there are beginnings, and there are ends, and there are also many ways of telling the same story' (249), this fictional account of the decline of old banking in the face of twenty-first-century financialized practices and associated corruptions offers the 2007–8 credit crunch as a moment in social, political and historical history that will be contested, represented and re-presented for decades to come. As De Goede asserts, a 'complex reality like a financial crisis has no unequivocal and immediate meaning': its meaning cannot be ascertained through any single 'objective' economic analysis. Instead, our understanding of such events depends upon 'political and cultural processes of articulation, mediation and sedimentation'.[64]

Examining individual narratives behind the international economic meltdown, Crunch Lit not only offers a plurality of representations of the financial crisis, but also asserts the role of literature in offering a significant intervention in mediating popular understandings of complicated economic events. Crunch Lit interrogates a wide variety of characters in every sector of twenty-first-century society – from bankers to homeowners, shopaholics to politicians – as complicit in the causes of the credit crunch, variously implicated in its events and disproportionately subject to its aftermath.

As Crosthwaite, Knight and Marsh reflect, the events of 2007–8 'were experienced as a crisis because they were confusing and chaotic. The causes and implications of the event appeared to be too complex, too impenetrable and too surprising to be understood.'[65] Mediating this disarray and the paralysis of the global banking system as it ground to a halt during 2007–8, Crunch Lit employs fictional representations of real-life events to emphasize both the trauma of market dislocation and the impact of a breakdown in global economics on the life of ordinary individuals. Mobilizing the crunch as a rich source of narrative drama and dramatic irony, these fictions chart a slow recognition of the intricately interconnected condition of global financial systems to expose the absence of an established emergency procedure for this kind of situation. Offering literary representations of the credit-hungry pre-crunch world of risk, securitization and over-leverage, the dramatic days during which credit systems froze and the aftermath of job losses that followed, Crunch Lit offers important representations of change – social, political, economic, personal, individual, collective, local and global – as a way of encouraging new understandings of and critical engagements with, ways forward from the 2007–8 financial downturn.

3

'Capital' cities

Space is the expression of society.
MANUEL CASTELLS[1]

The meaning of a 'capital' city carries new associations and implications in the post-millennial context of a Western world in economic downturn. Castells reflects that 'futurologists' have long predicted 'the demise of the city, or at least cities as we have known them until now'.[2] This demise has been offered as a product of the rapid expansion of world financial markets over the past hundred years. These new conditions have led many sociologists and cultural critics to ask 'what happens to place in a global economy?'[3] In response, globalization scholars have proposed that the city is destined to play a decreasing role in contemporary interactions with finance and globally networked capitalism. Central to this de-territorialization lies an 'essential sameness'[4] at the heart of globalized visions of the contemporary city. As Saskia Sassen argues, the 'dispersal capacities emerging with globalization and telecommunication [. . .] led many observers to assert that cities would become obsolete in the new economic context'. In this 'borderless world',[5] conventional geographic boundaries are less relevant and, as a result, the city loses its defining influence as a significant site.

Yet, in the twenty-first century, changes in the geography of the global economy have actually led to the rise of cities as zones of organizing influence. While the ongoing internationalization of economic relations may well mean less autonomy for a nation's cities, intense competition between cities remains and each enjoys unique social and political conditions and negotiates the growing interpenetration of local and global economies differently. Developments in the global economy are also presented in terms of territory, and place remains 'central to the multiple circuits through which economic globalization is constituted'.[6] In practice, nations continue to be defined by cities of varying powers and geo-economic strength is still an important factor in influencing voting decisions and asset distribution. Investment is the lifeblood of a city, but proximity also creates capacity for growth and demand. Concentrating similar industries in a central space creates a capital pull on talent, drawing people who want to work in similar sectors into a single space. This magnetism also creates choice, since the wide availability of similar services in a city conspires to drive up standards and competition, and can increase productivity. Functioning as an effective gateway to industries that service the financial sector, city space now functions as a flywheel of national economies and a significant site of reinvention and sustainability.

Porter proposes that the space of the city also remains essential to business success in the twenty-first century as a result of its continued role as the supplier of resources and its contribution to global competitiveness.[7] As a site of agglomeration for some of the central functions of networked economies, the city is characteristic of the internal differentiation, boundary crossings and border tensions that define globalization itself. Porter's argument reinforces an approach to the twenty-first-century city that recognizes a continued world order between global cities – one measurable by difference, as well as by similarities. During the twenty-first century, 'against all predictions, a significant number of major cities [. . .] saw their concentration of economic power rise'.[8]

Crunch Lit is concerned with representing the impact of financialization on business, domestic and virtual spaces in contemporary cities during and after the 2007–8 credit crunch. Critically reviewing the colonizing of the home and imagined 'alternatives' to the contemporary metropolis, new fictional representations of the financial crisis interrogate the changing relationship between the financial sector and the city in the twenty-first century. In epistemologies of the capital that trace the impact of financialization on place and space, culture and community, Crunch Lit writings highlight the critical possibilities of contemporary genre fiction to interrogate the influence of the financial sector on twenty-first-century societies. Exploring greater connectivity between cities and also the breakdown of social and political cohesion within them, these fictions consider the divergent states of visibility and marginality created by flows of finance across capital space. Offering representations of two-world capitals, jointly populated by those who run and those who service city space, Crunch Lit examines the architecture, residence and virtuality created in the contemporary city as a response to the forces of financialization. Charting the social, political and economic history of cityscapes, these fictions suggest that capitals remain distinct sites of social, political and economic power in the twenty-first century.

Financial architecture

In Crunch Lit, financial architecture functions as a metaphor for the influence of financialization over contemporary city space. Representing physical changes to the skylines of capitals as a metaphor for the increasing effect of finance on city life, Crunch Lit is concerned with re-presenting the metropolis as a contested site in the new millennium, one divided between competing layers of social, economic and political interests. Mobilizing financial buildings and architecture as the physical expression of an ideological and cultural colonization of the city by the financial sector, these novels foreground financial topographies as extensions of the increasing role of finance in London life during the years preceding 2007. The financial architecture of the city represents the power and history of both its past and present. In contrast to American financial fictions of the 1980s and 1990s that focus predominantly on Wall Street and New York, fictions addressing the 2007–8 financial crash examine experiences in and impacts of the crisis in the UK.

Traditionally a romantic symbol embodying the rise of New York in the twentieth century, the growth of the skyscraper on the London skyline offers a revealing commentary on the state of both the city and the nation in Crunch Lit fictions. A composite construction uniting the skills of financial, architectural and legal services, in this mixed-use offering of office, recreational and residential possibilities, the skyscraper is presented as the ultimate symbol of collaborative networking in the contemporary city. Nearly half of the world's skyscrapers have been built since the year 2000 and, in London as in many other cities, these buildings have come to represent the transcendence and ambition of the financial sector. As representations of economic optimism, the number of skyscrapers being built has historically risen prior to an economic crisis.[9] Reflecting on the rush to build ever-taller buildings in London, Lancaster argues that

> these buildings [...] are almost their own brand. Lorenzo Piano's Shard. Or what's known as the Gherkin, the Erotic Gherkin, a Norman Foster building which does look indeed like half a gherkin, half a penis, 40 stories high. It's from the idea of Frank Gehry's Guggenheim-Bilbao, which I think is a wonderful building. But I think it started a trend for the idea that the building is a sort of picture, an icon. It's not much to do with the place; it's not much to do with anything. It sums itself up and is its own logo, in a way. And we're seeing an awful lot of those, so I think that's going to be this moment – the idea of a slightly self-contained, self-reflexive, anti-humanistic building because they look worse when you put people in and around them. They're better without the humans. And when you interact with them you feel like one of those tiny model figures in an architect's diagram, and you're meant to. So there is an anti-humanistic aspect to those guys' buildings, and I think that's the kind of thing we'll look back on and say: oh well, that sums up that period.[10]

As an architectural statement of prosperity visualized on the skyline, the skyscraper represents both the literal and metaphor height of the financial sector. Products of an economy of space and also symbols of economic power, skyscrapers help to define the identity and status of London as a global economic player. The semiotic capacity of the constructions 'sum up' the post-millennial period of the credit crunch, speaking not only of a physical dominance over the skyline but also of the global reach of financialization at the start of the twenty-first century.

In Elton's *Meltdown* (2009), London's pre-crunch financial districts are represented as palaces of money, beautiful, awe-inspiring structures that function as symbols of the contemporary world.

Merchant banker Jimmy reflects that London's bank 'buildings were just so BEAUTIFUL. All black glass, mirrors and steel. Just like cars. Cathedrals to money. To success. To growth and expansion. This was the sort of thing that once upon a time they had only had in America. Now London had its own Manhattan and we were finally taking on the Yanks at their own game' (313).[11] Likening financial buildings to sites of worship, *Meltdown* critiques pre-crunch cultures of consumption and credit that came to dominate not only city life, but also global approaches to culture and value prior to 2007–8. The suggestion that London is not only competing with but also now rivalling New York as a global economic centre, is proposed as a sign of its vitality, but also functions to assert the prevailing identity of the city as a distinct player in the twenty-first-century financial world.

The development of ever-taller architectural tributes to financial power forms the central concern of the representations of city space in *Capital* (2012).[12] Representing the adventurous buildings and office-scapes that have changed the London skyline, the novel interrogates the power of the financial zone to penetrate surrounding areas and spread its architecture and influences. Often referred to as London's 'second city', Canary Wharf constitutes a relatively new clustering of financial services zones into a dedicated space renowned for the provision of world-leading financial services.[13] Describing the skyline of Canary Wharf, the narrative notes 'the early-setting December sun [. . .] making the towers, normally so solid-looking and un-ethereal, seem momentarily aflame with clean gold light' (18). Illuminated against the London sunset, the towers of Canary Wharf suggest the power of the looming financial organizations they house, presenting the skyscraper as a symbol of the strength and domination of the financial industry over London in the twenty-first century.

Faulks's *A Week in December* (2009) is equally concerned with city architecture as an expression of the power relationship between the financial sector and capital space.[14] Offering a representation of the increasingly financialized spaces of London – including the Westfield shopping centre, rumoured at the time of opening to be the UK's biggest new 'supermall' – the narrative represents the reality that this new consumer centre 'was not a retail park with trees and benches, but was a compression of trade in a city centre, in which migrant labour was paid by foreign capital to squeeze out layers of profit from any Londoner with credit' (1). Drawing connections between 'building a giant monument to greed and possession – Europe's biggest shopping centre, slap in the middle of the shop-lined streets of the world's most well-provided consumer city' (97), the novel critiques consumer culture as an extension of financial cultures of credit, and the impact of these cultures on the physical landscape of the city.

Opening with a panorama of the capital, *A Week in December* takes in an architectural tour of new buildings created by the financial industries in contemporary London. From the 'Emirates Stadium' (1) housing players from all over the world 'one Czech, one Spanish' (1), to the 'grey high-rises marked with satellite dishes, like ears cupped to the outside world in the hope of gossip or escape' (1) of Hackney and Bow, to the tiny, cramped dwelling of barrister Gabriel Northwood living in a Chelsea postcode but without a Chelsea income, Faulks presents the capital as a contested site. Within this space, 'The City' of London is isolated, immune from the inspection of society, and only connected to the rest of London by a single (notoriously wobbly) Millennium bridge over the Bank side of the River Thames.

With specialisms including private equity, carbon markets and maritime finance, London remains Europe's leading financial capital. The financial district of London, 'The City' is set apart in both name and geography, centred on a single district around St Paul's Cathedral. However, as John Lanchester asserts, 'The City' is, 'in terms of its basic functioning, a far-off country of which we know little.'[15] Crunch Lit seeks to make visible 'The City', shining a narrative spotlight on its architecture, occupants and practices to challenge the status and representability of financialization in the twenty-first century.

In Faulks's *A Week in December*, the financial district of 'The City' is primarily represented through the eyes of protagonist financier John Veals. His perspective on 'The City' is firmly financial, one defined by office buildings, historic banking sites and modern financial architecture. Veals's office 'is located in a 'tall, blank building in Old Pye Street – the only such block in an otherwise quiet, residential road in Victoria – with a view over to the miniature Byzantine domes and piebald brickwork of Westminster Cathedral' (9). As a symbol of faith, strength and a site of ideology, the cathedral occupies a significant position in this financial quarter, offering a reminder of the worship of credit and consumption that justifies the surrounding financial monuments to power.

Set against the 'cold December darkness' (14), the financial district operates cloaked from the rest of London life. Considering the distance of 'The City' from the rest of London, Veals wonders:

> What false picture of a city did these people have? [. . .] Their London was a virtual one, unknown to residents – Tower and Dungeon, veteran West End musicals and group photographs beneath the slowly turning Eye; but Veals believed it was important for him to be aware of other people, natives and visitors alike, however partial and bizarre their take on life. Since his own reality derived from numbers on a computer terminal, he thought it wise to keep an eye on flesh and blood; there might still be something he could profitably learn from them. (38–9)

Enjoying panoptic views of the city, Veals's position is one of estrangement and alienation from the lived reality of life on London's streets. Contrasting the fleeting unreality of tourist experience – centred on attractions and famous sites, cultural encounters and glimpsed photographs – with his own lived reality of the capital city, Veals observes competing 'users' of the city like a social scientist. Although he recognizes the value in acknowledging alternative experience and realities of London life, Veals's own understanding of the cityscape remains staunchly financial and 'derived from numbers'. Looking down on London, Veals observes 'buildings only, silhouettes on a river, units of economic function' (389). Reducing London to component parts of wider financial operations, Veals's perspective on the city constructs an understanding of 'financial architecture' as relating not only to the physical buildings and sites occupied by the financial sector in the contemporary city, but also to the systems and networks that constitute the frameworks that facilitate and further the domination of city space by the contemporary financial sector.

Town houses

Over centuries, an ever-growing sprawl of domestic dwellings and residential zones developed around the urban core of London.

These domestic spaces were originally populated by working-class residents whose trades serviced the city. However, from the mid-twentieth-century onwards, these sites were taken over by the growing middle classes, keen to escape city life. In the late twentieth and early twenty-first centuries, the occupants of these spaces altered again, as growing house prices pushed out many middle-class inhabitants, and bankers, footballers and investors took over houses that had recently risen dramatically in value. Appealing to the aspiration of financiers and economic immigrants to the city, the residential zones of London offer a tantalizing lifestyle choice for those wishing to live beside, but not in, the contemporary city. Shifts in the composition of communities caused by wealthier residents and rising property values not only led to the economic eviction of key workers, but to the transformation of residential spaces into newly financialized sites of social and political meaning. Offering representations of specific cities and staging experiences of life in different cities, the penetrating effects of financialization are indicated, interrelated and illuminated by Crunch Lit. In these urban imaginaries, representations of the impact of financialization on the city articulate and give shape to resulting tensions and draw attention to social problems as a response to inequality.

Faulks began writing *A Week in December* with a vision that it would be a 'modern Dickensian novel' featuring characters from different areas of London.[16] The guests at the dinner party that opens the novel are spread across London, yet they each experience the capital very differently. Uniting a range of contemporary city inhabitants – from Farooq and Nasim al-Rashid 'a chutney magnate and a large private donor to party funds' (5); Tadeusz 'Spike' Borowski, a Polish footballer ('But did he speak English? Would he behave? What did footballers like to do after dinner? "Dogging", was it, or "spit-roasting"? She wasn't quite sure what either of those things was,' [6]); R. Tranter, a book critic living in a 'bohemian' part of town; and barrister Gabriel Northwood, struggling to meet the financial demands of living in the city – the novel's opening 'big dinner' (4) offers a snapshot of pre-crunch London life. Mobilizing the domestic home as a political setting, Faulks employs the social occasion of the dinner party to examine a cross-section of London residents in the early twenty-first century.

The growing impact of financial immigrants in London is revealed by literary critic R. Tranter in his daily trip to the newsagent. He reflects that this journey is now reminiscent of:

> a walk through the history of the late twentieth century; here was the fallout of wars hot and cold; here was the collateral displacement of free markets and porous frontiers [...] His route to the high street took him through three near-identical roads of modest houses built for another London, a place long gone. He sometimes tried to picture those first tenants: manual workers who commuted to the smog-producing factories of Bermondsey or Poplar, then returned at night to their modest white enclave; but it was hard to imagine them now in these car-lined streets: the homogeneity was not in nature any more. (17–18)

Highlighting the connections between economic developments and shifts in population, R. Tranter's survey of everyday London life exposes a city in transition. Bearing the architecture of a time 'now long gone', his walk foregrounds the diversity and heterogeneity characterizing the contemporary city. Considering a shift away from earlier working-class communities and towards a more diffuse, fragmented experience of city living, the 'free markets and porous frontiers' of global capitalism are made visible on these residential streets that lack a sense of cohesion and community.

Bearing many parallels with Victorian London as a place where characters go to 'make their fortunes', *A Week in December* interrogates the state of 'the London dream' in the new millennium.[17] Throughout this week in December, readers are forced to confront a range of Londoners who do not enjoy home ownership or a stable sense of 'residence'. Concerned with the 'invisibles' of the city, those who work in and service city space but who do not occupy prominent roles in its landscape, the novel explores the changing ethnic, cultural and power relations of contemporary London. Schizophrenic Alan is 'released into a "care in the community" scheme when his asylum, "one of the original Victorian ones" is "closed by the government, bought by a property developer" and turned into "luxury apartments with state-of-the-art gym and sauna facilities"'(43). Examining change-of-use and the increasing domination of developers over London buildings, the novel offers a scathing critique of the impact of financial decisions on the most vulnerable members of city society.

Lanchester's *Capital* offers an equally damning perspective on the changing function of London's domestic spaces in the lead up to the credit crunch. The novel interrogates a pre-crunch obsession with property wealth and, like Faulks's *A Week in December*, features a spectrum of city inhabitants. Concerned with a lack of community and communication among London's new financial immigrants, the novel mobilizes a single residential road. Pepys Road is remarkable only for being 'an ordinary looking street in South London' (10), but one in which, as a result of the pre-crunch credit boom 'houses were now like people, and rich people at that, imperious, with needs of their own that they were not shy about having serviced' (6). Named after the great diarist Samuel Pepys who, having retired, moved out of London to a small village Clapham, in what was then the countryside, Pepys Road is offered as a 'kind of microcosm of London in the same way that the city is a microcosm of the wider world'.[18] Changes in the 'value' of houses on Pepys Road from working-class homes to multi-million-pound assets and symbols of status and wealth is the central concern of the novel.

The residents of the newly gentrified Pepys Road are a heterogeneous group, drawn to London to make money, or newly wealthy as a result of being long-time residents. The houses had originally been 'built for a specific market: the idea was that they would appeal to lower-middle class families willing to live in an unfashionable part of town in return for the chance to own a terraced house – a house large enough to have room for servants' (2). However, as the years went on 'Pepys Road began to climb the economic ladder [. . .] it tracked the changes in Britain's economic prosperity, emerging from the dowdy chrysalis of the late 1970s and transforming into a vulgar, loud butterfly of the Thatcher decades and the long boom that followed them' (2–3). As 'house prices slowly rose, the working classes, indigenous and immigrant, cashed in and moved out, usually looking to find bigger houses in quieter places, with neighbours more like themselves' (3). As the opening of the novel asserts, for 'the first time in history, the people who lived in the street were, by global and maybe local standards, rich. The thing which made them rich was the very fact that they lived on Pepys Road. They were rich simply because of that, because all of the houses in Pepys Road, as if by magic, were now worth millions of pounds' (4–5).

In an examination of the 'winner and losers' approach to society that Lanchester argues has been an effective 'slogan for British life in the last three decades',[19] *Capital* examines how new, wealthy inhabitants colonize a single London road. Adversely reshaping the demographics of the street, these newcomers enact a social, political and spatial reshaping of what was once a historically cohesive residential zone. From banker Roger Younts and his shopaholic wife, to the Muslim corner-shop keepers the Kamals, wealthy footballer Patrick Kamo, and Petunia Howe, 'the oldest person living in Pepys Road' whose 'grandfather had bought the house "off plan" before it had even been built' (11), the novel offers case studies of characters whose lives are adversely altered by rising house prices and the transformation of domestic residences into financialized assets.

By 2007, 'having a house in Pepys Road was like being in a casino in which you were guaranteed to be a winner [. . .] Britain had become a country of winners and losers, and all the people in the street, just by living there, had won' (7). Lanchester reflects that by the time of the credit crunch, London houses had become an

> ever more critical capital asset, there is a constant va-et-vient of renovation, a non-stop turmoil of attics being done, basements being dug out, skips being filled, scaffolding put up and everything knockable being knocked through. In a street two hundred metres long, there is at the moment one skip, three sets of scaffolding, two basement conversions, a loft conversion and two full renovations. Most of this activity is generated by the City people.[20]

For a society in which a house is 'the biggest and most expensive and most significant thing' (576) you can own, gentrification becomes a hegemonic process, as ever-wealthier residents buy up the houses in Pepys Road, adapting and modifying the buildings to meet their needs. The novel notes a new 'fashion [. . .] for people to install basements' (3–4), literally digging into city space. This process is described as a profoundly unnatural and damaging enterprise: 'the earth was spreading, vomiting, rejecting its own excavation, and far too much of it seemed to come out of that ground, as if it were fundamentally unnatural to reach down into the earth to take up more space, and the digging could go on forever' (7). Physically rejecting attempts to occupy more space, this process of digging down into the earth is presented as a metaphorical extension of the unending quest for accumulation and control that is characteristic of newly gentrified residential zones.

Critiquing a period in which house prices became central to the culture of liberal economies, Lanchester examines the financialization of domestic real estate through the haunting 'We Want What You Have' campaign. The campaign begins in the form of cards sent to the residents of Pepys Road, each featuring a picture of the front door corresponding to the recipient. The cards centre on the home as a site of value and a source of envy for those who cannot afford what the residents 'have'. As a sign of how significant the value of residential homes had become before the credit crunch, when Arabella Yount first notices the card, she dismisses it 'as some semi-criminal estate agent' that had finally confessed to a wish to sell her home for her' (46). In fact, 'We Want What You Have' is a profoundly anti-capital campaign, an expression of local resentment at rich residents displacing local inhabitants.

As the novel develops, the campaign escalates with 'incidents of graffiti in the street; "cunt" and "wanker" were spray painted on the side walls of the houses at number 42 and 51' (372), 'dog excrement in jiffy bags – reeking, horrible jiffy bags' arrive at houses and 'one night in late June somebody or somebodies [ran] a set of keys down the cars parked on the even-numbered side of the street – every car, all along the street' (372). Mutating into a blog and an interactive website – on which, when 'you clicked on the numbers you were taken to a photo of the house – sometimes the front door, sometimes a detail from the door such as a close-up of the number, or of the letter box, or the steps, or the doorbell' – 'We Want What You Have' repeatedly features photographs of Pepys Road front doors. These are gradually 'defaced by digital graffiti. Somebody had written swear words across the pictures; not all the pictures, just some of them; about one in three. The swear words focussed on very simple, very direct abuse: "Rich cunts", "Wankers", "Arsehole", "Tory scum", "Kill the rich" and so on' (352). At this point, Arabella and the other residents of Pepys Road realize that they are subject to a hate campaign.

This sustained assault is based on envy, but as Roger Yount notes, it is not envy 'in the reassuring, warming way in which he quote "liked being envied" but instead "like someone keeping an eye on you and secretly wishing you ill"' (279). Eventually revealed to be the brainchild of Parker, a jealous assistant to long-time resident Petunia's YBA (Young British Artist) grandson Smiffy, 'We Want What You Have' is an expression of social anger against the new power and wealth represented by Pepys Road. When finally accosted, Parker's defence against his actions – 'who do they think they are, you know? Do they think they're, you know, the kings of the world or something?' (570) – addresses wider tensions within newly gentrified residential areas of London, as those who 'want what they have' engage in expressions of resentment in response to wider issues of displacement and social invisibility caused by the financialization of city space.

Constructing a city at a 'peak moment of obliviousness',[21] the novel centres on the varied lives of 'fictional but precisely observed Londoners'[22] to offer count-points to the experience of the city's richer habitants through the challenge faced by poorer, immigrant inhabitants.[23] Contrasts between the narratives of those who live on Pepys Road and those who work there – such as traffic warden Quentina, nanny Matya and builder Zbigniew – draw attention to the continued status of London as an aspirational place. As Zimbabwean traffic warden Quentina wryly notes, you only notice parking issues in a country where life is good. While characters enjoy alternative communities in their workplaces, religions or cultural groups, significantly, they do not enjoy a community life based around the street in which they live or work.

An absence of non-economic interaction defines the exchanges on Pepys Road. Its inhabitants are 'neighbours' in spatial terms only; in reality, their lives barely brush against one another. This is underlined by the segmented narrative style of the novel that features 107 short chapters, each devoted to single characters whose lives rarely cross with others. Concerned with the 'sad fragility of modern life' in which 'self-contained parallel privacies'[24] exist within the same street, *Capital* depicts characters connected only by random encounters. Lanchester argues that:

> A lot of the time in modern Britain, certainly in urban life, we barely have any contact at all with the people around us. Add to that the divisive impact of the economic downturn and we are heading towards being a society in which the words 'We're all in this together' are precisely the opposite of the truth. My hunch is

that dividedness and fragmentation – which, as you imply, were on my mind when I wrote Capital – are likely to be increasingly pressing as themes: not just the 1 per cent and the rest but the tension between different generations and perhaps also between London and the rest of the country.²⁵

The residents of Pepys Road occupy the same street during the same time, but their experiences are hermeneutically sealed from one another as a result of a culture focused towards isolated urban living. Foregrounding a missing sense of community and the dominance of superficial, product- and appearance-based approaches to detached city living, *Capital* lays the foundations for a wider discussion of the impact of financialization on the environment.

In *Capital*, Lanchester examines how the evolving power of financialization reaches a point at which, at the moment of the credit crunch, everyone seems to know the value of everything, except one another. 'Capital' in architectural form is the one thing that binds his characters together – although they know the value of their neighbours houses, they are less interested in knowing the people living in them. As an expose of what can happen when a society becomes obsessed with acquisition, the growing social polarization between those who reside in Pepys Road and those who service their homes, is offered as a critique on the 'Wimbledonisation of the city',²⁶ in which property acquisition becomes an international game, one dominated by powerful, foreign players.

Examining the fragmentation of local communities caused by escalating pre-crunch house prices, Crunch Lit offers fictional studies of individuals whose lives are increasingly defined by the power of the postcode. These texts represent how and why rising property prices transformed 'homes' into assets that were subject to intense interest and competitive exchange in the pre-crunch period. In residential zones that are not of the city, but embody its values, the displacement of old communities and the impact of new socioeconomic demographics challenge the possibility of achieving a consensus, creating a dislocated and isolating experience for residents. Focusing on the impact of financialization through the pre-crunch housing boom and its effects on the topographical and social landscape of London streets, Crunch Lit represents the alterations to houses, communities and community relations that occur when the established socioeconomic identity of residential city spaces becomes another form of tradable asset.

Virtual cities

As well as examining lived experiences of the impact of financialization on city life during and after the 2007–8 financial crisis, Crunch Lit fictions also represent characters who attempt to find alternatives to the financialized reality of twenty-first-century city life. *A Week in December* features a range of characters who actively seek out virtual realities and opportunities for new models of city living. These virtual cities form important components of a virtual world that offers the flexibility of real-time communication. In a virtual realm, participants can reimagine or recreate city space and construct new communities. Experienced via avatars that create a miniaturization of experience, these immersive multimedia, computer-simulated environments combine elements of the real world and utopian elements of fantasy. Faulks's characters in particular increasingly interact with and within these virtual environments, attempting to escape the reality of London life and immerse themselves further in the environment of augmented reality as the novel develops.

Faulks was inspired to write about the role of alternative worlds after witnessing his own children fully immersed in virtual games. He recalls watching his son swap between viewing south London team Chelsea play football on television, while at the same time texting a friend and playing the virtual game *Football Manager* online. Faulks realized 'it was possible that the movement of his virtual team meant more to him that the performance of his real flesh-and-blood team'.[27] As a result, a 'theme began to emerge of how we are living in a world in which we have become detached from, or separated from, real life'.[28] This encounter informs the approach his novel takes to technological flights from reality, and in *A Week in December* Faulks interrogates 'the way [. . .] London, has become detached from reality' in the twenty-first century.[29]

The dehumanizing effects of the electronic age and the pull of the virtual are explored through a series of subplots that are just as powerful as the central boom-and-bust narrative of the credit crunch itself. Finding freedom in a virtual world, some characters are empowered to explore fuller lives, alternative personalities or identities via augmented multiplayer online games. Using the virtual to explore the politics of the dispossessed – from the radicalized religious reality of Muslim Hassan, to the fantasy gaming world of Jenni the tube driver, and footballer Spike who becomes so immersed in playing fantasy football he wonders 'which meant more to him: his real team or his fantasy?' (215)[30] – interactions with other worlds and altered states enable characters to explore different lifestyle options.

Representing the seductive power of fantasy and escape, Faulks's 'Parallax [...] alternative reality game' (3) bears many similarities to the real-life alternative-reality game *Second Life*, although Faulks's characters talk about non-computer events as happening 'in true life' rather than 'in real life'. Operating in a MUD (multi-user domain), characters inhabit the world of a MMORPGs (massively multiplayer online role-playing games), and move between 'YourPlace', an alternative version of Facebook, and Parallax as a 'parody of a human world' (47). Via these departures from the real, characters make attempts to escape the reality of a financialized contemporary society.

A London tube train driver by day and a Parallax addict by night, Jenni becomes disengaged from the reality of London life. The lack of freedom or access to the outside world created by the monotonous and mechanical routes and shifts of her job are in sharp contrast to Jenni's virtual 'maquette' (196), or avatar, in Parallax, Miranda Star. More confident and sexually aggressive, Miranda lives

> in a far nicer place: on the banks of the Orinoco, where she had built a house. In order to pay for this, Miranda had borrowed 200,000 vajos from a mortgage lender called Points West and had engaged to repay it at a rate of five percent interest over ten years. With Miranda's new job as a beauty therapist this was just about feasible. Vajos were on a fixed exchange rate with sterling in the real world, and Jenni had, cautiously at first, given her credit card details online to the Parallax Foreign Exchange, which was based on the island of Oneiros. (28–9)

Linking the virtual economy with the actual economy, Parallax mimics the concerns of contemporary economics and allows users to feed their virtual accounts with credits on a 'Uranium credit card, the highest rating' (29). Generated from real-life bank accounts, these credits can be used to build houses or buy products in the parallel world. Jenni reflects that the

> economy of Parallax is derived from that of the real world, but with a lesser sense of responsibility. The inventiveness of the traders was such that few people understood the securities they bartered, but the gains to be made were stupendous, while the losses, after a certain level, became either too complicated to compute or too subdivided by onward sale to pin on one person. If they were truly serious, they were absorbed by the Central Bank, and the resulting blip in the overall Parallax economy could be ironed out by raising game subscriptions, taxes and shop prices for the less sophisticated. The financiers' gains were theirs to keep, but their losses were democratically shared. (28–9)

Building a base of in-game resources via virtual assets, Parallax players are also susceptible to in-game crimes, in which their assets can be taken or their homes invaded. While these assets have no demonstrable value outside the confines of the gaming world, as a digital medium of exchange, the crypto-currency of Parallax satisfies a need to establish space and ownership. As a metaphor for a real world in which the gains of bankers are hoarded but the cost of their losses are footed by tax payers, the virtual economy of Parallax is uncomfortably similar to the financial systems underpinning 'TL' or 'True Life' (30). Parallax is used by Faulks to show how migration to virtual space can have economic effects in the actual world. The economy of Parallax might be fake, but it is implicitly connected to the real world via the power of purchase. Jenni finds that she still needs money to make a difference to her life and identity, even in a virtual world. No matter how 'alternative' these 'realities' appear, they operate on the same capitalist principles.

At the end of *A Week in December*, John Veals looks out over the London cityscape and realizes that it contains many of these virtual

> worlds of which he knew nothing [. . .] contained within the darkened streets, where febrile realities competed for attention: YourPlace, Parallax and Husam Nar; True Life, Stargazer and

Dream Team [. . .] What John Veals saw was buildings only, silhouettes on a river, units of economic function. (389)

As Veals's singular vision suggests, there is no escaping the financial, even in a virtual world. From Jenni's avatar in Parallax and Gabriel's dream of his ex-lover Catalina returning, to footballer Spike's fantasy football team and Finn's drug-induced dream-world, *A Week in December* suggests that, in the twenty-first-century city, 'we all live in our different worlds' (304). Through drugs, reality television, virtual markets, consumerism or alternative realities, characters seek to escape the reality of twenty-first-century city life. Proposing that contemporary society has 'lost touch with something' (308), and needs to 'get back to reality' (330), the final message – that 'our idea of physical reality is somehow misleading' (303) – encourages Gabriel to discard his mobile phone and Jenni to leave Parallax. However, their attempts are ultimately futile. The power of financialization proves that it can penetrate even virtual worlds in increasingly subtle and sophisticated ways, and the novel ends with a reassertion of the failure of an alternative, as characters recognize a need to withdraw from the virtual when the effects of the credit crunch force them to prioritize events in the real world.

While the real and virtual cities of Crunch Lit remain 'sites for the concrete operations of the economy'[31] they also 'concentrate diversity'[32] and offer a unique composition of social, political and economic factors that maintain their individual identities, albeit as part of a wider networked system and a broader hierarchy of geographies. Although in the twenty-first century 'complex, global processes connect the fate of communities to each other across the world in new ways',[33] this does not automatically signal the death of the city. Instead, these new conditions generate a range of new issues and tensions centred on identity, risk and responsibility, of how to monopolize on the opportunities of interconnectedness and mitigate associated problems.

Fictions addressing the 2007–8 financial crisis play a crucial role in representing topographical change, offering alternative, and often critical, re-readings of the unseen impact of financial practices on the physical, social and psychological landscapes of a place and its inhabitants. Presenting the city as a microcosm of the economic, social and spatial inequality dominant during the early years of the new millennium, Crunch Lit offers socioeconomic cross sections of the contemporary city to illuminate the impact of economic changes in the world of high finance on those in the city suburbs, or at the very bottom of the social ladder. From pressures on housing stock, to gentrification, the breakdown of community relations and the emergence of alternative realities as escape mechanisms, these fictions foreground the need for capital cities to offer a mixed ecology of natives and newcomers, not just financiers and foreign investors.

Representing a period in which houses ceased to be 'homes' and instead became another form of capital asset, these novels are characterized by a shared concern for the economic distancing created in cities by the forces of financialization. Representing the dominance of financial architecture, the transformation of domestic dwellings, the futile search for alternative realities and the fragmentation of social cohesion in the contemporary city, Crunch Lit offers a vital critical perspective on the influence of financialization over London life in the early twenty-first century. Mobilizing topography as a tool in a wider critique of financialization and the lack of a viable alternative, rising house prices and urban discontent in London are harnessed by contemporary authors in novels that consider not only what is wrong with capital but, perhaps, how it can be put right in the post-crunch period.

4

Masters of the universe

> *The monster is the true victim of the book*
> MARY SHELLEY[1]

After the height of the financial crisis, the blame game began. In the weeks and months after the crash, the focus of dominant media and political discourse fell firmly on bankers – and male bankers in particular – as being responsible for the economic crash. Prior to 2007–8, there had been several studies of the financial sector that aimed to examine the reasons behind and the impact of the prominent role of men in the industry.[2] Yet in the wider search for meaning following the credit crunch, media and political rhetoric singled out men as culpable and positioned the crash not as a crisis of financialization, but as 'a crisis of masculinity'.[3] In 2009, the National Council for Research on Women produced a report that argued 'the economic crisis was caused by [. . .] masculinity run amuck'. This claim was repeated in a number of mainstream press publications, including a now infamous article in *The Washington Post*, in which Barnard College President Deborah Spar called the credit crunch a 'one gender crash'.[4]

Variously dubbed the 'Man-cession' or the 'He-Cession' by media commentators, claims that an excessively 'masculine economy' was to blame for the credit crunch grew in the weeks and months following the summer of 2008. Reframing a crisis of financialization as a crisis of masculinity, this rhetoric deflected responsibility and attention away from economic systems and onto gender, protecting finance capitalism at the expense of its subjects. Representing the embedding of finance in social institutions as well as political and cultural economics, Crunch Lit fictions offer representations of the impact of financialization on society and individuals, institutions and behaviours. Capturing the transactional reductionism of financialization and its impact on professional and personal relationships, Crunch Lit mobilizes male bankers as monstrous metaphors for the reality of financialization, and representations of its tyranny over twenty-first-century society.

Expansion Vikings

The dominant narrative of male responsibility that was promoted by media and political commentators following the credit crunch is epitomized by the case study of Iceland, a country that can reveal many contributory factors to the crisis as a whole and, in particular, the gendered readings of responsibility that emerged in its wake. The narrative of the so-called *útrásarvíkingar* ('expansion Vikings'), or Icelandic businessmen, is a complex one. The years before 2008 saw Iceland experience the most rapid expansion of a banking industry in history. As symbols of a new-found economic optimism in the post-millennial period, the expansion Vikings were lauded as gatekeepers, opening the doors of Iceland to the twenty-first-century markets. Drawing on a national stereotype of bravery, pride in the nation, success and aggressive masculinity, these men set about asserting Iceland's new role in the world economy.

Redressing the power balance of the colonial process through success in the financial world, the expansion Vikings forged a new sense of national identity and independence for Iceland in the twenty-first century. As the latest economic supernova, the Icelandic stock market multiplied in size nine times from 2003–7, while the country's real estate prices tripled. However, as in other Western financial markets during this period, the promise of high returns blinded many Icelandic bankers to the risks they were taking. Their operations were often dubbed 'Whale Trades' because they were so vast, but the extraordinary complexities of these deals meant that it was beyond the capacity of any one individual to understand what was happening on the trading floors. Much like the Southsea Bubble or the Tulip Craze of previous centuries, a mania for money in Iceland was the product of a specific set of social circumstances and economic and political conditions. With the male, expansion Vikings behaving aggressively, 'greed, incompetence, feuding, revenge, and deceit: the themes of the ancient Viking sagas' were 'transplanted onto a modern age'.[5] 'Iceland', reflects analyst Lars Christensen, 'was the most extreme of everything'.[6]

A spectacular failure to refinance short-term debts meant that the expansion Vikings were not only unable to continue expanding, but could not even service the financial expansions they had begun. Icelandic author Halldor Guodmundsoon writes that 'coal miners used to put a caged canary in their pits. As long as the bird sang, the air was fine. The Icelanders were the canaries of international capitalism. And then the air started to disappear'.[7] A sudden and un-forecast withdrawal of credit produced the systematic collapse of all three of the country's privately owned commercial banks and pushed Iceland into a situation that became a microcosm of what would happen across the world. The ensuing 'kreppa' (the Iceland word for 'catastrophe') proved that the previous rules of 'small country, small problem' no longer held true in a global age. By the end of 2008, Iceland was 'the only nation on earth that Americans could point to and say, "Well, at least we didn't do that"'. In total, Iceland 'amassed debts amounting to 850 percent of their GDP. (The debt-drowning United States has reached just 350 percent).'[8] As Boyes notes, 'geological fault lines between American and Europe, the Mid-Atlantic Ridge, run through Iceland'.[9] When Iceland adopted the lifestyle and culture of financialization it also adopted its fundamental flaws. While the lifestyle was an illusion built on false confidence in the myth of expansion without limits, the culture of debt it generated was very real and grew quickly. As a symptom of a globalized financialized industry, the flat world theory became practice, as a domino falling in another continent set off a global chain reaction that wiped out an island in the North Atlantic.

The growing influence of the financial sector and its values in Iceland did not cause issues in the short term – the personal wealth of Iceland tripled between 2003 and 2006. But by 2008, each inhabitant of the country was on average $330,000 in personal debt as a result of their banks losing $100 billion. The Icelandic Prime Minister was widely reported as telling his population to stop banking and go fishing (a claim he later refuted)[10] but the simple fact was that not only Iceland, but also the world economy, could not just 'go back' to a more innocent, pre-crash state. Iceland has been left in a state of shock and disappointment at the failure of its expansion Vikings. Post-2008, the country was described by one resident as a place 'where the men are men and the women seem to have completely given up on them'.[11]

Many media and political commentators argued that gendered readings of the crash were necessary in its aftermath. In his popular blog, Professor of Peace and Conflict Studies Dan Smith suggests that the causes of the credit crunch lie in 'an overdose of self-confidence, a refusal to admit to problems, a taste for risk, limited knowledge of international finance [. . .] All the main players in the brief brilliance and quick disaster were men, behaving aggressively.'[12] Examining the Icelandic scenario as a case of 'too much, too soon', Smith highlights that the qualities that propelled the expansion Vikings to rapid wealth and success pre-2007 were ultimately the same qualities that doomed them to failure when credit froze.

The story of the expansion Vikings is significant, because this narrative was adopted by many political and media commentators as part of their attempts to explain the reasons behind, events during and consequences of the 2007–8 financial crash. In a now infamous blog post, BBC reporter Robert Heston – the journalist who broke the Northern Rock story – propounded gendered readings of the crash that, like Iceland, place the blame for events firmly at the feet of men in finance. Peston proposes that, 'every major non-geological disaster in history has been man-made, from climate change to the credit crunch and from warfare to genocide [. . .] Men's denial of vulnerability and the need to consume and acquire are intricately connected.' Concentrating on a 'masculine' tendency to put short-term gain ahead of long-term interest, Peston goes on to confess that:

> I routinely characterise the credit crunch as 'men behaving badly'–because it's almost impossible to find a woman to blame [. . .] The reckless chief executives of banks who went on a borrowing and lending binge: all men. The financial engineers who packaged up poisonous subprime debt and mis-sold it as AAA solid gold: they were long of Y chromosomes [. . .] The central bankers and regulators who slept while the dangerous financial party was in full swing: blokes. The finance ministers who didn't want to recognise that the surge in house prices was perilous, for fear of alienating voters: yup, it's my gender again.[13]

Dissecting the many 'masculine vices' that 'played a dominant role in fermenting the crunch', Peston's blog argues that the culture of the financial industry is instrumental to its appeal for men. He suggests 'the kind of complex mathematical modelling that underpinned so many of the toxic financial products – and of flawed systems for controlling risk – is also a peculiarly male practice. It's the equivalent of an obsession with computer games, or cricket scores or railway timetables: little worlds detached from the real world.'[14] These comments formed part of a wider post-crunch positioning of events as a crisis of masculinity, rather than of financialization. Commentators argued that, in what were already highly masculine environments, testosterone capitalism and transnational models of financial masculinity combined in the pre-crunch years to produce financial systems in which men made and enforced the rules and therefore had to be held responsible. The case study of Iceland and its expansion Vikings exemplified the fact that men had come to dominate the financial world at every level, and the potential consequences of this disproportionate influence over the industry.

The term 'masculinities' variously conveys the many definitions of being a man and the socially constructed origins of these definitions, as well as their tendency to change over time and differ according to location, race, class and age. Since 'masculinities' are socially, politically and economically historical and influenced by social change, they are also 'concerned, more than anything else, with power and its complex and polyvalent meanings and operations'.[15] Masculinity studies led by R. Connell has long considered gender and the influence of globalization, especially on hegemonic forms of masculinity. The connection between masculinity and competitiveness, especially on a global stage, is a long-standing one.[16] Connell argues that 'transnational business masculinity' – a model connected to those who run the leading institutions in the world economy including 'the business executives who operate in global markets' and 'the political executives who interact (and in many contexts, merge) with them' – is essential to understanding how masculinity is created and how it functions in a global arena. This model is 'marked by increasing egocentrism, very conditional loyalties (even to the corporation), and a declining sense of responsibility for others (except for purposes of image making)'.[17] Men have long been 'in charge' in the major cities of the global economy. On Wall Street, the bull statue functions not only as 'a symbol of unbridled capitalism' but also of 'the inherent masculinity of the financial services industry',[18] Tackling the aggressively competitive environment of a male-dominated financial sector, dominant post-crunch analysis focused on this toxic culture of hegemonic masculinity as the reason behind the crunch.

Literature across the ages has profiled the character of the banker as a deeply flawed and villainous creature, but in the twenty-first-century genre of Crunch Lit the character of the male banker takes on a new significance. As Kellaway reflects:

> Ever since Shylock demanded his pound of flesh from Antonio, bankers have been presented as loathsome figures in literature. Trollope and Dickens made them greedy, unprincipled villains; Tom Wolfe updated this model for the 1980s, adding sexual incontinence, coke habits and a taste for vulgar interior design. In the slew of new novels about the financial crisis, the bankers are all of the above, but blacker still.[19]

The years following the credit crunch gave birth to a range of Crunch Lit fictions that sought to engage with, and attempt to understand, the role of men in 2007–8. *A Week in December* by Sebastian Faulks (2009) and *Capital* by John Lanchester (2012) offer important interventions in these gender debates, representing male characters at the heart of the credit crunch.[20] Dissecting models of financial masculinity, the texts chart the social and economic fortunes of their respective protagonists, John Veals and Roger Yount, before, during and after the crash. While these fictions shy away from an explicit first-person perspective, they seek to give voice to a relatively silent actor in these global financial events—the investment banker.

Crunch Lit does not opt for the easy path of demonizing bankers, but instead chooses to confront the literary challenge of creating well-rounded and sympathetic characters, offering personal accounts of excess as metaphors for wider global systems. These novels enable individual stories of male bankers and their specific sets of circumstances to be read as representative of a much broader body of professional people subject to the pressures of financialization. As mediations on the power practices and relations between men in a specific set of organizations, settings and positions, Crunch Lit fictions explore the conditions and consequences of financial culture on twenty-first-century men. Examining masculinity across the sector, they present banker protagonists as victims of suppressed emotions, living lives dominated by work and able to speak only in the language of finance.

Vampire capitalists

The language of the Gothic and the monstrous quickly came to define the fallout from the financial collapse. In 2007, Goldman Sachs was dubbed the 'Vampire Bank' by *Rolling Stone Magazine*, a 'great vampire squid wrapped around the face of humanity, relentlessly jamming its blood funnel into anything that smells like money' ('at least vampire squids don't harm humans', a spokesman for the bank said).[21] Elsewhere, in an article pithily titled, 'Bite Club', *The Financial Times* reflected on so-called 'Vampire properties' – bank-owned foreclosed homes in the US housing market in which the previous owners continue to reside (estimated to be 250,000 in 2011), alongside 'zombie properties' – homes vacated by their previous owners but still in the midst of the foreclosure process (estimated at 150,000 in 2011). Characterized by the press as parasitical sub-humans, feeding on the entrails of the public purse, dominant media and political narratives situated the banker as a symbol of greed, power, illness and alienation – the ultimate post-millennial monster.

Franco Moretti claims that 'monsters are metaphors',[22] while Judith Halberstam argues that they can be best understood as 'meaning machines', capable of representing multiple issues in a single form. 'The monster', she argues, 'functions as monster, when it is able to condense as many fear-producing traits as possible into one body'.[23] This metaphorical capacity is an important part of what makes the creature so monstrous since its terror lies beyond a single plane of interpretation. As David McNally notes in his study *Monsters of the Market: Zombies, Vampires and Global Capitalism* (2012), 'the idea that something monstrous is at work in the operations of global capitalism is never far from the surface today'.[24] As the monstrous face of the financial sector, the banker became both a target and a scapegoat of post-crunch culture, and an uncomfortable reminder of the reality of financialized practices.

Since the nineteenth century, 'Gothic economies' have operated across cultural representations of finance, with numerous images of being consumed and drained by the vampire closely corresponding to contemporaneous economic images of decline and takeover. Marx drew upon the metaphor of the vampire on many occasions to describe the process of economic and ideological deconstruction and alienation. In *The Eighteenth Brumaire* (1851), the bourgeoisie 'has become a vampire that sucks out its [the smallholding peasant's] blood and brains and throws them into the alchemist's cauldron of capital',[25] while in *The Grundrisse* (1858), capital survives by 'constantly sucking in living labour as its soul, vampire-like'.[26] In *Capital* (1887), Marx describes the capitalist as a vampire nourishing itself upon labour, viewing this monster in terms of materialist mass culture and its modes of production and consumption. This powerful analogy – made some thirty years before the publication of Bram Stoker's *Dracula* (1897) – functions as a reminder of how common vampires were in nineteenth-century descriptions of global economic systems.

Marx employs *Capital* – as John Lanchester does more than a century later – to explain the vampiric nature of capitalism itself: 'Capital is dead labour which, vampire-like, lives only by sucking living labour, and lives the more, the more labour it sucks. The time during which the worker works is the time during which the capitalist consumes the labour-power he has bought from him. If the worker consumes his disposable time for himself, he robs the capitalist.'[27] As Halberstam notes, Marx uses his writings to describe capitalism as Gothic specifically 'in its ability to transfer matter into commodity, commodity into value and value into capitalism'.[28] Like both capitalism and colonialism, the vampire is impelled towards a continuous growth, an unlimited expansion of his domain: accumulation is in his nature. The stronger the vampire becomes, the weaker the living become: 'the capitalist gets rich, not, like the miser, in proportion to his personal labour and restricted consumption, but at the same rate as he squeezes out labour-power from others, and compels the worker to renounce all the enjoyment of life.'[29] Vampires make effective bankers: they have an insatiable thirst for the job, a lack of emotional empathy with their victims and a cyclical relationship of rapid trades and exchanges. Like vampires, the bankers of the twenty-first century survive on flows of economic lifeblood, exchanging currency, investing or spending. Just as the vampire is capital personified and must subordinate his private existence to the abstract and incessant movement of accumulation, the banker is also motivated by the desire for power and sacrifices a work–life balance to the dominance of financial priority.

Reminiscent of the age of colonial empire and imperialism, the twenty-first-century financial sector and its predominately male workforce are founded on principles of trade, conquest and acquisition. As Krishnaswamy argues:

> Masculinity is not only a foundational notion of modernity, but it is also the cornerstone in the ideology of moral imperialism that prevailed in British India from the late nineteenth century onward. The cult of masculinity rationalised imperial rule by equating an aggressive, muscular, chivalric model of manliness with racial, national, cultural and moral superiority. Modern masculinity was elaborated not only through an increasingly stricter demarcation between the sexes but also through a systematic 'unmanning' of minorities within and foreigners without Europe.[30]

Rationalizing superiority and justifying domination, the imperial practices of capitalism have historically centred power on a select male elite. Through this 'vaster paternalistic enterprise',[31] the financial empire of contemporary capitalism reproduces and reinforces the financial homosociality of its participants, pitting contending male fears and fascinations in a global arena. Via this form of gendered, financial colonialism, money becomes both the circuit through which male desire flows and the subject of objectification as a symbol of attainment.

Throughout history, imperial conquest and globalized financial systems have brought distant regions into close contact and assisted the export of Western masculinities and practices to the colonized world. Ling argues that Western 'hypermasculine capitalism' has the potential to reconstruct social subjects, spaces and activities 'into economic agents that valorize a masculinized, global competitiveness associated with men, entrepreneurs, the upwardly mobile, cities, and industrialization'.[32] The tropes of invasion, occupation and colonization in contemporary financial discourse outlined by Ling and echoed also in De Goede and Hooper's work are significant as they attempt to understand gendered responses to the credit crunch and position 'capitalist investment as a masculine conquest of virgin territories' wherein financial transactions are 'understood as the operations of masculine agents called on to act boldly in the face of panic, irrationality, and "exuberance"'.[33]

In Crunch Lit, the significance of money in the colonization process is explored through bankers' manipulation of imperial financial practices. The economic domination of financialization is positioned as an embodiment of the worst excesses of capitalism, a strategic desire to colonize the world by means of capital, rather than force. As foot-soldiers in this war, Roger Yount and John Veals are solitary and despotic, they will not brook competition. Their ambition is to subjugate the last vestiges of the liberal era and destroy all forms of economic independence. As 'vampiric capitalists', they are always on the look-out for hidden knowledge and greater power.

Paranoid monsters, living in fear of discovery and destruction, the bankers of these novels go to great lengths to ensure that their operations are hidden from public view. Going to extreme precautions to operate undetected and separated from the rest of society, money motivates capitalist protagonists to take risks, betray ethics and break rules. *Capital* emphasizes the 'element of deliberate mystification about the process' (16) of banking, one perpetuated by those involved in the industry itself. Roger Yount installs 'a machine generating white noise, which could be turned on to prevent conversation being overheard outside the room' (18) in an attempt to preserve the privacy of his trading space (the irony of this action is underscored when Roger finally loses his job because his deputy practises criminal embezzlement right under his nose).

John Veals is equally paranoid about being 'discovered' and takes extreme lengths to avoid detection. He 'spoke little because he was so aware of security risks. Although the office was regularly swept for bugs, he had trained himself never to say anything that he couldn't bear to have overheard' (9). John has 'six cellphones' (9), each of which connects him to a specific contact kept discrete from and ignorant of the other operatives in his web of connections. This web of intrigue also extends to illegal practices as Veals establishes a ghost-system for all email communications that operates outside the purview of accountability or official governance systems via 'an email service [. . .] neither stored nor checked by the authorities' (9).

It is not only the uncanny state of their work places, but also the Gothic mind-set evoked, that creates the cloak of invisibility necessary to frame both the dark spaces and practices of bankers in these texts. Operating undetected in places restricted to those outside of their immediate sector, these bankers literally work on the margins of society, and often late into the night or during weekends in their impenetrable office-block citadels far away from society and the reality of the global economies they serve.

The anti-hero bankers of these novels are engaged in a constant quest for power that leaves them isolated from others and leads them to become monstrous through the single-minded pursuit of money. They function as representations of the unrepressed greed of contemporary financial systems, holding a mirror to the damaged soul of the credit-hungry pre-crunch period. In these dark geographies of the financial world, banker protagonists sit safe in fortresses that facilitate transgression and decay. The gendered expectations of these architectural settings problematize public–private divides and offer the space of the financial sector as a political site in which financial masculinities can not only be played out, but also perpetuated. As men in positions of influence and power, these characters draw attention to the condition and consequences of a financial desire that becomes unregulated because it operates outside of conventional norms and in protected spaces. Highlighting the monstrous lived reality of financialization and its impact on identity, relationships, language and values, Crunch Lit novels position their banker protagonists in liminal spaces to foreground the dominance and distance of the financial sector from wider society in the lead up to 2007–8, and after.

Money talks

The language of money has historically been one of certainty, of tangibility and representation. Yet in the pre-crunch period the language of finance had, much like the systems it sought to represent, become more and more abstract. The 'monetary terms' circulated by politicians, economists and the media in the wake of the crisis meant little to the person on the street, and operated as exclusionary and obstructive to wider understandings of the causes and implications of the crisis. Christian Marazzi argues that the upper echelons of the financial economy are facilitated by the consolidation of a 'linguistic community'.[34] Exposing the shared language required to penetrate and comprehend the mechanisms and movements of the financial world, Crunch Lit profiles the power of language to frame masculine discourses of power and authority over finance in the pre-crunch period.

Over the past century, commentators have noted the increasing role of language in maintaining the 'masculine reification of economic and financial discourses'[35] as values of competence and professional prowess become transformed into vocabularies of conflict and conquest. The business world is often linked with the hyper-masculine, and this is transported into, and perpetuated by, the realm of linguistic exchange. Language based on metaphors from sport or the military and sexualized images of playing, hunting, racing or engaging in battles, dominates bankers' interactions in these texts. Veals and Yount are either on a 'winning streak' or must bear their losses 'like a man'. In a linguistic system that refuses to engage in cooperation or collaboration of exchange, language constitutes a significant part of 'doing the masculine' in Crunch Lit.

John Veals is a divisive figure whose name conjures associations of illegal activities and banned practices. Despite this, he is more than simply 'Dr Evil with an MBA'.[36] Veals is a problematic character who manipulates the loop-holes and grey areas afforded by lax regulatory systems and cultures of financial malpractice. Faulks recalls that he borrowed the name 'from a real estate agent. I liked the name "Veal" because it's a bit like venal, and of course veal is a kind of bloodless meat and these things to me suggested the character of John Veals. He is an extremely cold, bloodless, rapacious, calculating, ruthless, greedy son of a gun.'[37] Veals has a 'lack of grace' which 'meant that he was oddly direct, if foul-mouthed'. The narrative notes that this 'could be interesting' (7), and excuses his language as a symptom of his condition, that of being a powerful banker. In social situations, Veals's money literally speaks louder than words. At a restaurant 'John and his colleagues [. . .] didn't even look at the menu. They'd summon the waiter and tell him what they wanted' (31). Wielding words in a 'testosterone driven' (33) and combative fashion, Veals is 'a man obsessed by detail' (35) and this extends to his command over language. Adept at the slippery language of finance and the definite article of deception, Veals values his own interpretation of key industry terminology as the guiding principal for his actions. He argues that in banking there is 'a snobbery about being honest' and claims that the 'distinction between "legal" and "ethical" was of no concern to him–or to anyone else he'd ever met' (69). Minor differences in interpretations of financial and ethical terminology characterize Veals's exchanges, whether addressing the spectre of 'TAX' or confusion about whether 'profit had been capital, not income' (69).

Significantly, the male bankers of Crunch Lit even experience and express emotion using economic terms and references. Treating social encounters as transactions, and emotional relationships as fiscal vulnerabilities, they articulate profound feelings using the financial language they know best. When John Veals meets his future wife, he recalls that 'it felt as though all the reserves he'd held in various accounts had been drained, electronically, without his knowledge, presenting him with the paper statement – the first he knew of it – that all he owned was now vested in Catalina' (80). In what is perhaps the least romantic description of falling in love ever written, Faulks positions Veals as an absolute slave to the practices of banking. Unable to interpret social relations on any level other than that of the trading floor – and in this case a transfer of assets rather than emotions – Veals views his partner as 'a market he had yet to crack [. . .] he wanted to know her risk – her yield, her beta and her delta' (235). The words used in and outside of work by these characters are demonstrative of and symbolically denote some of financial masculinity's most regarded values: 'control, reason, strength, industry, courage, decisiveness, dominance, emotional control'.[38]

Pre-crisis, the language of bankers speaks of profit, risk and self-interest. The bankers of Crunch Lit begin the narrative firm in the belief that trading involves the 'creation' of money. The thrill and exhilaration they experience from this process overtakes the purpose of the act itself and addiction to risk and gain comes to dominate their lives. When he loses his job at the bank in the crunch, Roger Yount starts playing poker online to satisfy his need for risk (493) and, as a child, Veals learns his skills of speculation not from the banking world but from watching his bookmaker uncle. Fascinated by the element of chance and the ability of the player to control risk, Veals moves into banking where he finds that many of the same rules apply. Readers are told that 'Veals dreaded boredom' and 'missing any opportunity' (66). Risk ultimately plays a defining role in Veals's identity and success as a trader. He engages in trades only when 'his own reputation for skill and ruthlessness would be enhanced' (37) and, fixed to the multiple computer screens that cover his desk, thrives on attempting to control the constant movement and changes in the market.

Risk becomes attractive to Veals as a result of his circumstance and experience. At the beginning of the novel, his business success has left him in a position whereby 'even by doing nothing, no new trades at all, he could make many millions a year' (10). Despite working for 'twenty-seven years in finance' (10) the narrative points out that 'no one ever warmed to Veals' (12) since he acquired his wealth by 'putting on his own trades a fraction before exercising identical ones requested by a client' (12–13). Brushing off accusations with references to a 'fog of war' (13) and the excuse 'everyone did it' (13), Veals is not sympathetic to the credit crunch but frustrated that he is unable to profit from it. While 'he took no pleasure in being proved "right" eventually about the fall' (13), Veals does nevertheless use it to his advantage, to bolster his position and underline his control of perceived risks and is the last man standing at the end of the novel.

As titans of the City, bankers in Crunch Lit do not display the 'big swinging dick' verbosity of their 1980s predecessors, but instead adopt a more covert style of manipulativeness. As Karl Figlio points out, 'the stereotype is single-minded, self-aggrandizing, fiercely competitive and unconcerned about consequences beyond demonstrating superiority in achieving market advantage through the phantasy of creating wealth as if from nothing'.[39] Whether a natural predisposition to risk or an active choice to engage in risk for personal and professional gain, these bankers take risks which lead them to other risky behaviours outside of work including infidelity and gambling in a continual quest to recreate this buzz. In doing so, these novels explore how and why financial masculinity became defined by risk-taking, competition, irresponsibility and self-interest, creating in some bankers a 'narcissistic sense of being special, of being better than ordinary mortals'.[40] Each text reveals the addictive practices of their male banker protagonists to shed light on the results of normalizing the practice of risk within both the working lives of a profession and the practices of a global industry.

Working 9–5

The financial world has long been a site for 'a struggle between the world of personal love, intimacy, empathy, magnanimity and self-sacrifice and the terrible pressures of conspicuous consumption to achieve, possess and display'.[41] From their analysis of a range of management textbooks, Gee, Hull and Lanksheer concluded that 'fast capitalism' has produced men who have few loyalties to their employer as well as to other workers or friends but instead prioritize hierarchical rewards, technical competence and rationality, and are usually ready to move jobs, companies or countries to achieve a better position in the workplace.[42] Benyon echoes their findings, observing that the 'true company man takes on the cloak of masculinity with a vengeance by engaging in blood-on-the-carpet power games. "Hard" business success is everything, with intimacy reduced to an institutionalized homosociality, while genuine ("soft") relationships are placed firmly on the back burner.'[43] Set against a wider cultural push for greater profit and personal attainment across the twentieth century, self-interest in banking became 'not just a reflection of the neo-liberal economic consensus but also of masculine discourses within the business class elite that make the pursuit of ever spiralling remuneration almost obligatory'.[44]

In Crunch Lit, success means sacrificing social and familial relations as part of a wider pursuit of wealth, status and identity. A lack of emotional involvement with families, friends and co-workers extends to a suspicious approach to the social world in general and a defensive approach to life outside the confines of the corporate. A culture of competition, long working hours and rivalry for time means that the male bankers of these texts extend their financialized masculinity and privileging of business before people into the social sphere. Working long hours isolated from the domestic and disengaged from friends and family – even though they rely on these structures to facilitate their own lives—the bankers of Crunch Lit are intensely individualist. Older patriarchs, under constant threat of being replaced with young pretenders to their financial thrones, Yount and Veals are driven by a singularity of desire and become blinded by the pursuit of a single goal: the attainment of status and the accumulation of control, wealth and power. With little time for leisure, they engage with the principle of pleasure only through the satisfaction of financial trading.

Early in *Capital*, Roger Yount is characterized in extensive detail to outline the ethos of contemporary banking he represents: 'work hard, play hard, and take no prisoners' (16). As a merchant banker at 'Pinker Lloyd' in the City of London (15), a key expectation is that banking staff such as Roger should 'be in the office from seven to seven, minimum' (16) and sacrifice their life outside work in a display of dedication to the greater good of the company. Usefully, Roger has little interest in life outside of the office and fails to attempt to hide his indifference towards the domestic. This constitutes not only a growing source of irritation and offence to his wife Arabella, but also the ultimate motivation for her to walk away from their marriage. She reflects that Roger 'didn't cook except show-off barbeques on the occasional summer weekend at his silly boy-toy gas grill, and he didn't wash clothes or iron them or sweep the floor or, hardly at all, play with the children' (43). While 'Arabella did not do those things either' it is only Roger who goes 'through life acting as if they did not exist [. . .] it was this obliviousness which drove her so nuts' (43).

A Week in December also presents its banker protagonist as a 'creature whose heart beat only to market movements. He couldn't be happy as a man if his positions weren't making money.' For John Veals, 'the analysis of a potential position was therefore more than a business or a mathematical problem; it involved something painfully close to self-knowledge. His life depended on it' (14). As a result of this dedication only to banking, Veals has

> no interests outside the acquisition of money. He didn't play golf or tennis. He didn't support a football team. He threw all colour magazines in the bin. He went to the theatre or opera once a year if there was a certain and measurable financial advantage in doing so. He never went to the cinema and he thought television was a waste of time. A personal shopper bought his clothes. His idea of dinner was sausages and frozen peas, though he was prepared to sit it out over foie gras and Japanese beef if there was a purpose to the tedium. He disliked alcohol, though kept the cellar well stocked for Vanessa (268).

Perhaps the most scathing comment on Veals's ruthless and relentless quest for greater profits is that 'the Veals family didn't need much income: John had no power boats or polo ponies; no collections of

Sumerian stone tablets or early Picassos; no mortgage, no hobbies and no interests outside work' (11). Fuelled by the desire to acquire money as a route to power, pride and prestige, John Veals becomes alienated from the core principle of the very thing he trades—value. In prioritizing the fiscal over the emotional, and trading above his relationships, Veals loses sight of balance and normality. He works weekends 'without interruption' (9) (including Sunday since the 'Muslim Sunday is a working day' in which to capitalize on his 'markets in Dubai', 389). The only friendships he actively nurtures are those with 'people in the ratings agencies' (67) that will offer him professional benefit. His wife Vanessa recognizes that John 'just regards social life as a waste of time' (100) but, like Arabella in *Capital*, is deeply hurt and frustrated by her husband's blatant and shameless prioritizing of the professional over the personal. She sadly confesses that, 'I could forget everything if I could just once see him laugh' (101).

Centring his existence on work and the practice of risk, control and accumulation, Veals participates in social life with extreme reluctance. Like Yount, he hates 'holidays because they kept him from the markets and he had nothing to do beside the pool because he didn't read and he had never learned to swim. He disliked travelling and claimed he'd done more than enough of it in the course of his job. The cultures, languages, arts and buildings of other countries were of no concern to him.' (268). His wife admits that, 'John had never, so far as [she] was aware, read a novel. He found all forms of music irritating and immediately instructed cab drivers to turn off their radios. He disliked art galleries, though thought the financial aspect of modern British art to be of minor interest [. . .] The only activity, the only aspect of human life, that interested John Veals was money' (269). Focusing on business as his sole source of identity and interaction, Veals is isolated from the rich cultural and social worlds of London through which the rest of the novel's characters move.

The development of the global banking sector, influenced by the growth of neoliberalism over the past thirty years produced a culture among male financial workers in which relationships are little more than another form of transaction and social and emotional life is disregarded since it cannot be measured in numbers. Faulks's omniscient narrative observes that in the years leading up to the credit crunch, 'bankers had detached their activities from the real world [...] they did take precautions to minimize the possibility of any contact with reality [...] a very limited sense of "the other"; a kind of functional autism was the ideal state of mind' (102–3). Drawing attention to a lack of emotional intelligence and failure to engage with every other non-work-related element of life, his wife becomes sidelined in favour of more time spent in the office. Veals is simply 'not interested in women' and 'personally found the dividend of carnal pleasure a brief and poor return for the hours of tedium he'd invested' (235). Interpreting emotional and physical intimacy through the prism of financial exchange, Veals demonstrates a profound inability to engage with a variety of networks and varying relationships.

His feelings for Olya (320), the porn star Veals regularly ogles online, is a situation more akin to his job as a financial trader–one of pursuit, exchange, control and gratification–involving none of the emotional intelligence or finer subtleties and selflessness of marital or familial bonds. This is underlined by the narrative when Veals eventually meets Olya at his wife's dinner party where she attends as the 'plus one' of a famous footballer. Back-footed, Veals struggles to comprehend his lack of control over the intrusion of the virtual into reality. He tries to reassure himself that this 'girl was from another world. She wasn't real; she was a screen fantasy, a laptop dancer' (370). Confronted with a situation that is far removed from the virtual fantasy accessible on his computer screen and at his command, Veals scans Olya in detail and notices changes to her appearance and weight, and then looks 'back below the tablecloth to the safety of his phone's illuminated screen' (370) to compare this with her online pictures.

Making apparent the implicit connections between economic and sexual life as dual forms of exchange and control, the economic and social power of money marks out the clearly defined roles of Veals and Olya as part of a wider financial industry. In virtual form, Olya is anonymous, another porn star who can be accessed at will and controlled like a market risk to pleasure Veals on his terms. In reality, Olya is problematic because she shatters the fantasy of the computer screen, destroys the distance, and brings Veal's private virtual world into the everyday life of the dinner party. Much like his virtual trades on the financial markets, Veals uses and abuses Olya's online profile for his own ends without thought to the reality behind his actions. As a metaphor for the fantasy finance of bankers and banking practices in the lead up to the crunch, as well as a further underlining of performative gender roles in the financial sector, the meeting of Veals and Olya functions as an effective foreshadowing of the realization of virtual exchanges that arrives in the form of the financial crisis.

'Stuff is not enough'

Post-crunch, commentators were quick to blame morality – or lack thereof – in the dealings of bankers and financial institutions in the years leading up to 2007. Dominant narratives placed the blame for the crash not on the bankruptcy of a financial system, but 'the intellectual and moral failure of those who were in charge of it: a failure for which there is no excuse'.[45] As a result, the moral potential of Crunch Lit was outlined by several critics. As John Lanchester argues:

> Art, especially the powerful form of the novel, can point the way. But let's have done with the satires and send-ups – it's been done ad nauseam, literally we are sick with it – and let's get serious. We need a road map and our moral voice back. A good place to start is that sinking spell, the 'sudden, vertiginous loss of self' – in actuality, a call to moral reckoning – or, even better, the activating rage a morally reckoned character feels at seeing the boat in which we're all passengers being hammered and scuttled. From there, we chart our way upward.[46]

Appearing in a period during which society seemed to be calling for a new morality in money, Crunch Lit was offered as an example of the role of art in offering important inventions in and representations of, our relationship with finance in the new millennium. In the wake of an 'economic earthquake' Crunch Lit calls for us to 'rethink the role of the markets in achieving the public good'.[47] These texts suggest that the crunch should actually be seen as the product of a wider ideological failure at an institutional level, 'the worship of economic growth for its own sake [. . .]. The main moral compass we have now is a thin and degraded notion of economic welfare, measured in terms of quantity of goods'[48] fundamental to the philosophy behind financialization.

The morality of the financial sector forms a key concern of Crunch Lit. Fiction is used to explore the credit crunch as a metaphor for a wider spiritual crisis, one created by economic changes but with its core in economic ruin as the logical end point of a longer term fascination with and enslavement to consumption and materialism. Disengaged from reality and resistant to opportunities to re-enter society, the one-track approach of these banker characters becomes self-perpetuating and internally corroborating. The bankers of Crunch Lit are 'loners', separated by their subscription to the principles of individualism and 'reinforced one another's belief [...] reinvigorated in their faith – convinced they needed nothing and nobody beyond their own fantastic circuitry' (103). Trapped in an endless cycle of virtual exchange, risk and accumulation, the men at the centre of these narratives create a system of norms and expectations, sustained by their blessed isolation.

Examining the effects of a financial downturn on real people in real terms, Crunch Lit examines the emotional impact of the crisis, the spectre of losing money and the contemporary reworking of the fall, a reversal of economic fortunes with unseen social, political and moral implications. The dangers of corporate capitalism are explored by these novels not simply in terms of economic implications but impacts on social systems and psychological composition. Illusion and decay is seen to manifest itself at every level of these worlds, as corruption and collusion of the trading floors leaks out into the private lives of characters and wider fictionalized society. Offering more than simply a good versus evil take on the relationship between the City and society, Crunch Lit offers both a representation of and interaction with a world in which crises and struggle have become a permanent feature of everyday life.

The crisis in late-capitalism epitomized by the credit crunch is framed and narrated in these novels through a crisis of the personal. Accustomed to operating in financial systems where unhappiness or discontent are understood as failure, Yount and Veals are forced to examine their personal and professional lives in the wake of the credit crunch. Roger Yount ends *Capital* dissolved of his financialized masculinity, unemployed and disillusioned by capitalism itself. He develops a longing for a simpler way of life, a return to nature and a more fundamental demonstration of his masculinity, away from finance and aligned instead with the physical world. Noting the authenticity associated with manual, outdoor work, in the brief moments Roger escapes the office and London – most often for a country shoot with customers or colleagues – he fleetingly dreams of a life in which he can 'retrain as a teacher and they would move out of London, somewhere like this where you could walk and breathe and see the sky, and the kids would go to the local school and Arabella would look after them [. . .] then one day he would look at himself in the mirror and see a different man' (99).

Rejecting the city and all that it represents, Roger attempts to revitalize his identity, crafting a new narrative to create a sense of belonging and purpose in an ever changing and increasingly unstable world. This desire for self-transformation, redirecting his efforts into a social purpose and retreating back to nature, returns as a way for Roger to reframe his identity in a post-crunch world. At the end of the novel, Roger's unemployment and growing realization of the true impact of financialization stands as a metaphor for society as a whole in the post-crunch years. Thrown off the corporate treadmill, Roger has a chance to reflect, reconsider his position and acknowledges that he 'was done with the City. He was done with the commute to work, with pin-striped suits [. . .] done with earning twenty or thirty times the average family's annual income for doing things with money rather than with people or things. He was done with London and money and all that. It was time to do or make something different' (573). His anxiety comes from a sense of discontent, highlighting the fragility of his identity post-trauma and the search for new certainties in a troubling and alienating world. The need for personal as well as professional fulfilment is suggestive of a new-found sense that a life devoted solely to financial gratification can no longer sustain an individualized form of empowerment. The motivations for this change are 'not only for economic reasons – for them of course but not only for them – but because this just wasn't enough to live by. You could not spend your entire span of life in thrall to the code of stuff. There was no code of stuff. Stuff was just stuff. You couldn't live by it or for it. Roger's new motto: stuff is not enough' (575).

The novel situates this change of priorities and realignment of values within a wider global shift in thinking in the wake of the crunch. Roger notes that the change 'was sinking in with people everywhere [. . .] it gradually dawned on them that hard times were moving in like a band of rain' (574–5). His mantra-like incantation that forms the closing sentences of the novel–'I can change, I can change, I promise I can change change change' (577) – offer a very different philosophy for life going forward from the financial crisis. Less a spiritual quest than a response to the changed conditions of the global recession and the strains of austerity to make sense of individual lives newly framed by reduced choice, he acknowledges the need for 'change' due to a shift in perceived value – stuff is literally no longer enough – and, as a result, the novel leaves Roger searching for a move forward, away from a life focused purely on finance, and towards one centred on values of family, home and ethical experience.

However, in fiction, as in reality, redemption is not always achieved. The desire for change articulated by Roger Yount is the antithesis of the conclusion presented by Faulks's *A Week in December*. Standing in his office, surveying the skyline of the City of London, Faulks's banker protagonist ends the novel with a controversial reflection that:

> I have mastered this world [. . .] I am a man alive to the spirit of his time, the one who hears the whispers on the wind. A rare surge of feeling, of something like vindication, came from the pit of his belly and spread out till it sang in his veins. As he stood with his hands in his pockets, staring out over the sleeping city, over its darkened wheels and spires and domes, Veals laughed. (390)

In choosing to end his novel with the image of a banker laughing over the skyline of the City, Faulks underscores both the Gothic leanings of his text and the social satire it offers twenty-first-century readers. Representing the credit crunch as an experience rather than an education, the detached, lack of remorse displayed by Veals is expressed as a vindication of his own self-belief and continued faith in financialization. This lasting image is representative of the continued domination and control of the financial sector over society. As this ending suggests, not all the big boys have been humbled as a result of the crunch.

Homo economicus

Economic theory has long operated with the *homo economicus* as an autonomous, rational, self-interested calculator of cost-for-benefit analysis that will, in turn, produce an efficient and self-regulating market – or so the theory goes. The credit crunch blew this baseline presumption out of the water, reminding everyone from psychologists to economists that men can be the very opposite of rational. Financialized masculinities are represented by these novels as implicit in, rather than wholly responsible for, an economic catastrophe with consequences that will continue to have a global reach for years to come. Depicting governments, home owners, bankers, retailers and consumers united in a shared desire to facilitate ever-greater levels of credit, these novels offer a literary analysis of causes, events and blame that is profoundly plural. Adopting an explanatory style, with a host of characters that exist to ask questions about the crash (to enable the elucidation and explanation of key concepts and perspectives) the educational function of Crunch Lit penetrates characterizations. These models of masculinity present divergent destinies for twenty-first-century masters of the universe, but ultimately come to the same conclusion – that, in reality, they are masters of nothing except illusion.

In his investigative travel journalism exploring the global causes of the credit crunch, Michael Lewis speculates that the financial crisis was 'created by the sort of men who ignore their wives' suggestions that maybe they should stop and ask for directions'.[49] Following the financial collapse positive discrimination sought to respond to such claims by placing women in positions of greater political economic power. In Iceland, women were deliberately appointed in executive roles at the newly nationalized Icelandic banks and in government there was a conscious increase in the number of new female cabinet ministers. As part of a widespread 'blaming' of men for the economic crisis, this positive discrimination was a reaction to public criticism of the young male expansion Viking bankers whose 'eyes became bigger than their stomachs'. 'Now', one Icelandic government official reflected, 'the women are taking over [. . .] its typical, the men make the mess and the women come in to clean it up'.[50]

The result of these fictional interventions is not ultimately the appropriating of blame to any one gender, but the message that diversity and representation in the financial sector is the only positive next step in helping the economy to recover and also in changing the culture of financial organizations and the image of the industry as a whole. As Jacki Zehner, president of the Jacquelyn and Gregory Zehner Foundation, argues, regardless of their gender, what should really matter is that 'the people who were on the ship when it went down are not the same people being put on the new ship'.[51] What can be taken from the Icelandic approach to the banking crisis is not to up-end the perceived problem, apportion blame and bring in the women, but to recognize the crisis as one of hyper-individualism, as the product of a variety of social, political and economic factors that conspired unchecked across the world for decades to produce a generation of bankers and banking practices that were motivated by personal gain and regulated with the lightest of touches. Christine Lagarde, France's finance minister, writing in *The International Herald Tribune* proposes that in future the financial sector should perhaps be run by both 'Lehman Brothers and Sisters'.[52]

One positive result of the 'he-cession' is the unforeseen ways in which it has created 'points of agreement among people not typically thought of as kindred spirits, from behavioural economists to feminist historians', and literature is an important part of this ongoing conversation.[53] Crunch Lit is significant because it makes an important contribution to the wider, collective process of understanding the financial crisis as culturally mediated, represented and projected as a multifaceted social, political and economic phenomenon, a site from which to move forward towards a more equal and accurate examination of how financial practices – which should be disinterested in gender – are in reality deeply rooted in gendered cultural practices.

Tackling a historic 'masculinization of an industry' exploring how, why and with what effect blame ended up being placed on men, requires a thorough review of social, political and economic practices, but also of cultural representations.[54] By asking what makes the financial sector so male-dominated, and by examining literary representations of finance, Crunch Lit offers a vital contribution towards a wider project of creating opportunities for understanding the causes and effects of the crunch and in allowing the development of a more integrated consideration of the way forward. Challenging narratives that claim the first major economic downturn of the twenty-first century was a crisis of gender, Crunch Lit offers representations of bankers who fall victim to the profit and loss values promoted by the cultures of financialization that they represent. Through a pronounced focus on this loss, fiction representing the credit crunch presents the world of work – a relatively underrepresented setting in contemporary fiction – in a new light.

Awareness, analysis and visibility are offered by Crunch Lit as key starting points in the task of new writings to aid our understanding of the crunch. Employing wit and clarity as key elements in its characterization of city boys, Crunch Lit mirrors nineteenth-century narratives of the rise and fall, with tales of ambition thwarted and business battles won and lost. Considering why it is so difficult to find a positive image of business and businessmen in twenty-first-century fiction, Crunch Lit not only explores the political reasons for this generic bad press, but also the political function of characterization in genre fiction. Using exaggerated characterizations to prove a political point, Veals and Yount are not offered as realist representations, but as representative figures that speak of bigger problems endemic to the financial sector before the crunch. Through these characters, Faulks and Lanchester conduct an exploration of the conditions of pre-crunch finance, a limited awareness of the looming disaster, and an obsession with conspicuous consumption and professional domination.

Post-crisis values of risk awareness, emotional intelligence and 'profit with principles'[55] promoted in theory by *Capital* are problematized in practice by *A Week in December*. Framed by performative elements and perpetuated by imperial discourses transported into the financial sector of the new millennium to ground practices in glorious associations of adventure and conquest, the true horror of the vampire capitalists of Crunch Lit is that they will prey on anyone and anything without consideration of consequence. Ultimately, the ghost-system of fantasy assets, off-balance-sheet figures and zombie real estate they generate fails because it cannot find short-term life-blood to sustain its own Gothic systems. These Gothic monsters of capitalism hold a mirror to the lived reality of financialization but ultimately they are presented as associated victims of its impact on gender, employment and social value in the pre-crunch period.

Interrogating expressions of financialization and its impact on gender identity, from the language of spending to the self-deluded, isolationist and paranoid state of financial masculinities, in Crunch Lit male bankers represent not only the madness of money but also money as madness. Using Veals and Yount to offer representations of the effects of financialization on men in the early twenty-first century, Faulks and Lanchester represent corporate leaders committing illegal and morally corrupt acts of irrational exuberance, refusing to engage in socially or economic productive behaviour and with a shared work ethic represented as workaholism that leads to the breakdown of their personal relationships. Both Yount and Veals, like the financial institutions they direct, consider themselves 'too big to fail'. These male protagonists lead novels fascinated not only with financialization but with its impact on gender roles and identity and question the male banker as a controversial, and problematic, monster for the post-millennial period.

5

Recessionistas

The real victims of the credit crunch? Women.
RUTH SUNDERLAND[1]

In the wake of the 2007–8 financial crisis media debates framed the credit crunch as a feminist issue, one that reignited debates about gender, debt, divorce and the workplace in twenty-first-century society. In Crunch Lit fictions, post-crash tensions between gender, consumption, debt and employment are played out through the character of the 'Recessionista'. The 'Recessionista' represents experiences of female characters that have previously been defined by a lifestyle based on consumer credit and the consumption of material goods. Recessionista fictions are authored by women, for women, explicitly targeting a female readership in their mobilization of chick-lit stylized cover jackets and titles. Placing the Recessionista at centre stage as protagonist, these novels are suggestive of the ways in the financial crisis led to a new sense of self and professional purpose for a 'chick lit' generation disillusioned with their previous way of life.

For the Recessionista, a pre-crunch lifestyle of cocktails and heels is eschewed in favour of financial practicality, as 'shopaholic' heroines confront a harsh new reality, forced into a position where they must take stock of their lives and start again from the midst of financial ruin, divorce or a major career change. In these new financial fictions, female protagonists refuse to hide from the credit crunch but instead tackle it head-on; offering cautionary tales of what can go wrong when the 'yummy mummy' is forced to go slummy. Exploring how, why, and with what effects, female characters challenge unemployment, debt, divorce and destitution, Crunch Lit offers alternative representations of the impact of financialization on women during and after the credit crunch.

The lipstick effect

In previous recessions, men were hardest hit by job losses but, in 2009, media reports claimed that women would be the main victims of the 2007–8 credit crunch. Since women occupied a majority of roles in the sectors hardest hit by the new millennial global economic downturn – including retail services, local government and the public sector – media sources asserted that they would likely bear the brunt of the financial crash. Ros Altmann, a former economic adviser at Downing Street, argued that 'in the 1980s it was actually an opportunity for women to get on the job ladder in a way they hadn't done before, and that really drove growth, boosting family incomes which benefited the economy. That is all about to change.'[2] Newspapers were also quick to report that twice as many women as men were losing their jobs.[3] In the UK, 53,000 women lost their jobs in the year to October 2008, while the gender pay gap increased from 17 per cent in 2007 to 17.1 per cent in 2008 on the basis of mean full-time hourly earnings.

These media narratives were enforced by social studies that framed the damaging effects of the credit crunch on women's lifestyle choices. In feminist blog *The F Word*, Carolyn Roberts conducted a small-scale survey of press headlines. She found a depressing range including:

> the reassuring news that the credit crunch is not affecting cosmetic sales (apparently because women would rather go without food than makeup – or more accurately, women shopping on a beauty product website – so no possible bias there then); a cosmetic surgery company's announcement of a 135% increase in breast augmentation procedures, with the tasteful statement, 'as the economy is going bust, UK women are boosting theirs'.[4]

These were accompanied by a range of articles on ways to 'beat the credit crunch' and strategies for continuing to dress stylishly and have expensive haircuts while on a budget. Roberts concluded that 'even in recession, a woman's appearance is perceived as her most interesting facet. Articles aimed at women assume that our interest in finance begins and ends with whether we can still afford to buy lipstick'.[5]

Women's magazines represented the recession with articles promoting frugality or exploring the impact of spending reductions on the fashion industry. Coined by Leonard Lauder, the chairman of cosmetics firm Estée Lauder in the 2001 recession,[6] the 'lipstick effect' was seized upon as a way of understanding women's reactions to the changed conditions of the post-crunch period. Referring to the increased sales of expensive make-up products during times of recession, the lipstick effect claimed to explain how economic recessions influence women's consumer behaviour. As a countercyclical indicator of economic conditions, it suggests that lipstick sales inversely correlate to financial well-being.[7]

In December 2008, *Harper's Bazaar* featured on its front cover 'Affordable Luxuries', 'Great Finds for all Budgets' and 'Stylish steals'. In the same month, US *Vogue* featured articles on 'Reality Chick: 181 Exceptional Gifts From $5 to $500' and 'Smart Investments 24K Fashion & Beauty', while US *Elle* published the 'Gift Guide: Cheap and Chick!' advice for 'Friends with Money: How to Deal When You're the Broke One'. Promoting crunch-inspired fitness plans (including the use of workout DVDs and gym balls to avoid costly gym memberships), profiling readers learning to make homemade cocktails and outlining the apparent rise in the popularity of dinner parties and home cinema nights as an alternative way of socializing through the recession, print media represented the fallout from the crunch as a specifically gendered experience.[8] Post-crunch, female readers were promised more time with their (now unemployed) partners, weight loss (thanks to a distinct drop in the number of restaurants visited), greater food economy (with no spare cash for luxuries or waste) and a renewed appreciation for the little things in life. Obsessed with credit crunch diets (based on own brands and lower fat alternatives), cut price holidays and 'credit crunch Christmas' plans, the message of the press was clear: women should expect to suffer as a result of the global economic downturn.

Recessionistas

Fiction and the publishing industry were not immune from these debates. In 2008, *The Guardian* reported that 'the credit crunch is already driving big deals for books with a financial flavour', while Joel Rickett, Editorial Director for Viking Press, reflected that 'every publisher is now scrambling for finance and business books – these are areas that have been under-served for many years'.[9] At the 2008 World Book Fair in Frankfurt, interviews with industry insiders suggested that 'publishers were remarkably upbeat, focusing on the positive – that people will want to read about the downturn – rather than panicking about their prospects'.[10] These new publications included 'prettied up financial guides' and banking 'memoirs', but the most successful new addition was a series of new 'fictional tales of women who, armed with outrageous credit card limits, spent beyond their means, found themselves at rock bottom and lived to tell the tale'.[11]

Across the latter half of the twentieth century, women's fiction offered important representations of shifts in female employment and lifestyle. The 'sex and shopping novels' of the 1980s that emerged under the political regimes of Thatcher in the UK and Reagan in the United States often represented female protagonists obsessed with luxury and glamour and achieving self-presentation through the power of purchase. Promoting individualism and independent enterprise as the dominant ideals of their period, 'sex and shopping' heroines were characterized by personal ambition and a rejection of any perceived value in the notion of a sisterhood. During the 1990s, these trends developed into a new genre of fiction, 'chick lit'. Led by the emergence of Bridget Jones as a literary and social phenomenon, the heroine of the chick lit novel, like those of the 'sex and shopping' fictions of the previous decade, had a career and was financially independent but did not define herself through her work, instead using employment to fund her lifestyle choices. As Philips argues, chick lit heroines take 'great pleasure in conspicuous consumption [. . .] and the opportunities afforded by the multiplication of consumer goods for women who are in a position to afford them'.[12] Yet these women are often deeply unsatisfied, and engaged in a seemingly fruitless search for a love interest to fill a perceived void in their lives that capitalist consumption cannot satisfy.

In the wake of the credit crunch, chick lit authors claimed that the recession had brought about the death of their genre. In 2009, Plum Sykes, author of *Bergdorf Blondes* (2004) and *The Debutante Divorcee* (2005), argued that she would 'not set another book in modern-day America because of the credit crunch', arguing that the crunch 'just doesn't work' as a context for social comedies. For Sykes, the crunch brought with it the last 'sex and shopping book as a publishing phenomenon' because it made chick lit seem 'out of date [. . .] because of the economic reality'.[13] However, other chick lit authors, such as Sophie Kinsella, refute claims regarding the 'death' of chick lit and instead reinvigorate the genre to confront the changed conditions of the post-crunch world. Her successful series of *Shopaholic* fictions follow the fate of protagonist Becky Bloomwood as she learns economy and frugality in the face of financial disaster.[14] Kinsella reflects that the credit crunch created a choice for chick lit authors, and, while some turned away, she decided to 'embrace it. I could have thought: "Oh no, financial crisis, run away, this is all a bit serious and scary and nasty." But I had the opposite instinct. I felt like this is what this character is all about, and I should write about it. There is a sort of gallows humour. We are a nation of shoppers, and I think you have to go with that. I think it was always a mix of funny and painful.'[15]

From the foundations of 1980s 'sex and shopping' novels and 1990s 'chick lit', the Recessionista emerged as a new female protagonist for the post-crunch period. The term 'Recessionista' was established by Crunch Lit as a term for those who have their life choices removed by the crunch and who are forced into alien social, economic or emotional circumstances. The character of the Recessionista is 'the biggest story' of the post-crunch period in fiction according to Jonathan Segura, deputy editor at *US Publishers Weekly*. He argues that 'it would be impossible to write contemporary glitzy women's fiction without taking the recession into account' and predicts a future 'flood of new fiction dealing specifically with the big meltdown'.[16] Author Avis Cardella suggests that Recessionista fictions can be understood as a reaction against earlier chick lit novels that represented an earlier 'fantasy world that so many young women were living during the '90s and early 2000s', one that propagated a 'fantasy of being the single young woman who can do it all, have it all and spend it all, which in the end, just wasn't true'.[17]

As part of a wider expression of female dissatisfaction with gendered representations of financial experience in chick lit, author Michael Silverstein proposes that post-crunch 'audiences are hungry for stories of women in heroic economic roles, succeeding in what was formerly the men's club of the financial world'. However, as Silverstein goes on to argue, a concern with money, romance and social context is not a new feature of chick lit, in fact 'these issues have been and will continue to be the themes we see in storylines, as they're the ones women can readily connect with'. Jason Ashlock, co-principal of Moveable Type Literary Group in New York, supports this thesis, reflecting that 'so-called chick-lit titles have always been a way for female readers to grapple with common personal traumas [. . .] it just so happens that the great personal trauma of the moment is the economic crisis, and the fallout of the end of indulgent lifestyles filled with high consumer debt and overt materialism [. . .] [these novels] reflect that [. . .] in times of crisis [. . .] they resonate, and the metaphors become clearer when they hit closer to home.'[18]

Devoted to profiling the development of this genre, website Chicklit.com was quick to identify the Recessionista as a source of vitality for post-2000 women's fiction. Considering the impact of the credit crunch on the genre, it exclaimed 'from *Confessions of a Shopaholic* to *Recessionista* within 10 years. Who would have predicted that?'[19] Keshini Naidoo, commissioning editor at Avon (which published *Hedge Fund Wives*), argues that the character of the Recessionista 'perfectly fits the mood of the times'. Naidoo argues that traditional chick lit of the 1990s could never hope to survive in the new circumstances of the post-crunch. She suggests that 'after the downturn in the economic climate, blockbusters that glorified excessive, conspicuous consumption threatened to look both in poor taste and deeply out of touch with what readers are experiencing'. Naidoo suggested that while some readers are keen to avoid characters who simply shop and spend, 'there is still a thirst for glamorous fiction that details an aspirational lifestyle', but also an increasing market for novels 'that show the tarnish behind these gilded lifestyles' partly fuelled by 'a sense of *schadenfreude* on the part of readers'.[20]

Early Recessionista fictions draw upon their author's experience of life inside major financial institutions at the time of the financial crash and use fiction to critically reconsider the cultures and practices common to the pre-crash financial world. Mobilizing the intimate first-person-narrative voice of chick lit, these novels suggest that the 'financial crisis has not rendered chick lit redundant as a form of social commentary'.[21] Featuring a range of 'privileged protagonists who are forced to belt tighten'[22] as the crunch bites, the subjective journey of the protagonist becomes part of a wider story of a society reorientating itself to a new way of living in the radically altered social, economic and political reality post-2008. In her 2010 novel *The Recessionitas*, Alexandra Lebenthal mobilized a popular media term and applied it to three fictional female protagonists in New York and their experiences of events during and after the 2007–8 credit crunch.[23] Comprising a potted history of the financial crisis and a regular *precis* of hedge funds and trading practices, the novel draws on Lebenthal's experience as a bond seller at her family's company to offer intelligible definitions and applications of financial terms and practices to the general reader. As the crisis takes hold, each woman's life is adversely affected by events beyond their control, forcing them to engage with the economic. As the novel develops, the personal fall of corrupt bankers and their out-of-touch wives comes to mirror the crashing markets as both tumble to new lows and are forced to reassess their *modus operandi* in a post-2008 world. Mimi is the wife of a prominent trader caught in a legal scandal, Renne is an assistant to a hedge fund manager and Sasha is in charge of an asset-management company in the city. Using the traditional chick-lit settings of Manhattan and the Hamptons, the novel adds the financial crisis as a narrative agent that shapes the lives of the rich and powerful in New York.

Bond Girl (2012) develops these concerns, following the fate of graduate Alex Garrett in her first bond sales job at Cromwell Pierce, a large, fictional brokerage firm on Wall Street.[24] Author Erin Duffy wrote the novel after being made redundant by Merrill Lynch during the 2008 financial crisis. Drawing on her experience of life inside a major financial organization at the time the crunch hit, Duffy returned to work as a trader after writing the novel, but later became a full-time author. In the novel, protagonist Alex has dreamed of being a trader since she was a child and, following in her father's footsteps, she rises through the ranks to Associate Trader. On the way, she is exposed to regular abuse as a result of her gender, ranging from verbal assaults to inappropriate advances from clients and work-place politics between female staff. She is also asked to fulfil increasingly ridiculous tasks in order to prove her 'worth' or 'submission' to managers (including wheeling a $1,000 block of cheese across New York to their offices). When the crunch hits, Alex is forced to consider the values of her profession, and must choose between a life on Wall Street or a more equal, and perhaps less profitable, life away from the high-tension and pressure of the Cromwell Pierce trading desks.

Crunch Lit profiles the Recessionista as an active response to 'the recession and its attendant woes',[25] with darkly funny tales following women succeeding despite the impact of divorce, debt and the consequences of a culture of credit. Targeted at audiences who, post-crunch, have little sympathy for the shopaholic protagonists of chick lit, the Recessionista more accurately represents the post-crunch reality experience of readers. Forced into a position in which she must take stock of her life and start again after the crunch causes debt, divorce or a major career change, the Recessionista is used by Crunch Lit authors to explore opportunities for female agency and transformation brought about by the 2007–8 financial crisis.

Debt

From the horror of owing money, to the burden it places on individuals and societies, both debt and sin are often discussed in the form of financial metaphors. Debt is also the subject of many popular proverbs – people can 'pay a debt to society', be made aware that 'crime doesn't pay, carry out a 'debt of honour' or the hope that 'death pays all debts'. In literary history, debt has frequently functioned as a central plot device informed by the context, events and shared memories of its period. As Margaret Atwood argues, 'without memory there is no debt. Put another way: without story, there is no debt'. In terms of structuring a story 'debt happens as a result of actions occurring over time. Therefore, any debt involves a plot line: how you got into debt, what you did, said, and thought while you were in there, and then – depending on whether the ending is to be happy or sad – how you got out of debt, or else how you got further and further into it until you became overwhelmed by it, and sank further from view.'[26]

Western society is heavy with metaphors of debt and informed by the language of debt or owing. Debt, Atwood argues, is 'like air' – we are surrounded by it and therefore 'never think about it unless something goes wrong with the supply'.[27] Attitudes towards debt are 'deeply embedded in our entire culture'[28] and are a product of that culture. Debt carries with it connotations of shame and social judgement. From the debtors' prisons and workhouses of the nineteenth century to the credit card companies and payday loan advances of the new millennium, 'Debt is the new fat'[29] of the twenty-first century, a source of anxiety, stigma and debate but also an increasingly important element of personal identity.

In her account of the financial crisis and its fallout, Atwood writes about these poisonous activities brought about by readily available credit and its specific effects on women:

> There are accounts of shopaholic binges during which you don't even know what came over you and everything was a blur, with tearful confessions by those who've spent themselves into quivering insomniac jellies of hopeless indebtedness, and have resorted to lying, cheating, stealing and moving cheques between bank accounts as a result.[30]

The consequences of this binge and purge model is 'a penance imposed – snip, snip go the scissors on the credit cards – followed by a strict curb-on-spending regime; and finally, if all goes well, the debts are paid down, the sins are forgiven, absolution is granted, and a new day dawns'.[31] In her study *Sheconomics*, Karen Pine supports Atwood's claims with survey evidence that suggests 70 per cent of women shop to cheer themselves up and that many commit 'financial adultery', hiding purchases from their husbands.[32] More than half of women questioned by the survey said they hit the shops when they feel low, with one in five admitting to buying something during such a spree that they will never wear or use. Meanwhile only 46 per cent of the same women were preparing adequately for retirement, compared with 55 per cent of men.[33] Further, 48 per cent of women said they felt frightened by the credit crunch, while almost two-thirds (65%) expressed feelings of anxiety or worry. Pine also found that one in four women said that economic circumstances were making them sad or depressed, and while only 9 per cent claimed to feel happy, 31 per cent were 'optimistic' about the future.[34]

Through the character of the Recessionista, Crunch Lit authors focus on 'debt's harmful behaviour'[35] and the effects this can have on the psychological, professional and social standing of women. In these novels, the shadow of the credit crunch means that the fictional wives of bankers, hedge fund managers and private equity partners are forced to curb their designer habits and cut back on their spending. The female characters in Ben Elton's *Meltdown* (2009) are serviced by a range of private chefs, nannies and personal shoppers prior to 2007.[36] Employed commercially in the private sector or domestically as mothers, these women are fuelled by an addiction to the lifestyle and luxuries that money brings. Accustomed to having 'somebody to sort out their kids and somebody to sort out their lightbulbs' (13), they are consequently hit hard by the fallout from the credit crunch, an experience Monica likens to a Greek tragedy (44) in which she is thrown into a metaphorical 'fall' from fortune. This tragedy culminates in the horror of being forced to send her child to a state school when the private school pursues her and her newly redundant husband for unpaid school fees.

In Lanchester's *A Week in December* (2009), banker's wife Arabella Veals is defined only by her wealth and purchases in the pre-crunch period.[37] Consumed by doubts about her own existence, she needs 'occasional reminders that she was still actually there, and it was this unconscious need which underlay this habit of needing to look at her reflection' (45). Fellow bankers' wife Vanessa Yount experiences similar doubts about her pre-crunch identity in *Capital* (2012).[38] These doubts produce a 'brutally lonely [. . .] relentless, remorseless pounding of solitude. It was like the sea; it never stopped' (268). Significantly, both women console these concerns by running to retail. In contemporary society, as Rob Shields argues, there is 'a need to treat consumptions as an active, committed production of self and of society, which rather than assimilating individuals to styles, appropriates codes and fashions, which are made into one's own'.[39] Both Vanessa and Arabella use shopping as a form of escapism in the pre-crunch period, distracting themselves with a seemingly never-ending quest to define themselves through their purchases. Elsewhere, in *Hedge Fund Wives* (2009), Recessionista Marcy sadly reflects that she is drawn to shop because 'the saleswomen treated you the way you wish your husband still did' (136).[40] Faced with doubts and a perceived void of purpose, consumption as a form of agency offers these women a familiar and easy means of constructing a sense of self during the period before 2007–8.

While this conspicuous consumption is a target of criticism in Crunch Lit, it also proves a catalyst for change following the financial crash. Confronting the rapid drying up of ready credit to fuel their habits of consumption, Recessionistas have to curb the excesses of spending sprees and credit card bills that follow a pre-crunch culture of credit. For the Recessionista, the credit crunch functions as an occasion to halt a historic reliance on credit and consumption and instead forge a new life free from the controlling confines of debt. As Susie Mesure suggests, the Recessionista has 'cut up her credit cards, taken her kids out of private school, and, gasp, even thinks about finding a job to try to plug the gaping hole in the family finances'.[41] Formerly accustomed to tackling doubts through the power of purchase, in the wake of the crunch, Recessionistas reconsider the sources from which they draw their identity, define themselves and their purpose. In a post-crunch world, consumption as a form of agency no longer offers these women an easy means of constructing the self.

In *Confessions of a Reluctant Recessionista* (2009), Cassie goes on shopping sprees with her credit card to get over losing her job, the difficulty of finding work and splitting up with her partner.[42] Shopping takes the place of working in her day-to-day life but also offers a new sense of purpose, focus and identity – an option denied to her by the depressed employment market of the twenty-first century. However, these identity-searching spending sprees also position Cassie in a huge amount of debt, which forces her to consider the reasons behind her spending habits. The objects she purchases and the bills documenting her actions effectively make visible her problem to friends, who stage an 'intervention'. She is instructed that 'You can't just spend your way out of every problem you ever have' (99), and Cassie realizes the need to go on an 'anti-extravagance drive' (105) and to live within her means. She reasons that, 'for as long as I was unemployed, for as long as this blasted recession lasted, I was going to have to stop living like a rich person' (149). This involves experimenting with new sources of identity via a 'clothes swap party' (165) in which participants can literally 'try on' alternative identities and adopting a general 'Less Is More spirit' (166), more in keeping with the economic times. Rejecting a previous reliance on 'totems of excess', Recessionista fiction follows heroines as they battle with the trauma of a loss of consumption and the new identity options it brings.⁴³

Set in the American State of New Jersey, the State that has the most shopping malls in any one area in the world – *The Penny Pinchers' Club* (2009) follows the fate of Recessionista Kat, an interior designer who mimics the lifestyle and spending habits of her wealthy clients.⁴⁴ Accustomed to living beyond her means, Kat is the opposite of her frugal, economist husband. When Kat finds suggestive emails from her husband Griff to a PA, and discovers that he has a secret bank account containing money syphoned from their joint account as a marriage 'bailout' fund, Kat begins to surreptitiously prepare for a divorce and a future alone. With just seven months to raise $15,000 – the amount she estimates she will need to start again – the novel follows her experiences of 'penny pinching', including cancelling cable TV and kicking her $240-a-month Starbucks habit. When these fail to make an impact, she joins her local 'Penny Pinchers Club'. This budget-conscious group of individuals are a world away from her usual friends, but share the same need to make savings and changes to their spending habits. Breaking historical habits of reliance on her husband and credit, Kat mobilizes her own capacity to earn and save as a restorative response to her changed conditions. Finding happiness through hardship, Kat, like her other fellow Recessionistas, is granted a renewed sense of personal perspective and individual agency in the wake of the financial crises.

Confronted with reduced circumstances, a crisis of self and professional and emotional breakdowns of relationships, the women of Recessionista fiction do not run to retail like their chick lit ancestors. Instead, they use life-changing events as catalysts for awareness-raising activities. Moving through an arc of anger and denial to depression then acceptance, characterized by motifs of empowerment and realigned values, these women rediscover the value not only of money, but of people and behaviour in the wake of the credit crunch. Overthrowing practices of credit, purchase and consumption, in favour of saving, self-awareness and recycling, the Recessionista mobilizes the changed conditions of the post-crunch period to liberate herself from the constraints of debt and regain control over her finances and future.

Divorce

During the post-crunch period, the complicated relationship between love and money was subject to new magnification. The credit crunch had a significant impact on divorce rates in the UK and the United States. Divorce rates had increased rapidly in 1993 in the wake of the 1990–2 recession, and did the same in the early 1980s. Following the 2007–8 credit crunch, divorce rates rose by a 5 per cent in the United States, after five consecutive years of decline. As a change in circumstances motivated one partner to leave and separate the marital finances, the 'credit crunch divorce' became a familiar feature of post-2008 society. Statistics emerged suggesting that those who lost their job had an increased chance of losing their partner, while a woman losing her job was increasingly likely to lead to partnership dissolution the longer the partnership had lasted.

Significantly, the credit crunch had different impacts on the marriages of the very wealthy and the very poor. The financial crisis led to an increase in the divorce rate between wealthy individuals and a decline among the less well-off. Poorer couples were unable to tolerate the costs of divorce and as a result many stayed together, or continued to cohabit while separated, unable to afford the cost of renting alone. The credit crunch put disproportionate pressure on the 'super-wealthy', and the number of divorces between couples with assets of $10 million or more increased dramatically after 2007. A 2009 survey by *Divorce On-line* detailed a 50 per cent increase in the number of divorces between December 2007 and 2008, with women filing in 60 per cent of cases. Four out of ten cited unreasonable behaviour, with many blaming the financial irresponsibility of their husbands. The economic climate also caused further complications for the assessment of marital assets, as volatility in relation to shared investments and pensions, doubt over property values and an increased risk of redundancy led to disagreements regarding values.

The collapse of the financial system is echoed in Crunch Lit by the breakdown of personal relationships, but, for the Recessionista, the breakdown of a relationship often leads to a personal breakthrough in awareness and personal direction. When Cassie is dumped by her boyfriend trader Dan at the beginning of *Confessions of a Reluctant Recessionista*, she is forced to re-evaluate her situation and lack of ambition in the workplace, making a shift from a large corporate organization to an independent specialist start-up company where she earns her stripes and is rewarded with promotion. Breaking with her trader boyfriend leads Cassie to a realization that the financial world is 'shallow and consumerist, they're obsessed with money and cars and clothes and things. Things, things, things. The men are pigs and the women know that unless they fit in with the boys they'll be harassed to within an inch of their lives, so most of them end up being pigs too' (201). An important part of this recognition is Cassie's reignited sense of ambition and passion for her own career. Despite working in the financial industry for all her professional life, a relationship breakdown and newly unemployed state make her realize that: 'I was never interested in how the markets work, how the traders make their money. I didn't care what a derivative was or whether Bank X merged with Bank Y and what the implications of that would be. My mother was right. Mothers usually are. I had to get myself a job in a field that I was at least vaguely interested in' (205). As a result, Cassie explores a wide range of career options, including temping (difficult in times of economic downturn), walking dogs for money, and volunteering. She finally hears about an admin role in an independent wine company through one of her dog-walking contacts and works hard to get promoted. At the end of the novel we are told that she is 'moving on to greater things' (313), away from the city, traders and designer Louboutin shoes.

The *Ex-Mrs Hedgefund* (2009) follows the journey of another transformed Recessionista, Holly, whose husband works as one of the 'hedgies' at the fictional Comet Capital.[45] With an ex-career as a music writer, Holly has a happy life being a stay-at-home parent to her son. It is only when she discovers evidence of her husband's infidelity that she finds herself swiftly divorced, with an expensive home but no income. The majority of the novel is focused on Holly's dating life and quest for a new sense of self and direction in a post-crunch, post-divorce world. As the narrative develops, readers are encouraged to see that 'Holly is experimenting not only with men, but also with her authentic self as she learns to finally stop silencing her inner blue-blood voice and let out her real thoughts, feelings and comments.'[46] Holly reassembles herself post-divorce to reinvent her life and purpose away from the charity dinners and fundraisers of the 'Hedgefund Wife' towards a career as a journalist and re-engagement with her professional life. It is only then, argue these fictions, that our heroines find true happiness, self-fulfilment and, notably, stable equal relationships. Pre-publication press for *The Ex-Mrs Hedgefund* centred on the very industries and sections of society that the text attempts to satirize. *Vogue* hosted the launch of the novel in 2009 while a preview in *Vanity Fair* praised the way the Kergman's tale goes 'for Wall Street's jugular'.[47] Highlighting the novel's 'prescient title',[48] leading women's magazines celebrated the Recessionista protagonist as a champion of female strength and resourcefulness in the wake of the credit crunch.

The financial recompense of a separation or divorce is presented as a significant form of consolation and empowerment for the Recessionista. The paratext of *Hedge Fund Wives* (2009) advertises the tale as set deep 'in the throes of the credit crunch' and the financial downturn dominates the text but the novel is equally framed by the divorce of the protagonist and the emotional as well as financial fallout from the crunch. Marcy, a heroine newly arrived in New York as the wife of a hedge fund manager from Chicago, finds herself 'surrounded by hedge-fund wives' in a city where there is, initially at least, 'nothing but the promise of pleasure' (1). However, as an outsider she is also 'deeply afraid of the other wives' (3), especially when she is educated into the 'seven kinds' (13) of hedge fund wife – the Accidental, Westminster, Stephanie Seymour, Former Secretary, Socialite, Workaholic and Breeder. She is also given a set of 'HFW rules' (including '"Never ask him about work. If he wants to talk about it, he will"') and 'never talk about your own problems' (44–5) which make her realize that 'I didn't fit the mould at all' (45). Instead Marcy remains detached as an observer and notes how the other wives 'lived in a bubble [. . .] [were] delusional and completely removed from reality' (65).

As an ex-financier, Marcy is quick to realize that economic conditions are changing in the lead up to the crunch. While the other wives in her social circle turn their heads and ignore the signs, she confesses that:

> Although no one spoke of it, the economy had begun to sour and every day brought fresh tales of falling fortunes. Most of the women assumed that their vast monetary reserves would protect them from having to alter any aspect of their enviable lives, but

of course they were wrong. Wealth is relative by nature, and if one day you have a hundred, billion dollars and the next you have only fifty, the things that were once within reach [. . .] are suddenly out of it. Under such circumstances, it's not long before a marriage built around material possessions and predicated upon the shared responsibility of their care and maintenance, begins to crumble. (2–3)

As the reader's eyes on this world, Marcy reminds us that the 'long run of American prosperity was coming to an end' (32) and that this would be most sharply felt in 'hedgefundlandia' (39). When the crunch hits, Marcy's husband John develops a cocaine and painkillers addiction to cope with the pressure, but refuses to allow Marcy to return to work, considering a working wife to be a reflection on his financial shortcomings. Marcy is unable to understand her husband's desire to make 'money for the pure sport of it', but wishes he could instead 'manufacture a product' or create something real. Instead, she watches as 'they partied despite the darkening economic clouds, despite the millions of foreclosure signs popping up across the country like little red flags. A storm was coming, but no one wanted to see it, least of all, of course, the wives' (67). Marcy admits to 'feeling worried about the world in general' (171) on several occasions, even before the revelation that her husband has cheated on her and impregnated another 'Hedge Fund Wife' while supposedly trying for a baby with her. The behaviour of Marcy's trader husband, and this betrayal by a fellow 'Hedge Fund Wife', motivate her to take stock of her pre-crunch life in New York, refocus herself, and return to the world of work following the financial crisis. She ends the novel with her own business, pregnant with another child and, conveniently, married to a billionaire. Freed from the constraint and financial dependence of marriage, the Recessionista is released into a new world of independence, employment and self-realization. Forced to craft a new identity, career or relationship, the credit crunch becomes a landmark occasion in the lives of women formerly troubled by lifestyle, money worries or self-esteem issues. Engaging a period of crisis as a chance for reform and regeneration, the Recessionista emerges from credit-crunch divorce as a new, stronger individual with direction, identity and aspirations beyond the confines of marriage.

Entrepreneurialism

Highlighting the challenges faced by women working in enduringly male-dominated employment sectors before the credit crunch, fiction focuses on the underrepresented character of the female trader or banker to emphasize the isolated and problematic role of women in the financial industry pre-2007. In Elton's *Meltdown*, traders opine that there are 'not many women in our game' (124) and this absence is represented across the genre. *Capital* includes one token female trader, Michelle, who is analysed by boss Roger Yount in terms of her appearance and manner rather than her performance. He reflects that:

> Female traders [. . .] went super girly and manipulative, or were more alpha males than the alpha males. Michelle was the second type. She was about thirty and came from Bristol. She had a uniform: pin striped trouser suit, worn with lots of make-up and very short, almost cropped hair. She was deliberately abrasive and swore conscientiously, painstakingly, as if she had taken a course in it. And yet there was a femininity to her too; her clothes were always slightly too tight, as if her womanliness wanted to burst out to contradict the rest of her persona. When Roger wondered about it, which he quite often did, he would speculate about her weekend and holiday self, whether it was gentler and softer. To see her cursing and rowing at work was to wonder if she spent the weekend lying on a chase lounge, having her toenails done while eating Turkish delight and watching *Sex and the City*. (282)

Unable to decode Michelle or her apparent motivations for entering such a masculine and male-dominated profession, Roger reframes her with a stereotypical feminine alter-ego, prone to girlie binges outside of office hours. *A Week in December* represents a similar landscape in which 'occasional female City staff' appear as either 'painted creatures' or calculating whores 'determined to work their way through every member of certain trading teams' (235). In Silver's novel, as a PA in the same organization, Cassie literally looks in from the outside and explains to readers that there are a 'handful of women on the floor [. . .] They have to work seventy-hour weeks in what is sometimes an unbearable environment – the stories you hear about misogyny and bullying in the City are fairly accurate. The pretty girls spend their time fending off the unwanted advances and the less pretty girls have to put up with incessant cruel remarks' (24). Cassie's trader friend Ali has apparently resigned herself to 'being one of the boys, which is virtually a job requirement when you do what she does, that she sometimes forgets the impact she makes on the opposite sex' (2). While some women de-sexualize themselves on the trading floor men consume female traders as a spectacle in these novels, analysing them in an attempt to decode why women would end up in such a masculine environment.

This hostile and limiting employment context is confronted by the character of the Recessionista in the post-crunch period. In Crunch Lit, women respond more quickly than men to the changed conditions of the crunch, adjusting their lifestyles and employment accordingly. Spotting gaps in the market and identifying opportunities for acquiring new skills, Recessionistas insert gender into a wider rewriting of employment practice post-2008. Exhibiting financial and professional prowess, they display resilience and stress-resistance that enables them to succeed during a period of economic uncertainty.

Unleashing the business woman within, the credit crunch offers an occasion for professional success and the promotion of sustainable personal finance. The Recessionista recognizes the period following financial crisis as a time to approach the world of work with job satisfaction at the top of her priority list. Following the credit crunch, the Recessionista looks on the positive side of changed conditions and proves more stress-resistant than the men that surround her. Confronted with job-losses or the need to pursue paid employment as direct result of the financial crisis, the Recessionista re-engages with the post-crunch employment contexts of the twenty-first century as an opportunity for change. Adopting new roles, careers, or establishing their own business, the post-crunch world is seized by the Recessionista as a site of opportunity and advancement.

In *Confessions of a Reluctant Recessionista*, a change of job brought by post-crunch redundancies motivates Recessionista Cassie Cavanagh to rediscover her personal ambition. Cassie is 'just a lowly PA' at investment bank Hamilton Churchill, who initially defines herself through her relationship with trader Dan rather than with her own career. The role of the PA suits Cassie at the start of the novel, since it does not carry 'the responsibility of buying and selling millions of pounds worth of stock, of trying to call the market, to sort the good tips from the bad, trying to please my clients while also pleasing my bosses'(3). In the wake of the crunch, Cassie is sacked, not only before male workers but before other, less experienced female workers. This final insult makes her reassess her career ('I didn't really have a dream career. I'd never really given it all that much thought') and her thinking that as long as she earns 'enough money to keep me in shoes, cocktails and the occasional weekend away in Paris or Rome, I really didn't mind that much what I did' (61).

The Recessionista also mobilizes the changed conditions of the post-crunch world to empower other women, and men. In *Hedge Fund Wives* Marcy is 'screwed over' for promotion by a female colleague in her old bank before 2007 and asks 'Why is it that women turn against each other like that? We should be supporting each other, not masterminding each other's firings' (300). This question echoes across Recessionista fiction as women use the post-crunch period and circumstances to support, rather than constrict, other women. As a result of the credit crunch, the Recessionista not only realizes her own entrepreneurial capacity, but mobilizes this and her own financial resources to empower others. *Meltdown*'s Lizzie works her way up in the service sector, selling sandwiches to bankers in the City too time-poor to leave their desks for lunch, before building a catering and food business that makes her millions. As Jimmy reflects in the wake of his own post-crunch housing woes, 'Lizzie was still rich. Her money was REAL. Concrete. It was secured by actual concrete STUFF [. . .] She hadn't built her fortune on the shifting sands of the futures market but on foundations hewn from the solid, timeless rock of people's love of posh things, fabulous design and exquisite nibbles' (60). When Jimmy and his wife need post-crunch financial support to service their huge mortgage, it is Lizzie who offers him a rescue package in the form of a loan when his own business interest is threatened by the declining mortgage sector.

The pronounced focus *Hedge Fund Wives* takes on matters of employment, independence and sisterhood were core to the aims of author Boncompagni in creating a Recessionista novel. She argues that 'I'm a big believer that all married women should keep working and networking even if they don't "have" to, because not only will their husbands respect them more for it, but they will respect themselves more for it, too [. . .] One of the main themes of *Hedge Fund Wives* is how foolish it is to depend on a man for your emotional and financial security' (358). Responding to the changed conditions of the post-crunch period, other Recessionistas seek to monopolize on the new contexts and demands created by an economic recession. Gigi makes her living as a freelance food writer; although she comes under criticism for being 'out of step with the economic climate, but also insensitive to the rising cost of food and gourmet food in particular' (126); she, unlike the banking men in the novel, listens and adapts to the post-crunch period, creating a new series of cookery books that tackle issues facing the austerity consumer.

Later in the novel, Marcy uses the proceeds from her divorce to set up 'Demeter and Co. [. . .] a female friendly working environment. We instituted several companywide policies to make it easier for the moms on our staff to balance motherhood and work, which has given us some of the best employee retention rates on Wall Street. We also offer several internships for high school students from middle-to-low income families, and have sent a handful of our most promising interns, including Gemma, through college via the scholarship program' (346–7).[49] Boncompagni argues that she wanted to use Recessionista fiction to 'depict life in New York after a stock market crash or other cataclysmic economic events that plunged the city into a recession [. . .] if these businesses went belly up, so would the good times [. . .] women whose lives revolved not around status but money and the consumption of material goods'.[50] She suggests that times of great economic volatility like the 2007–8 credit crunch 'are rich with drama, and I was excited about exploring how a market turn would affect the personal lives of a handful of characters'. Deliberately setting her novel in 'a period of tremendous uncertainty', the author was conscious that 'the economic downturn would change the dynamics'[51] of her text, enabling her to explore the ways and means by which female characters could not only respond to but also direct the redistribution of capital and control in the wake of the financial crisis.

Demonstrating flexibility and capacity for personal and professional growth, an openness and willingness to change, the Recessionista shows courage in making decisions and taking risks in the post-crunch period. As a signal of a new culture in Crunch Lit, women move into the workforce in leading or more prominent roles, or take on new responsibility for their own employment and income. No longer reliant on the finances and career of their partners, the future of women's entrepreneurship is promoted by these fictions through tales of women literally 'starting up' again and coping with the changed demands of the post-crunch period.

Women on board(s)

Following the credit crisis, media rhetoric positioned women as the victims of a financial crisis caused by men. As 'quite literally a man-made disaster, a monster created in the testosterone-drenched environment of Wall Street and the City', the credit crunch was offered by these discourses as the logical product of a male-dominated banking sector.[52] In her analysis of the unseen impact of the crunch on women, Ruth Sunderland argues that 'to the many thousands of female workers who have lost their jobs the recession may well look like a case of highly-paid men creating a mess, and low-paid women suffering the consequence'.[53] Gillian Wilmot also used her column in the *Financial Times* to speculate that if women had occupied more top positions in the banking world, then the credit crunch might never have happened. She argues that, in general, 'the more financially rewarding the task the more men' and as a result, the credit crunch marked a particularly 'lethal combination of testosterone, complexity and greed'.[54] In 2007 women held 13 executive directorships on the boards of Financial Times Stock Exchange (FTSE) 100 companies, or 3.6 per cent of the total. There were 110 female non-executive directors, 14.5 per cent of the total.[55] This lack of representation at the highest levels of the sector at the centre of this crisis became the subject of widespread debate centring on gender inequality at the heart of financialization in the wake of the financial crash.

Post-crunch, many female financial leaders united in calls for reform and review, and took the opportunity to outline potential paths forward involving greater gender equality. Nadereh Chamlou, a World Bank senior adviser, suggests that the credit crisis offered the world a unique opportunity to 'insert gender into the re-writing of the rules'. She outlined the need for 'new people at the table – people who are not associated with the past' and for a clean slate to be drawn in the sector.[56] Dr Barbara Casu Lukac of the Cass Business School also argues that 'regardless of the financial meltdown, attitudes towards women working still need to change; there is a need for family friendly and flexible working schedules as well as affordable and reliable childcare'. She claims that 'banking is still a predominantly male industry, particularly at the top'.[57] To prove the potential of having women involved in high-level finance, one expert highlighted the fortunes of French bank BNP Paribas, whose stock fell just 20 per cent in the crunch; 39 per cent of BNP managers are women, whereas in Credit Agricole, the largest retail banking group in France, whose managers are just 16 per cent female, stock had fallen by 50 per cent.[58]

In Crunch Lit, the Recessionista protagonist echoes these contextual calls for greater gender equality, economic education and visibility in business boardrooms following the 2007–8 financial crisis. Formerly defined by the structuring influences, practices and frameworks of debt, traditions of marriage or obligations of employment, the Recessionista mobilizes the changed contexts of the post-crunch period as an opportunity to enact self-transformation. Navigating the credit crunch, directing their own careers and cultivating successful personal and professional relationships, the Recessionista is significant in representing an alternative social, political and economic narrative on the impact of the credit crunch and its aftermath. The heroines of these novels do not always end up with more money as a result of the economic downturn, but do achieve a more developed sense of self and a renewed focus on their own identity and purpose.

Focusing on the empowering influence of a liberation from credit, a marital partner or a 9–5 job, female characters reduce their reliance on others and become self-sustaining and self-aware. Even *Cosmopolitan* magazine suggested that Recessionista fiction is finally 'something good [. . .] to come of this recession after all. Bring on the tales of women who are drowning in debt, unlucky in love and actually have to go to work to earn a living'.[59] Offering irony, agency, independence and economic acumen as key to surviving the crunch and its aftermath, the women of these novels are not represented as homogeneous but diverse and responsive to the after-effects of the crunch. Embracing changes brought about by the financial crisis including debt, divorce, unemployment and re-employment, the Recessionista uses the crunch as an opportunity to reorient her life and lifestyle, empowering others and taking a new, active role in authoring her own future.

Confounding media narratives of victimhood, unemployment and financial ruin, Recessionistas stand independent of their male counterparts and mobilize cultural and economic capital for social good, empowering themselves and others to ensure that diversity and sustainability become the foundations for future success. In the Recessionista, contemporary Crunch Lit authors have achieved a deeper connection to a situation that more accurately represents the situation of post-crunch readers. Post-2008, reinvention becomes the key to survival not only for the Recessionista, but also for the genre of 'chick lit' itself. The Recessionista is significant not only for making visible and analysing the relationship between gender and financialization in the twenty-first century, but also because she offers a model for the potential of the financial world as a hitherto underused setting in contemporary women's fiction. Faced with shrinking finances and fallouts from diminished incomes through divorce, the crunch and unemployment, the Recessionista draws upon reduced resources and transforms misfortune into motivation to exercise previously unrecognized skills and abilities. Championing the Recessionista as bringing a taste of reality to a chick lit in danger of extinction, 'recession-proof'[60] Crunch Lit fictions of female solidarity and agency call for less heels and more financial awareness in literary representations of women in the twenty-first century.

6

Financial performance

If there's a crisis, one can be sure there is always someone prepared to turn it into a drama.

JENNY ARMSTRONG[1]

From television drama and film documentary, to workplace and home improvement reality shows, stage and screen writings sought to reframe the financial crisis. These new writings tackle the dual problem of how to represent finance and its future in the new millennium, providing active interventions in a highly contentious period of recent history, as well as new examinations of the changed conditions of the period following the financial crisis.

Staging the crunch

Confronting the events of the credit crunch through music, movement and the spoken word, stage representations sought to improve audience understandings of the contexts informing events, encouraging a symbiotic relationship with financial education in its aftermath. Offering the contemporary stage as a place to consider the re-evaluation of cultural concepts and the improvement of political awareness, drama, comedy and musical theatre set about establishing new representations and understandings of the credit crunch. Concerned with making a drama out of a crisis, stage writers used the crunch as the basis of new productions. Reinvigorating theatre with a range of plays that tackle the recession, their works offer a vital connection between what happens on the stage and in the wider world, creating new perspectives on, and understandings of, the conditions and contexts of this highly contentious period.

In 2007, critic Charles Spencer wrote of his fears that the theatre would 'become an increasingly unaffordable luxury as the credit crunch got worse, and people woke up wondering whether they would get through the week without being summoned to collect their P45'.[2] In fact, the theatrical world not only survived, but thrived in the wake of the credit crunch. As the *Society of London Theatre*'s Nica Burns reflects, 'when times are hard, people are more likely to spend what little money they have on being cheered up' by a visit to the theatre.[3] Twelve months later, Spencer was forced to use his weekly column in British newspaper *The Telegraph* to concede that people were actually 'going to the theatre in amazingly large numbers. I can't remember ever being as busy as I have in the past five months'.[4]

The predicted 'Broadway Plague' bemoaned by critics such as Spencer actually translated into more savvy, rather than fewer theatre-goers. Writing in 2008, critic Michael Billington argued that there remained 'a huge hunger for good drama' in the wake of the credit crunch, 'whether it takes the form of re-imagined classics or new writing with a sharp political edge. There is no evidence to suggest the credit crunch has affected that one jot.'[5] Straight dramas and musicals faired equally well following the financial crisis, with theatres at near capacity and satirical shows such as *Avenue Q* (2003–) and *The Book of Mormon* (2011–) running for long periods on both sides of the Atlantic. Bankers formed the cast of *Blow Up! The Credit Crunch Musical* (2009) a comic tale of failure in the financial system narrated by a disgraced German financier, Max Klein (played by actor Charlie Talbot in a dreadful, but comic German accent) who relates his fall from grace with the help of an Oompah band dressed in lederhosen and Tyrolean hats. In 2013, a musical version of twentieth-century novel *American Psycho* (2013) launched in London. The production mixed 1980s music with original songs, using choreography to deflect the more graphic violence of the novel. Underscoring its relevance to the post-crunch context, a press release for the new musical emphasized an intention to put 'Patrick Bateman centre stage as an anti-hero for our time' and offer a 'satirical commentary on capitalism, resonating as strongly now as it did two decades ago'.[6] Although writer Duncan Sheik admitted that he initially thought it 'was the worst idea for a musical ever', critics generally responded positively to the musical's sleek 1980s sheen, with hi-tech designs by Es Devlin.

In the autumn of 2009, David Hare's *The Power of Yes* opened in the National Theatre's Lyttelton Theatre. Hare recalls that National Theatre Director Nicholas Hytner told him that the 'National Theatre had to have a play about the financial crisis'.[7] His drama *The Power of Yes* is not a play as such, but an attempt to tell a story: the story of the credit crunch as recounted by the people at its heart. The drama opens with the line: 'This isn't a play. It's a story. It doesn't pretend to be a play. It pretends only to be a story.' The subtitle – 'a dramatist seeks to understand the financial crisis' – offers another clear reference to its self-conscious status as a piece of verbatim theatre. In its capacity to discuss contemporary issues on stage, verbatim theatre offers writers a powerful form for political critique. Using extracts and language from original sources to re-examine a recent event or current issue, the playwright often interviews a range of individuals directly involved, and uses their testimonies to build a play based on real-life experiences. Hare had previously written verbatim theatre about contemporary issues including the war in Iraq and privatization. Verbatim theatre enabled Hare to address his aim of 'clarity. I want a non-professional audience to understand an incredibly complicated subject, and no longer feel excluded when it's reported on television'[8] For *The Power of Yes*, Hare set about interviewing a variety of people about the crunch, including many chief players in the crash such as George Soros and Ronald Cohen. He then used their words to inform his play, through a cast of 24 (named and unnamed) bankers, financial journalists, industrialists, academics and lawyers.

In *The Power of Yes*, Hare significantly extends his use of the verbatim form to comment on the process of creation, including himself as a character on stage ('the author'), drawing attention to the play as a conscious construct of exacting research methods. The illustrated programme accompanying the 2009 production even contains a timeline of the financial crisis, resonant quotations selected by the author, sketches of two influential figures – Maynard Keynes and Ayn Rand – and an extensive reading list of secondary texts for audiences to consult after the show. At the start of the play, one of Hare's interviewees points out that 'the author' faces a difficult task in attempting to dramatize the events of the financial crisis, and wonders whether it is possible to 'stage' the stock market. As a literal expression of a desire for 'facts', the play even featured a blackboard on stage, giving the production a lecture-like approach. *The Power of Yes* is a very informative piece of drama but was criticized for doing little more than dramatizing journalism, and sadly proved very dull to watch. As Ruth Sutherland argues, the play 'doesn't work as drama. It's more like a lecture given by two dozen speakers'.[9] Andrew Haydon's review also reflected that 'given how pressing the issues are, it is strange how uninteresting [. . .] *Yes* manages to make them'.[10] Mediated through 'the author' character on stage, the narrative of *The Power of Yes* is subject to a sustained information-overload, leaving audiences heavy on facts, but light on entertainment.

The crisis in the financial world translated more successfully in the field of stand-up comedy. Christopher Stevens argues that 'the best gags are forged in hard times', and historically the British 'have fought back against every economic downturn [. . .] with a sense of humour. In the Depression of the Thirties, the energy crisis of the Seventies and 2007–8 current credit crunch, stand-up comedy has flourished.'[11] Comedy has always been quick to respond to contextual social, political and economic affairs and accordingly the credit crunch became a significant source for stand-up comedy in the years following 2008. As a form of satire and relief, but also an important source of education, comedy attempted to respond to and combat depressing discourses of austerity. Confronting the crunch through humour, some comedians wrote material encouraging audiences to learn through laughter, while others altered the production and marketing of their stand-up shows in response to the changed conditions of the post-crunch period.

At the 2009 Edinburgh Festival Fringe, the world's biggest comedy festival, the credit crunch was cited as the reason behind a boom in stand-up comedy ticket sales, as well as a proliferation of new 'free' shows. The number of free shows at the Edinburgh

Fringe increased by a third in 2009, while some venues launched daily cut-price ticket offers in an attempt to respond to the pressing financial circumstances of theatre-goers.[12] Among the shows staged were many original comedy productions that directly addressed the financial crisis, including Daniel Atkinson's one-man show *The Credit Crunch and Other Biscuits* (2009) and Frank Skinner's *Credit Crunch Cabaret* (2009). Uniting a range of well-known performers for a ticket price of only £10, the *Credit Crunch Cabaret* asked comedians to perform for a fraction of their usual rates to reduce ticket costs. Skinner was motivated to get involved in the project after losing a 'few million' pounds of his own savings during in the 2007–8 financial crash after investing heavily in American insurance company AIG, that later had to be bailed out by the US government.[13] Prior to the 2009 Edinburgh Festival, Skinner claimed that the show meant that he would end up making 'less [money] than I was on when I performed at the [London comedy venue] *The Comedy Store* in the 1980s, but I think this is important [...] Comedy is the best way to forget what's going on in these dark, depressing days, but it costs about £30 to watch a big name in the famous venues so I'll do it at an affordable price. Hopefully it will spread to other cities.'[14] Speaking to changed concepts of 'value' in the post-crunch period and finding something to laugh about in the toughest of times, the comedy industry boomed throughout the period following the financial crisis.

Comedy also provided a form by which performers could use the stage as 'an opportunity to put the boot into those suited and booted high earners that everyone loves to hate – the merchant bankers – and highlight their unfortunate cockney rhyming slang couplet'.[15] In the UK, the 2008 UK pantomime season witnessed a revival of the banker as a stage villain. Jon Bradfield, the writer of *Dick Whittington*, at the King's Head Theatre, Islington, North London, decided to make the show's traditional baddy 'King Rat' a banker and property developer. Bradfield was inspired to turn to the world of finance because 'people are gob-smacked by what has happened in the financial markets, and taking a humorous look at it is one way of coming to terms with it [...] Many of the scenarios will be familiar to audiences who have followed the trajectory of the property bubble and the credit crunch.'[16] Soon bankers began appearing in stage comedies and in stand-up comedy sets as a new face of deceit and target for ridicule.

Combining elements of drama, musicals and comedy, Lucy Prebble's *Enron* has arguably been the most successful and acclaimed piece of theatre about the financial crisis to date. *Enron* premiered at the Chichester Festival Theatre (from 11 July to 29 August 2009), before London transfers to the Jerwood Downstairs at the Royal Court Theatre from 17 September to 7 November 2009 and then the Noël Coward Theatre from 16 January to 14 August 2010 (after a cast change on 8 May). Commissioned in 2006 before the credit crunch, the play dramatizes the story of Texan energy giant, Enron. Enron traded derivatives in many key areas including electricity, telecommunications and paper. *Fortune Magazine* named Enron the most innovative company in the United States for five consecutive years from 1995 to 2000.

However, it was the company's 'mark to market' accounting – in which it counted as current profits monies from deals that were not due to arrive for some time in the future – that created a situation 'so spectacularly and so systematically and so magnificently, reekingly wrong that it was in its way almost a thing of beauty'.[17] When Enron's essentially corrupt accounting was finally exposed, the revelation rocked its shares value which crashed from $90 to absolutely nothing. Enron tricked the stock market and the rest of the world into thinking it was making money, deceived key investors and politicians and was even implicated in the machinations in the electricity industry that led to the blackouts that blighted California during the year 2000. Enron executives lied about profits and kept the company's debt off balance-sheets, making the business appear far more successful than it really was. The extent of this culture of deception was only made clear when Enron filed for chapter 11 bankruptcy in December 2001.[18]

Prebble's *Enron* combines vaudeville and a mad-cap focus on enjoyment and learning about the 'other' world of finance. Its strapline – 'there was a warning: and its name was Enron' – makes clear connections between the legacy of Enron and the following financial crisis. Examining contemporary faith in finance, the characters in *Enron* cite the *Financial Times* as their religious text of choice, orate in the style of evangelic preachers and seek to convert others into financial believers. Ventriloquizing real-life players in the financial crisis such as Jeffrey Skilling, the play features financiers dancing with light sabers, engaging in work-outs using office equipment and singing songs about credit in barbershop quartets. Incorporating culturally knowing intertextual references to Hollywood movies (including *Jurassic Park* and *Star Wars*) and injecting twenty-four-hour rolling news into the unfolding drama on stage, *Enron* even choreographs the events of 9/11 using witness statements from traders, with projections of television news footage as a backdrop.

The many theatrical devices mobilized by the production – from three blind banking mice, to corporate raptors, and the 'Tweedle-Dee and Tweedle-Dumb' Siamese-twin 'Lehman Brothers' – collectively achieve an effective balance between documentary and fiction. According to the programme accompanying the production, these devices 'help to make accessible the corporate complexity of America and the World', but they also conspire to produce a confusing, and at times, contradictory chorus of voices and opinions on events.[19] Critics praised this combination, arguing that stylistically *Enron* stands 'in refreshing contrast to David Hare's quasi-verbatim response to capitalism's *annus horribilis*, *The Power of Yes*'.[20] A voyeuristic investigation into corporate ambition, the play executes a dramatic examination of why and how financial malpractice happens, as well as the role of both individuals and organizations in these practices. Combining classical tragedy and slapstick comedy, this multimedia morality tale for modern times generates new perspectives on the period leading up to the credit crunch.

Using magic and puppetry to suggest that capitalism itself is just another form of illusion or trick, Pebble's *Enron* offers accessible explanations of complex financial ideas and practices, telling a wider story about widespread post-crunch concerns – morality, ethics and active choices about right and wrong. Prebble argues that 'there is something human, something personal, even emotional, about a financial bubble. [. . .] A marketplace is just a group of people behaving, after all. Just like a workplace, or a family.'[21] Drawing on the credit crisis as a shared phenomenon, the theatrical world she creates uses the stage to re-present the causes, events and consequences of the credit crunch. While Enron was a triumph of style over content, in *Enron* the play both content and style unite to produce a cultural representation of a crisis that effectively highlights 'the gap between perception and reality' that Enron was able to manipulate so effectively.

Encouraging a new awareness of value as a constantly shifting, and highly political abstraction in the post-crunch period, drama, comedy and musical theatre offer original insights into the contemporary world, demonstrating a capacity to actively engage audiences in current affairs and in doing so make a complicated event such as the credit crunch seem relevant and comprehensible. As critic Jenny Armstrong argued in 2009, 'if you want to understand the financial crisis, you should go to the theatre'.[22] Raising awareness among the public, strengthening knowledge and inclusivity in current affairs and promoting financial citizenship, the stage adopted a profoundly political role during the fallout from the financial crisis. Responding both to the changed contexts of theatre and new audience trends in the financial downturn, drama, comedy and musical theatre emerged as dynamic forms in which new writings could consider the social, political and economic causes and consequences of the credit crunch.

Crunch TV

While production timeframes in the film industry meant that it was relatively slow to respond to the financial crisis, television stepped in to fill the void of understanding that characterized the post-crunch period. Because television 'moves much faster' and 'the production costs are lower',[23] the TV industry boomed, drawing new audiences and new kudos to the small screen. Producing rapid, relevant and innovative productions that addressed not only the causes of the crunch, but events during 2007–8 and their long-term consequences, television responded by creating a range of new programmes and genres.

Radio and television dramas representing events during the financial crisis were soon followed by a made-for-television feature examining the consequences of the crash for both bankers and members of the public. Described by critic Rachel Cooke as 'a searing exploration of the financial and moral fallout of economic collapse – and one of a growing number of examples of how culture is reflecting the times'[24] *Freefall* (2009) was the 'first television film to tackle the financial crisis and its human consequences head on'.[25] Directed by Dominic Savage and premièring on BBC Two on 14 July 2009, critics celebrated the 'horrifying relevance'[26] of the film and its emphasis on the crunch as a collaborative product of wider cultures of credit.

Freefall follows the experiences of the credit crunch from both sides of the CDO market. Following the fortunes of two old school friends, 'Diamond' Dave Matthews who works for a ruthless mortgage firm selling discounted mortgages to customers with bad credit ratings, and Jim Potter, a shopping centre security guard who lives on the same council estate where the pair grew up, *Freefall* offers opposing representations of the reality of the credit crunch. Operating using illegally obtained lists of people who cannot get credit, Dave targets renters with promises of home-ownership, white goods and a new way of life, all thanks to the new sources of credit he can offer them. Dave specializes in selling mortgages regardless of whether customers can afford the repayments, and opens the film closing deal after deal with confused customers who are clearly being mis-sold products that will rise in price after an initial period.

Set alongside their story line is the story of divorced city banker Gus, who makes millions selling tranches of CDOs over the phone in the City of London. Gus lives to trade and is represented literally orgasming at his own success. The floor-to-ceiling glass offices Gus works in overlook the City of London, and camera angles frequently frame Gus surveying his kingdom. The scenes set in his office represent the speed and impenetrable language and practices of the trading floors. Gus's own philosophy on the ethics of their business – that traders are liberating the market and empowering people to own things they wouldn't normally be allowed to own – positions his actions in the context of democratization, rather than exploitation. As Gus explains mortgage CDOs to his daughter, it becomes clear that *Freefall* is attempting to make the core problem at the heart of this film intelligible, while at the same time illustrating its far-reaching effects across different sections of society.

These competitive traders and unethical brokers are set against the honest family man Jim. When the pair reignite their friendship after a chance meeting, Dave's stories about his success and material wealth make Jim dissatisfied with his own life. When Dave sells his friend a mortgage to 'enable' Jim to leave his council house, Jim's main objection is that he, unlike Dave, lives a lifestyle that may be modest, but is importantly debt-free. As a security guard in a major shopping centre, Jim is a permanent witness to the spending culture of the pre-crunch period and, under Dave's influence, becomes normalized to obtaining the same credit that he sees other customers using. Despite his wife's protestations about their inability to repay the mortgage, the pair are assured by Dave that although the payments will increase after the first-year probation period, that increase is unlikely to be above £100 a month. At this point, the film shifts forward in time one year to 2008. With mortgage rates up and Jim facing an increase in payments of £300 per month, he is forced to work extra shifts, eventually falls asleep on the job, and is sacked.

As a result of defaulting on payments, the mortgage company repossesses the house and the couple are also confronted with a new capital debt, since house prices have fallen and left them in negative equity. As Jim's mortgage unravels, the CDOs being traded by Gus also start to fail. Unable to sell the tranches of mortgages he has been stockpiling, Gus is left losing millions every minute. Finally sacked from the bank, Gus is unable to cope with the reality of not being able to trade, and kills himself. In stark contrast, Jim and his family move back to a council flat and begin again, working hard to carve out a debt-free life for themselves. Only Dave ends the film unaffected, having transferred his manipulative selling techniques to the field of solar energy following 2008.

Shot in a combination of fly-on-the-wall and static camera work, the aesthetic of *Freefall* situates the film in a context of social reality and documentary making. Dominic Savage argues that the film is 'essentially about greed that in many ways had got out of control. It is a film that reflects our obsession with wanting more, wanting everything, the desire in many of us to gain the world, but in doing so, potentially lose our souls. *Freefall* reflects those complexities, needs and conflicts that I believe exist in us all.'[27] As research for their roles, actors were introduced to the character's real-world counterpart with whom they spoke and improvised lines to add to the narrative. Some of the drama's smaller roles – such as estate agents and debt collectors – were even played by real-life professionals to add authenticity to the fictionalized drama. As the first TV film dedicated to examining the credit crunch, *Freefall* offers an important intervention in small-screen representations of the financial crisis. Situating its characters and their human responses to the contraction of mortgage markets in the shadow of wider global financial developments, this television drama foregrounded a new appreciation of the causes and consequences of the credit crunch. *Freefall* highlights the glamourous appeal of credit culture, the terrifying reality of over-exposure to debt, and the alignment of ethics and weakness on trading floors that culminated in greed taking priority over principles. As the first feature-length small screen analysis of the role of mortgage debts in creating the credit crunch, the film offers a significant representation of what happens when housing is transformed into a financial product and status symbol, rather than a human necessity or right in the twenty-first century.

Other Television drama attempted to tackle the 'unrepresentability' of the financial crisis through a series of fictional re-imaginings of events based on news and boardroom testimonies. In the UK, the BBC commissioned two productions dramatizing the rise and fall of the now infamous Lehman Brothers. *The Last Days of Lehman Brothers* (2009) was broadcast by the BBC on 9 September 2009. Filmed in London, written by Craig Warner and directed by Michael Samuels it was shown as part of the BBC's *Aftershock* season, a series of programmes marking the first anniversary of the collapse of American investment bank Lehman Brothers. A collaboration between the factual and drama departments of the BBC, the film drew upon off-the-record accounts from those involved in the collapse, as well as recorded interviews with the management of the bank to tell the story of 'the biggest bankruptcy in history'. Shot over a short time frame (five weeks for scriptwriting, two for filming and five for editing), the film closely followed the broadcast of *Freefall* but, unlike Savage's drama, focuses solely on insider experiences of the credit crisis.

The film follows chief executive of Lehman Brothers, Dick Fuld, as he attempts to strike a last-ditch rescue deal for the bank. Set in the three days leading up to the declaration that the company was no longer considered 'too big to fail', the TV show fictionalizes the voices behind the CEOs of Wall Street, the Federal Reserve and the US government, and follows the fate of a business and a nation, as public money is withdrawn and the financial crisis enters a significant new stage. Despite describing herself as a 'financial idiot' before the research process for the show began, producer Lisa Osborne quickly came to see that the credit crunch 'had all the material for a great drama. Yes, it was about finance, but it was about so much more besides. It was a disaster movie, it was Apollo 13 with the titans of Wall Street racing against the clock to save the stricken bank; it was a Greek tragedy with Lehman's chief executive brought down by his own tragic flaw; it was Twelve Angry Men with solutions sought in smoke-filled rooms.'[28] Using the drama inherent to the financial crisis to tell personal stories of the people bearing witness to these era-defining events, the television drama drew upon documentary evidence, combined with fictional re-imaginings of individual responses and responsibilities to offer a new representation of a now infamous event at the heart of the 2007–8 financial crisis.

In radio drama *The Day That Lehman Died* (2009), director John Dryden and writer Matthew Solon take a longer timeline, charting the collapse of one of the oldest and largest investment banks in the world on 15 September 2008. Considering how and why this collapse sparked the beginnings of the global recession, the radio drama contextualizes events with a firm focus on the global aftermath of this company's failure, as well as the drama and tragedy of those in charge at Lehman Brothers during 2007–8. The drama explores the sources of financial tensions that began in America and how they spread to rest of the world. It opens in 2007 with Lehman Brothers riding high, achieving unbroken records of profit and 'making the world a richer place'. Fourteen months later, the narrative shifts forward to profile a crisis meeting between banks. Centring on a single weekend in September 2008 as a critical point of no return, when controlled panic and the predicted collapse of the financial system came to a climax, the drama mobilizes fictionalized characters based on real people to offer human reactions and responses to the realization that a major US bank is about to go bankrupt.

Under extreme pressure, Lehman attempts to raise fresh capital but is repeatedly told by representatives of the US Federal Reserve that 'there will be no federal bailout'. Refusing the offer of a public solution to a private sector problem, the Federal Reserve turns the problem of Lehman Brothers over to the financial industry and its representatives and asks that they make a decision about the company's future by Sunday night. Set against the clock, the racing time of this 'very long and challenging weekend' and its tensions are played out in a series of phone calls and boardroom conversations between industry and government figures. Fuld remains spectral in this process, a voice on the end of a telephone line railing against the perceived unfairness of the decision to allow his company to fail while other financial institutions are bailed out. Confident that the financial crisis is 'a tropical storm that will pass' and that a deal will be made, Fuld refuses to listen to early warnings and will not accept that bankruptcy will happen.

With the eyes of the world watching, the audience listens in voyeuristically to phone calls between bankers and the Federal Reserve as they attempt to understand and mediate the outcome of the Lehman case. Burdened by a legacy of toxic loans and black holes, Lehman proves impossible to save and despite several buyout offers, nothing comes to fruition. Fuld struggles to cope with the lack of options available to his company, and will not tolerate the 'compelling and inescapable reality' of bankruptcy. The competing voices in this drama make it clear that Fuld is responsible for exposing Lehman to high levels of risk and, unlike Bear Stearns or AIG who are saved by the Federal Reserve, Lehman falls victim to the principal of moral hazard – 'those who take action should be responsible for the consequences of those actions' – engendered by Fuld's management.

During the final hours of Sunday it becomes clear that there is no other option than bankruptcy. Fuld initially refuses to file, and then hopes to delay the filing in the hope than an alternative will be found but, at the culmination of the drama, after 158 years of trading, the vote to file for bankruptcy goes ahead. The misery at Lehman is set against the celebrations at Bank of America and Meryll Lynch, as managers celebrate their merger as a sign of strength and prowess for the future. The drama closes with a statement outlining the millions of job losses brought about as a result of the financial crisis, the number of bank rescues and a warning that the debts incurred as a result of this period will have to be 'paid back by generations to come'. Ending with a profile on the long shadow cast by the legacy of the 2007–8 financial crisis, *The Death of Lehman Brothers* offers a fictional case study of an organization whose fate has come to define the fallout from the financial crisis.

Other new writings mobilized the Internet as well as television to position the millennial crisis of credit as a key concern of contemporary drama. *Crisis in the Credit System* (2009) documents events at an away day for a major investment bank as they run a brainstorming and role-playing session for employees, asking them to create strategies for coping with the contemporary financial climate. As a result of their role-plays, the financial workers discover wider truths about the economic and the personal in a period of confusion and conflict. Scripted and directed by artist Melanie Gilligan, and commissioned and produced by Artangel Interaction, *Crisis in the Credit* System was the result of extensive research and conversation with major hedge fund managers, key financial journalists, economists, bankers and debt activists. Using fiction to communicate ideas or realities omitted from documentary accounts of the crisis, the short, television-style episodes aimed to represent the dislocated sense of anomie created post-2008.

The true horror in these television and radio dramas is the interconnectedness they illuminate between the financial ruin of the banks and society. These dramas are concerned with debt, and as a result they focus on human desire and human fears. Profiling the social costs of a financial disaster, each drama reappraises contemporary relationships with money and the encompassing extent of the line of responsibility that emanates from the speculation by the banking sector into public legacies of financial chaos. Critiquing the greed of brokers as well the greed of the general public in subscribing to ever-greater levels of debt and risk, television dramas about the 2007–8 financial crisis provide important new representations of the events of the credit crunch, as well as new understandings of its legacy for contemporary society.

The impact of the credit crunch was not only articulated in the subject of TV and radio dramas, but also inspired the production of new television programming post-2008. Programme production responded to the events of 2007–8 with a range of reality and entertainment programmes that took the contemporary workplace and home as their central concerns. Profiling the working lives of frontline staff as well as boardroom executives, these shows proved popular and, equally importantly, cheap to produce in a period of austerity. From the rise of call centres as the factories of the contemporary world (*The Call Centre*, 2013–), to the operations of British Airways (*The Nations Favourite Airline*, 2014–) and estate agents (*Under Offer: Estates Agents on the Job*, 2014–), television responded to a new audience hunger for the inside story on business. From entrepreneurism in *Dragons Den*, to winning employment in *The Apprentice*, and turning around the fate of the High Street (*Mary Queen of Shops* (2007); *Mary Queen of Charity Shops* (2009), new 'celebrity' business experts descended onto TV screens 'like guardian angels with MBAs' to 'solve' the problems of the post-crunch period.[29]

Production companies also commissioned new programmes promoting self-sustaining lifestyles and austerity practices as part of a wider modification of behaviour following 2007. In the wake of the credit crunch, television was forced to move away from the worship of conspicuous consumption and represent a new drive for conscious consumption. Charting a transition from greed and acquisition towards recycling and 'upcycling', television 'moved with lightning speed to reflect our current realities'. As television critic Stephen Pile observed in 2008, 'suddenly frugality rules. Ration books will be next.[30] In response to this new frugality, the television makeover format underwent a transformation to maintain relevance with audiences facing a post-crunch age of austerity.

'Property-porn' programmes that promoted house buying, second home acquisition and home improvement thrived in the pre-crunch period. The most famous and highly viewed 'property-porn' programme in the UK was a Channel 4 show called *Location, Location, Location* (2000–), and its sister show *Relocation, Relocation* (2004–11), that focused on the purchasing of second homes, often overseas. Presented by Kirstie Allsopp and Phil Spencer, the format follows 'Kirstie and Phil' as they try to find the perfect home for a different set of buyers each week. When the bottom literally fell out of property market following the 2007–8 credit freeze, so-called property-porn shows such as *Location, Location, Location* declined in popularity. Failing to represent the new reality faced by the viewing public who were now unable to get credit for one home, never mind two, *Relocation, Relocation* was axed in 2011, while *Location, Location, Location* was forced to reframe its original, frequently repeated, claim that 'house prices always go up'.[31]

The story of *Location, Location, Location* is an effective case study for the post-crunch period in British television. Critic Nancy Banks-Smith described the fate of the show as a 'tragedy of Shakespearean proportions. One minute Phil Spencer and Kirstie Allsopp are a charmed couple making *Location, Location, Location* and *Relocation, Relocation* and so forth. The next his property search agency implodes owing half a million – possibly because no one is searching for property any more – and she turns up on telly sneaking stuff out of skips.'[32] This latter reference was a satirical swipe at Allsopp's new austerity-angled shows – including *Kirstie*

Allsopp's Homemade Homes (2009–11), *Kirstie's Handmade Britain* (2011) and *Kirstie's Fill Your House For Free* (2013) – that directly responded to the crunch by relaunching Kirstie as a domestic goddess for recessionary times. Less concerned with acquiring newer, bigger, better homes, than with making the most of existing spaces and resources, the shows feature lessons on how to cross stitch, how to decorate a cake and how to recycle fabrics and clothes as part of an overall attempt to reduce household expenditure.

Recycling the format of the television makeover show as a small screen reaction to a contextual 'trend for parsimony', as one of the first examples of the post-crunch genre of 'thrift TV' Kirstie's show was quickly followed by other programmes keen to cash in on austerity as a marketing device. Reaching a pinnacle in the success of the *Great British Bake Off* (2010–) cookery show and the return of 1970s home economics guru Mary Berry as host, the years following the crunch witnessed a return of the domestic to British television screens. In their promotion of home economics and housekeeping, these programmes also raised important debates about the gendering of responses to the crisis. Journalist Liz Jones protests that 'men aren't admonished to spend their free time doing craft [. . .] it's a conspiracy, all this craft and *Great British Bake Off* propaganda. To keep women tied to the Aga when times are tough and jobs are scarce.'[33] Promoting a retreat to the security of the home and the skills of the domestic during a period of perceived crisis, post-crunch British television programming not only represented recessionary attitudes in the viewing public, but also offered austerity as gendered entertainment during a period of economic uncertainty.

Describing the 'mind-numbing cultural diet'[34] of post-crunch television makeover shows featuring baking, crafts or sewing, TV critic Stuart Jeffries argues that 'what's especially striking about the New Boring is how much of it is tied to our anxiety about recession'. First coined by music critic Peter Robinson,[35] 'The New Boring' is used by Jeffries to articulate the rise and effects of craft, creativity and upcycling in television makeover shows as a response to the recession. Considering 'the unstoppable rise of baking shows in the proving bowl of recession Britain', as well as the 'conservatism, vapidity and comfortism' characterizing this visual output, Jeffries suggests the implications of thrift TV are political. Chastising Allsopp as 'the poster girl for the New Boring' and her fellow presenters as 'insufferable toffs' with 'reactionary agendas', Jeffries proposes a 'political purpose to Allsopp's eulogy to the crafts [. . .] let's get busy with our darning needles rather than revolting against those, including Allsopp, who are cashing in on people's anxiety about money to bore us'. Criticizing 'thrift TV' as a genre developed to keep the viewing public 'diverted through the austerity years rather than rising up', Jeffries argues that the real message of these new makeover shows is 'Keep Calm, Proles, and Crochet Your Way through the Recession'. Arguing that these shows actually conspire to create 'a boretex', his tirade suggests that the new post-crunch genre of 'thrift TV' is profoundly counter-revolutionary, encouraging viewers to submit to discourses of austerity and an 'overwhelming narrative of recession Britain' as one of 'political quiescence and cultural conservation.'[36]

Focusing on a transformation of pre-crunch 'politics of aspiration' – in which the discussion of class became refracted through the prism of consumption rather than production – television sought to screen the events of the crunch and document its impact on the lives of ordinary viewers in a new period of austerity. Articulating the drama of the crisis in finance as well as its effects on everyday life, television tackled complex social, political and economic issues through a pronounced focus on the changed circumstances of its viewing audience. In doing so, it not only engaged in contemporary debates about austerity, identity and the legacies of 2007–8, but also foregrounded the relevance, agency and critical power of new programming and writings for the small screen in the twenty-first century.

Crunch film

Across the Atlantic, the credit crunch had a profound impact on Hollywood. The film industry responded to the fallout from the financial crisis with significant reductions in production costs. Studios began to search for competing locations and tax breaks in their overseas shoots and resorted to 'Credit Crunch Casting', employing cheaper actors as an alternative to big-budget names.[37] In 2009, former Sony (SNE) Pictures Chairman Peter Guber even lamented the post-crunch state of the film industry, complaining that 'no one wants to lend money these days for an asset that will take months to create'.[38] In the same year, Paramount announced that it was cutting the number of films it was releasing each year to just twenty, as a reaction to post-crunch conditions.

The 'Nightmare on Wall Street' also had a direct impact on the content of films entering production, many of which chose the credit crunch as their subject. In the context of reduced budgets, limited funding and an audience desire for facts, the documentary proved a powerful form in which to represent events before, during and after the crunch. From *We All Fall Down: The American Mortgage Crisis* (2009) (mapping housing in the United States from the 1930s to 2008 to consider why people fell into the trap of taking on mortgages that they would later fail to service debts on) to *Inside Job* (2010), Charles Ferguson's Academy-award-winning five-part documentary that questions who is really looking after money in the global markets, and Lauren Greenfield's *The Queen of Versailles* (2012) – a documentary following businessman David Siegel and his wife Jackie who are part-way through building a 90,000-square-foot palace (that would have been the biggest house in America) when the economy collapses – the documentary became a medium through which to study those individuals who helped created the crash, as well as people whose lives were forever altered by it. Perhaps the most infamous of this suite of crunch documentaries is Michael Moore's *Capitalism: A Love Story* (2009). Moore uses his documentary to profile individuals who have lost their home or jobs as a result of the crunch and also examines the financial practices that contributed to these conditions. According to Moore, 'this film has got it all: lust, passion, romance and 14,000 jobs being eliminated every day'.[39] Satirizing the dramatic taglines of Hollywood movies, his documentary takes a far more measured response, connecting individual suffering to the practices of corporate business.

While television had a head start in the race to represent the financial crisis, the film industry followed pace with a host of movies depicting the drama of the crunch. The crisis of 2007–8 produced a new wave of cinematic productions that sought to represent bankers through feature-length documentary as well as fictional big-screen dramas. These documentaries and films take diverse perspectives on the crisis: some feature personal stories of unemployment and suffering, while others offer fly-on-the-wall exposés of financial practices and fast-paced, testosterone-filled big-screen dramas centring on the executives at the heart of unravelling economic systems. The post-crunch period was not the first time the world of finance had been committed to the big screen. During the boom decades of the 1980s, movies including *Bonfire of the Vanities* (1990) and *Wall Street* (1987) established the banker and the greed of the financial world as dynamic concerns of screen culture. Fuelled by *Wall Street*'s 'greed is good' mantra and the intersection of Thatcherite and Reaganomics ideologies, Oliver Stone's protagonist 'Gordon Gekko' became an anti-hero for the period. Thirty years on, Hollywood again turned to the world of finance for a new source of drama.

In the years following the 2007–8 financial crash, financial features about insider banking practices, corruption and unemployment proliferated. HBO's made-for-television film *Too Big to Fail* (2011) examines the aftermath in Wall Street and Washington after the Bear Stearns collapse, following key players as their professional and personal lives unravel. Although the film ends with an epilogue reassuring viewers that the markets did stabilize post-crash, the final statistic that ten financial institutions hold 77 per cent of all US banking assets and have been declared 'too big to fail' constitutes a very disturbing conclusion. At movie theatres, features including *Plunder: The Crime of Our Time* (2009), *Frontline: The Warning* (2009) and *American Casino* (2009), suggested that the film industry appeared committed to confronting the credit crunch on screen. Existing movie franchises, such as the 2012 DC Comics film *Batman Dark Knight Rises* also employed financial corruption at the core of their post-crunch narratives, and the crunch even inspired a sequel to era-defining 1980s film *Wall Street*: *Wall Street: Money Never Sleeps* (2010).

The new film revives 1980s icon Gordon Ghekko, following his release from prison for insider trading, and follows his journey promoting a new book that predicts the upcoming financial crisis. Contextualizing the events of 2007–8, the film shows how Ghekko, like the markets, evolves and responds to changed conditions and practices. Heading up a hedge-fund-inspired business in London, Ghekko functions as a stark reminder that the roots of the current crisis have connections to the financial practices that originated during the 1980s and the culture of greed they promoted. In an interview to promote the film, director Oliver Stone suggested that he was inspired to revive the character and make a sequel by the rising power of hedge funds from 2006 onwards, but that '2008 gave it definition, a sense of karma, that there had been some reckoning in this system. Crime and punishment.'⁴⁰ The tagline for the sequel, voiced by the film's notorious antihero Gordon Ghekko – 'somebody reminded me I once said "greed is good". Now, it seems, it's legal' – speaks directly to a post-crisis audience outraged at the activities of bankers. Critically reviewing the events of 2007–8 and their connections to the legacy of 1980s policies of deregulation and individualism, the latest instalment in this film trilogy offered a timely representation of the evolution of credit culture in contemporary society and on screen.

Perhaps the most commercially successful credit-crunch movie to date is J. C. Chandor's *Margin Call* (2011). The film chronicles twenty-four hours in the fall of an organization loosely modelled on Lehman Brothers. Shot over just three weeks in a single location, the film effectively captures the tight, claustrophobic and unrelenting atmosphere of the financial crisis. The term 'margin call' is used in finance to describe a broker's demand on an investor using margin to deposit additional money or securities so that the account is brought up to the minimum maintenance margin. Margin calls therefore occur when the account value depresses to a value calculated by the broker's particular formula. Charting the early stages of what would go on to become the 2007–8 financial crisis, *Margin Call* follows a group of traders who discover that their company is very exposed to the toxicity of the new mortgage-backed securities market. In an attempt to avoid losing a large amount of money when the values of these assets fall, they set about executing margin calls in the form of a secret 'fire' sale to rid the company of its toxic asserts before the markets begin to unravel.

Writer–director J. C. Chandor's debut feature is a tragedy – not only a tragedy of personal events in individual lives, but also a tragedy of the pre-crunch signs of an approaching crash that went unnoticed in the years before 2007–8. As Condor argues, 'the tragic flaw of capitalism is that the more money you have, the easier it is to make money. That's why it has to be regulated.'⁴¹ Making 'a vague stab at unravelling some of the massive mathematical miscalculations behind the crash', while refusing 'to demonize individuals', *Margin Call* examines a plurality of contributors to the crunch.⁴²

Although these crunch films attracted press attention, they were largely commercial flops. Paul Dergarabedian, a box-office expert at the website Hollywood.com, argues that crunch movies simply came too soon after the trauma of the crisis. He suggests that 'you can have movies that are topical but come too soon – when the wound is too fresh – as it was after 9/11' and that 'in the wake of the global recession, the question is "how soon is too soon" to talk about Wall Street.'[43] While many critics agreed with director J. C. Chandor's claim that through film and wider culture 'we do need to engage' with the realities of finance in a post-crunch world, they also highlight the dangers of his film and others in appearing to sympathize with Wall Street. When representing the drama, tension and racing pace of events in the financial crisis on film, it seems difficult to avoid glamorizing the banking industry. As film critic Stephen Dalton argues, 'ultimately, American cinema just can't help glamorizing wealth and success, even the kind of wealth and success that bankrupts the entire world [. . .] even in the midst of apocalyptic meltdown, film-makers continue to pay craven homage to the American Dream fantasy of unlimited wealth and infinite growth. In other words – business as usual.'[44]

The success of Scorsese's 2013 film *The Wolf of Wall Street*, commercially at the box office and critically at the Academy Awards, would initially appear to support Dalton's claim. Released into a context of post-crunch recession and cut-backs, *The Wolf of Wall Street* depicts the journey of Jordan Belfont, the 'real Wolf of Wall Street' during the 1980s. Some critics accused *The Wolf of Wall Street* of an imbalanced focus on the dark glamour of the hedonistic behaviour of financiers as they juggle sports cars, yachts, drink and drug habits. In the week of its general release, newspapers highlighted the number of businesses paying for special staff-screenings of *The Wolf of Wall Street* and muted the protagonist Belfont as a new form of folk hero for contemporary financiers. The London office of recruitment company Spencer Ogden caught the attention of the press when it asked its staff to attend a special screening of Martin Scorsese's movie in 1980s trader-inspired fancy dress.[45] The level of corporate interest in *The Wolf of Wall Street* was furthered by a viral email that circulated around businesses during the week following the film's release. The email reassured business readers that while 'the release of *Wall Street* (1987) and its sequel *Money Never Sleeps* (2010) coincided with major falls in stock indices', in the week that saw the release of *The Wolf of Wall Street*, 'the FTSE has been on the verge of hitting an all-time-high'.⁴⁶

While *The Wolf of Wall Street* neither condemns nor celebrates the practices in operation in the pre-crunch years, like many other cinematic representations of the pre-crunch period it does encourage a degree of self-reflection in audiences. As Bowler notes, in contemporary cinema 'bankers have replaced gangsters or cat-stroking Bond villains in secret lairs as the characters we love to hate'.⁴⁷ DiCaprio's Belfont is charismatic and attractive, but ultimately highlights the seductive appeal of finance capitalism and its appeal to audiences as well as bankers. Although some critics argue that 'no dramatic film-maker has yet managed to pin [the crunch] down' subsequent decades will likely benefit from further representations of the financial sector and the events of 2007–8 on film. Yet, in focusing only on the vilification of bankers on screen, critics run the risk of missing an essential point. Dutch anthropologist and writer, Joris Luyendijk, argues that it is not the banker characters in these films but 'the financial system itself which is sick [...] when you look at the financial industry, it is hard to find the villains [...] We like the idea of financiers as parasites and as psychopaths but it is more unsettling than that.'⁴⁸ The true horror of the crunch film is the reality of financialization and its impact on societies and individuals, practices and values that it reveals.

Like other new writings that seek to represent the credit crunch, Crunch screenplays do not offer intimate portraits of bombastic and dynamic financiers in order to glamourize or encourage explicit empathy with these individuals. Instead, these works represent protagonist male bankers as the product of the systems they serve. Charting the financialization of values, ethics, languages and relationships in the financial sector and beyond, films representing the 2007–8 credit crunch not only interrogate narratives of male responsibility for the financial crash, but also profile bankers as the face of a financialized system that effects every member of society. Implicating the audience in the contexts they represent, Crunch Films offer not only important and timely interventions in ongoing debates about the representability of contemporary finance, but also about the future of financialization in a post-crunch world.

Financial journalist and author Gillian Tett argues that there is an intrinsic value in new writings for stage and screen that seek to represent the 2007–8 financial crisis. She argues that representations of the credit crunch on stage, and across the small and big screens are of 'profound value' and that 'we need a lot more' of them. Bemoaning coverage of the crisis that has mostly, in her words, involved 'blame attribution and finger-pointing', she suggests that future writings must

> challenge this Hollywood-isation. In the past, novels have done us great service in revealing the pain that often gets hidden away, the misgivings, the sheer social cost of financial disaster. *The Way We Live Now* [Trollope's novel about the financial scandals of the 1870s] and *The Grapes of Wrath* [Steinbeck's great novel of the Depression] should be required reading for bond traders everywhere.[49]

A commitment in new stage, television and film writings to visualize the financial crisis articulates an increasing realization that understanding the impact of financialization on culture and society has never been more urgent than in the post-crunch period. As BBC Business reporter Tim Bowler attested in 2009, 'for writers and film makers, the world of finance has proved a rich source of stories, because ever since the credit crunch of 2008 it has become clear that decisions made by financiers affect us all – like it or not'.[50] The authors generating this work and the audiences consuming it are united not only by a shared need to seek narratives about the events of the credit crunch, but also a desire for directions forward from it. Suggestive of the ways in which culture can contribute to knowledge, the worlds of stage and the screen have functioned to offer an axis of representation concerning the pervasive role of financialization in contemporary society.

Exploring events before, during and after the credit crunch, post-2008 stage, small- and big-screen writings offer audiences new perspectives on the financial crisis. Highlighting the role of money, new concepts of value and changed behaviours in financiers and consumers, these representations offer significant perspectives on the events and aftermath of the credit crunch, as well as an educational function in fostering greater financial awareness. As Cultural Studies academic Marceline Block argues, new writing for stage, television and film 'matters because it reflects, expresses, and validates the spirit of our epoch'.[51] Reinforcing the power and purpose of performance in contemporary society, Crunch Lit writings for stage and screen offer multidimensional representations of, and interactions with, the contexts, events and consequences of 2007–8.

Interrogating the nature of finance in a post-crunch context, stage, television and dramatic representations of the 2007–8 financial crisis foreground the significance of writing in interpreting, re-presenting and problematizing contemporary issues. As active interventions in global debates and conversations, the ideas and attitudes central to these works are also central to economies and societies. They suggest that new genre writings can point to other notions of value, highlighting the representational element by undermining, reframing or challenging received conventions and boundaries. This can also lead us to look at the financial world in a new way, drawing attention to the fictions behind financial systems and promoting a new awareness of our relationship with money and its role in the contemporary world.

Conclusion: The future of finance

The credit crunch of 2007–8 made visible the impact of financialization across society, culture politic and the economy in the twenty-first century. More fundamentally, it revealed a new narrative: that savers, spenders and lenders were variously implicated in its international circuits of influence. The recognition that contemporary global capitalism cannot be dismissed or escaped has led to a fresh desire to engage with and understand it. As Pym and Kochan argue:

> It will be several years before anything like a complete understanding of current economic events is possible. But the severity of the crisis has pushed economics to the top of the public agenda. The crunch had a profound effect on the financial awareness of the general public and the infiltration of economic discourse and language into culture and society. People who had not previously felt the remotest curiosity about financial matters are now curious, not to say deeply concerned, and want to know more.[1]

The problem of what happens after the credit crunch, of how to 'correct' identified flaws in our financial systems and cultures, to improve public financial literacy and engineer a new relationship between the social and the economic, is a profoundly collective one. Financial crises are crises of representation. As Ferguson argues, the 'financial markets are like the mirror of mankind, revealing every hour of every working day the way we value ourselves and the resources of the world around us. It is not the fault of the mirror if it reflects our blemishes as clearly as our beauty.'[2] The future can only be confronted with an agenda and an agency that seeks to engender enduring change, emotionally, intellectually and physically. The scale of the crisis offers hope for change and draws attention to the cultural politics of genre: in each of the representations discussed by this book, apathy and inaction are not options.

The way forward raises important economic, social, political and moral questions for twenty-first-century societies. The consequences of the credit crunch will affect societies for years to come. In their response to the crunch, the governments of the UK and the United States transferred the debt bubble from a private to a public sector problem. While banks were given huge sums of money to be bailed out, public spending was reduced in a desperate attempt to balance the books. Following 2008, austerity cuts were enacted across Europe that sent many countries into an economic slump. In the UK alone, the crunch was responded to with 'a near-total freeze on government spending, public-sector job cuts, companies laying off every worker they can to save costs, and in turn a dramatic upward spike in unemployment'.[3]

The consequences of the crunch were geopolitical in terms of both the scale and extent of the impact that contracting markets and liquidity had upon every country in the world. But if individuals simply begin to borrow again to work their way out of debt, there is every chance that they will establish the foundations of a new crunch in the future. As Žižek reflects:

> It is unlikely that the financial meltdown of 2008 will function as a blessing in disguise, the awakening from a dream, the sobering reminder that we live in the reality of global capitalism. It all depends on how it will be symbolized, on what ideological interpretation or story will impose itself and determine the general perception of the crisis [. . .] The danger is thus that the dominant narrative of the meltdown won't be the one that awakens us from a dream, but the one that will enable us to continue to dream.[4]

Admitting that something is not working is a vital step towards recognition and an impetus to change. By 2009, 'the financial world had become overwhelmed by a sense of having lived through something – and of having survived it'.[5] However, as Callinicos warns, if the post-crunch response is to 'steam ahead as if nothing has happened' then a similar crisis will happen again because the 'illusions have survived the bonfire'.[6] Encouraging us to stop dreaming, cultural representations of the 2007–8 credit crunch form part of a wider dialogue about the need to move towards a new system, one governed by tighter regulation, intelligent finance and an end to the mystifications that have masked the operation of the financial sector to date. Brought in on the sea of change that followed, in the United States, President Obama spoke to these calls for an alternative and to the renewed importance of the relationship between nationhood and finance. At ground zero in terms of rebuilding trust in bankers and the financial industry, the present period is an opportunity to reshape and direct our relationship with money for the next stage of the twenty-first century, to represent the events of the crunch, the role played by it and its impacts on place and space, gender and culture, individuals and nations.

Improving financial literacy, enhancing awareness of the internal mechanisms of contemporary finance and critically reviewing the impact of financialization on twenty-first-century society, Crunch Lit foregrounds the need to think carefully about contemporary uses of capital, and the possibility of making capital our servant, rather than our master. In 2010, the Archbishop of Canterbury in the UK, Rowan Williams, used an open lecture to tell the public that the credit crunch has taught us that 'economics is too important to be left to economists'.[7] This led to calls for culture to 'renew its commitment to critique in the public interest and in a multidimensional framework of analysis' and to extend this to the role of financial capitalism in the twenty-first century.[8] As Boyles argues, the message that should be taken from any representation of this economic crisis is that, in future, 'we should all be watching'.[9]

The debate does not abate. Competing representations of the credit crunch continue to engage in an ongoing dialogic exchange to author events before, during and after 2007–8. The financial world has long been a source of fascination for writers, and this intensified in the wake of the credit crunch. In the post-crunch period, money has been mobilized by writers of fiction, stage drama, musicals, comedy, television and movie screenplays as a means of protest and an expression of discontent with the capitalist system, as well as a means of offering new educational perspectives on events. Contemporary writers have used these forms to forge new understandings and mediate new realities of life after the credit crunch and, in doing so, have made vital steps in a wider process of redefining the social, political and economic 'value' of culture in a post-crunch context. Drawing attention to dynamic and interrelated facets of literary form, these works constitute a corpus of writings that critically represents the power and influence of financialization in the twenty-first century. Across this corpus, value is interrogated as complex, abstract and pervasive, tangible and intangible, visible and invisible and implicitly related to the power, desire and control of the financial sector.

Literature is foregrounded by this study as an effective means of cultural resistance – a site for the struggle over the legitimacy of reality. Rewriting events, literary representations offer fictionalized micro-histories of a highly contested period that engage in a dialogic interaction with the lived fallout from the crisis. In the words of Morson and Emerson, 'wholeness is always a matter of work; it is not a gift, but a project'.[10] Only by studying these representations and adding them to our existing body of knowledge can we begin to create a holistic and comprehensive account of the conflict. Such literary works are significant because they influence and shape understandings of the period presented. As Jauss argues, 'literary works differ from purely historical documents precisely because they do more than simply document a particular time, and remain "speaking" to the extent that they attempt to solve problems of form or content, and so extend far beyond the silent relics of the past.'[11]

Perhaps it is only at such moments of crisis that literature can find a space within the dominant culture to present alternatives and contest prevailing hegemonic discourses. The period post-2008 proved such a moment at which counter-representations in writing could break through and confront media accounts of the crisis. The sense of urgency in these writings reflects a wider feeling that authors were living through a major historical event. Each work constitutes a fragment in a much wider conversation, documentation and articulation of the crisis and the period that followed. Using writings not as a form of imaginative escape from the chaotic and confusing reality facing global economic systems but as an exercise in critical understanding and reframing, they suggest that contemporary genres can be relevant and revealing in their social and political purpose.

Collectively, Crunch Lit highlights the interconnected state of finance and society during and after the credit crunch. Reframing our relationship with and understanding of contemporary finance, these works transgress the boundaries of established narratives on finance and instead offer critical and alternative standpoints on the financialization of society in the new millennium. In literary examinations of what went wrong, why, and where the finger of blame should be pointed, writers foreground the financial ignorance of the pre-crunch period, the drama of events as credit froze and the benefit of hindsight afforded to cultural interventions created in the post-crunch period. Offering accessible contexts and intelligible representations of hitherto seemingly unpresentable events, they foster new communities of understanding, reframing the period of economic freedom preceding the crunch. From the rise of finance during the 1980s, to the fast finance of the 1990s, and the emergence of a financialization in the new millennium, new literary representations of the 2007–8 credit crunch remind contemporary audiences that value does not begin, and end, with the economic.

NOTES

Preface

1 Brian Walters, *The Fall of Northern Rock* (Petersfield: Harriman House, 2008), pp. 6–7.

Introduction

1 John Louis DiGaetani (ed.), *Money: Lure, Lore and Literature* (London: Greenwood Press, 1994), p. xv.
2 DiGaetani, *Money*, xv.
3 Geoffrey Hosking, *Trust: Money, Markets and Society* (Oxford: Oxford University Press, 2012), p. 13.
4 G. R. Krippner, 'What Is Financialization?', mimeo, Department of Sociology, UCLA (2004), p. 14.
5 Robin Greenwood and David Scharfstein, 'The Growth of Finance', *Journal of Economic Perspectives*, 27(2) (2013): 3–28, 17.
6 L. P. Rochon, 'Financialization and the Theory of the Monetary Circuit: Fiscal and MonetaryPolicies Reconsidered', *Journal of Post Keynesian Economics*, 35(2) (2012): 167–9, 167.
7 G. Epstei, 'Financialization, Rentier Interests, and Central Bank Policy', manuscript, Department of Economics, University of Massachusetts, Amherst, MA, December 2001, p. 1.
8 Charlie Brooker, *Newswipe: Series 2 Episode 1*, BBC Two, 25 March 2009.
9 Andy Haldane in Paul Crosthwaite, Peter Knight and Nicky Marsh (eds), *Show Me the Money: The Image of Finance 1700 to the Present* (Manchester: Manchester University Press, 2014), p. 34.
10 Elaine Showalter, 'Money Matters and Early Novels', *Yale French Studies*, 40 (1968): 118.
11 Kevin McLaughlin, 'The Financial Imp: Ethics and Finance in Nineteenth-Century Fiction', *Novel: A Forum on Fiction*, 29(2) (Winter 1996): 165–83, 165.
12 McLaughlin, 'The Financial Imp', 165.
13 Mary Poovey 'Writing about Finance in Victorian England: Disclosure and Secrecy in the Culture of Investment', *Victorian Studies*, 45(1) (2003): 1.
14 Barbara Weiss, *The Hell of the English: Bankruptcy and the Victorian Novel* (London: Associated University Presses, 1986), p. 14.

15 Kurt Heinzelman, *The Economics of the Imagination* (London: University of Massachusetts Press, 1980), p. xi.
16 Nicky Marsh, *Money, Finance, and Speculation in Recent British Fiction* (London: Continuum, 2007), p. 17.
17 Cedric Watts, *Literature and Money: Financial Myth and Literary Truth* (New York: Harvester Wheatsheaf, 1990), p. 198.
18 Watts, *Literature and Money*, 3.
19 Sathnam Sanghera, 'Confessions of the Man Who Caused the Credit Crunch: There's a New Kid on the Crunch-Lit Block – but the Books Don't Get Any Better', *The Times*, 20 April 2000, p. 8.
20 Alex Preston in Crosthwaite, Knight and Marsh *Show Me the Money*, 128.
21 Sebastian Faulks, *A Week in December* (London: Hutchinson, 2009), p. 307.
22 Niall Ferguson, *The Ascent of Money* (London: Penguin: 2009), p. 16.
23 Margaret Atwood, *Payback: Debt and the Shadow Side of Wealth* (London: Bloomsbury, 2008), p. 2.
24 Peter Carty, 'This Bleeding City, by Alex Preston', *The Independent*, 5 March 2010. http://www.independent.co.uk/arts-entertainment/books/reviews/this-bleeding-city-by-alex-preston-1916148.html.
25 Stuart M. Kaminsky and Jeffrey H. Mahan, *American Television Genres* (Chicago: Nelson-Hall, 1986), p. 17.
26 First coined by Betty Rosenberg, a prominent Library Science educator, who also wrote a book *Genreflecting: A Guide to Reading Interests in Genre Fiction* (Libraries Unlimited, 1982), the term was used by lending libraries to enable users to explore a database of related texts and navigate their way through vast choices and selections. Building on a recognition of readers as 'genrefluent' and well versed in the conventions and tropes of genre, these strategies aimed to help readers find books that extended their interests in other genre-based works.
27 Jacques Derrida, 'The Law of Genre', *Critical Inquiry* 7(1) (1980): 55–81, 61.
28 Robert Stam, *Film Theory* (Oxford: Blackwell, 2000), p. 14.
29 Jane Feuer, J., 'Melodrama, Serial Form and Television Today', *Screen*, 25(1) (1984): 4–16, 144.
30 Tzvetan Todorov, *Genres in Discourse* (Cambridge: Cambridge University Press, 1990), pp. 18–19.
31 A. Fowler, 'Genre', in Erik Barnouq (ed.), *International Encyclopaedia of Communications, Vol. 2* (New York: Oxford University Press, 1989), p. 215.
32 John Frow, *Genre: The New Critical Idiom* (London: Taylor and Francis, 2006), p. 1.
33 Douglas Kellner, 'Television Images, Codes and Messages', *Televisions*, 7(4) (1974): 4.
34 Stephen Neale, 'Questions of Genre', in Oliver Boyd-Barrett and Chris Newbold (eds), *Approaches to Media: A Reader* (London: Arnold), pp. 460–72, 463.
35 David Buckingham, *Children Talking Television: The Making of Television Literacy* (London: Falmer Press, 1993), p. 137.
36 Christine Gledhill, 'Genre', in Pam Cook (ed.), *The Cinema Book* (London: British Film Institute, 1985), p. 137.
37 Stam, *Film Theory*, 128–9.
38 Derrida, 'The Law of Genre', 62.

39 Frow, *Genre*, 68.
40 Tony Thwaites, Lloyd Davis and Warwick Mules, *Tools for Cultural Studies: An Introduction* (South Melbourne: Macmillan, 1994), p. 104.
41 David Duff, *Modern Genre Theory* (London: Longman, 2000), p. 2.
42 Todorov, *Genres in Discourse*, 19–20.
43 R. Coe, L. Lingard and T. Teslenko (eds), 'Genre, Strategy, and Difference: An Introduction', *The Rhetoric and Ideology of Genre* (Cresskill, NJ: Hampton, 2002), p. 6.
44 John M. Swales, *Genre Analysis: English in Academic and Research Settings* (Cambridge: Cambridge University Press, 1990), p. 58.
45 Hugh Pym and Nick Kochan, *What Happened? And Other Questions Everyone Is Asking about the Credit Crunch* (London: Old Street Publishing, 2008), p. 1.
46 Pym and Kochan, *What Happened?*, 6.
47 Zizek in Gregory Sholette and Oliver Ressler (eds), *It's the Political Economy, Stupid* (London: Pluto Press 2012), pp. 14–31, 17.
48 Naomi Klein in Michael Winterbottom (dir.), *The Shock Doctrine*. Revolution Films (2009).
49 Frederic Jameson, 'Postmodernism, or the Cultural Logic of Late Capitalism', *New Left Review* (146): 53–92, 58.
50 John Lanchester, *Whoops!: Why Everyone Owes Everyone and No One Can Pay* (London: Penguin, 2010), p. xv.
51 John Lanchester, 'Credit Crunch Can't Work in Fiction', *BBC Today Programme*, 29 September 2010. http://news.bbc.co.uk/today/hi/today/newsid_8486000/8486730.stm.
52 Alex Callinicos, *Imperialism and Global Political Economy* (Cambridge: Polity, 2009), p. 17.
53 Paul Crosthwaite, *Criticism, Crisis and Contemporary Narrative: Textual Horizons in an Age of Global Risk* (London: Routledge, 2011), p. 5.
54 Crosthwaite, *Imperialism*, 161.

Chapter 1

1 John D. Bone, 'The Credit Crunch: Neo-Liberalism, Financialisation and the Gekkoisation of Society', *Sociological Research Online*, February 2011, <http://www.socresonline.org.uk/14/2/11.html>.
2 Bone, 'Credit Crunch'.
3 Bone, 'Credit Crunch'.
4 Jerry A. Varsava, 'The "Saturated Self": Don DeLillo on the Problem of Rogue Capitalism', *Contemporary Literature*, 46(1) (2005): 80.
5 Sam Whimster, 'Yuppies: A Keyword of the 1980s', in Leslie Budd and Sam Whimster (eds), *Global Finance and Urban Living: A Study of Metropolitan Change* (London: Routledge, 1992), p. 76.
6 Michael Schaller, *Reckoning with Reagan: America and its President in the 1980s* (Oxford: Oxford University Press, 1994), pp. 49–52.
7 Martin Amis, *Money (Penguin Modern Classics)* (London: Penguin, 2000).
8 Anthony Giddens. *The Consequences of Modernity* (London: John Wiley and Sons, 2013), p. 63.

9. Via what Marsh describes as 'the novel's critique of the mystification of finance capitalism', Amis reveals John Self to be the personification of money during the 1970s and 1980s (Nicky Marsh, 'Money's Doubles: Reading Fiction and Finance Capital', *Textual Practice*, 26[1]: 124).
10. Tom Wolfe, *Bonfire of the Vanities* (London: Vintage Classics, 2010).
11. Wolfe argues that the 'book only showed what was obvious to anyone who had done what I did, even as far back as the early Eighties, when I began; anyone who had gone out and looked frankly at the new face of the city and paid attention not only to what the voices said but also to the roar' (p. xxvii).
12. Brett Easton Ellis, *American Psycho* (London: Picador, 2006).
13. D. J. Taylor, *A Vain Conceit: British Fiction in the 1980s* (London: Bloomsbury, 1989), p. 15.
14. Caryl Churchill, 'Serious Money', in *Plays Two* (London: Methuen Drama, 1990), p. 287.
15. John Lanchester, 'The Today Programme', *BBC Radio 4*, 29 September 2010, http://news.bbc.co.uk/today/hi/today/newsid_8486000/8486730.stm.
16. Don Delilo, *Cosmopolis* (London: Picador, 2013).
17. Manuel Castells, *The Rise of the Network Society* (Oxford: Blackwell, 2000), p. 465.
18. Jerry A. Varsava, '"The Saturated Self": Don DeLillo on the Problem of Rogue Capitalism', *Contemporary Literature*, 46 (1) (2005): 78–107, 104.
19. Varsava, '"The Saturated Self"', 85.
20. Barrie Axford, *The Global System: Politics, Economics and Culture* (London: Palgrave Macmillan, 1995), p. 120.
21. Blake Morrison, 'Future Tense', *The Guardian*, 17 May 2003, http://www.theguardian.com/books/2003/may/17/fiction.dondelillo.
22. John Lanchester, 'Credit Crunch Can't Work in Fiction', *BBC Today Programme*, 29 September 2010, http://news.bbc.co.uk/today/hi/today/newsid_8486000/8486730.stm.
23. Sabin Willet, *Present Value* (London: Random House, 2004).
24. Adam Haslett, *Union Atlantic* (London: Atlantic Books, 2011).
25. William Skidelsky, 'The Privileges and Union Atlantic', *The Guardian*, 20 June 2010, http://www.theguardian.com/books/2010/jun/20/the-privileges-union-atlantic.
26. John D. Bone, 'The Credit Crunch: Neo-Liberalism, Financialisation and the Gekkoisation of Society', *Sociological Research Online*, 14(2): 11, <http://www.socresonline.org.uk/14/2/11.html>.
27. Philip Tew, 'Alexithymia and a Broken Plastic Umbrella: Contemporary Culture and Martin Amis's *Money*', *Textual Practice*, 26(1): 99–114, 112–13.
28. Frederic Jameson, 'Culture and Finance Capitalism', *Critical Inquiry*, 24(1) (Autumn 1997): 27.

Chapter 2

1. Paul Crosthwaite in Paul Crosthwaite, Peter Knight and Nicky Marsh (eds), *Show Me the Money: The Image of Finance 1700 to the Present* (Manchester: Manchester University Press, 2014), p. 4.

2 Hugh Pym and Nick Kochan, *What Happened? And Other Questions Everyone Is Asking about the Credit Crunch* (London: Old Street Publishing, 2008), p. 6.
3 John Lanchester, *Whoops!: Why Everyone Owes Everyone and No One Can Pay* (London: Penguin, 2010), p. 8.
4 FCIC, 'Conclusions of the Financial Crisis Inquiry Commission', *Financial Crisis Inquiry Commission*, January 2011, https://web.archive.org/web/20110304020317/http://c0182732.cdn1.cloudfiles.rackspacecloud.com/fcic_final_report_conclusions.pdf.
5 Crosthwaite, Knight and Marsh, *Show Me the Money*, 4.
6 John Lanchester, *Capital* (London: Faber, 2012).
7 Graham Turner, *The Credit Crunch: Housing Bubbles, Globalisation and the Worldwide Economic Crisis* (London: Pluto, 2008), p. 26.
8 Turner, *Credit Crunch*, 26.
9 Lanchester, *Capital*, 187.
10 Lanchester, *Capital*, 19.
11 Lanchester, *Capital*, 4.
12 Pym and Kochan, *What Happened?*, 12.
13 Pym and Kochan, *What Happened?*, 9.
14 Richard Bitner, *Confessions of a Sub-Prime Lender: An Insider's Tale of Greed, Fraud and Ignorance* (London: Wiley, 2008).
15 Margaret Atwood, *Payback: Debt and the Shadow Side of Wealth* (London: Bloomsbury, 2008), p. 8.
16 Turner, *Credit Crunch*, 30.
17 Turner, *Credit Crunch*, 30.
18 Pym and Kochan, *What Happened?*, 20.
19 Pym and Kochan, *What Happened?*, 24.
20 Pym and Kochan, *What Happened?*, 67.
21 Ben Elton, *Meltdown* (London: Black Swan, 2009).
22 Sebastian Faulks, *A Week in December* (London: Hutchinson, 2009).
23 Cartwright quoted in Joshua Lustig, 'The Obscure Object of Financial Fiction', *Open Letters Monthly*, 2011, http://www.openlettersmonthly.com/the-obscure-object-of-financial-fiction/.
24 Pym and Kochan, *What Happened?*, 15.
25 Pym and Kochan, *What Happened?*, 13.
26 Justin Cartwright, *Other People's Money* (London: Bloomsbury, 2011).
27 Lustig, 'Obscure Object'.
28 John Maynard Keynes, *General Theory of Employment, Interest and Money* (Delhi: New Atlantic, 2006), p. 142.
29 Jonathan Dee, *The Privileges* (London: Corsair, 2011).
30 Jonathan Franzen, 'The Priviledges: A Novel', *Random House*, http://www.randomhouse.com/highschool/catalog/display.pperl?isbn=9781588369208&view=print.
31 Lanchester, *Capital*, 4.
32 John Lanchester, 'Credit Crunch Can't Work in Fiction', *BBC Today Programme*, 29 September 2010, http://news.bbc.co.uk/today/hi/today/newsid_8486000/8486730.stm.
33 Lanchester, *Capital*.

34 Lanchester, *Capital*, 200.
35 Adam Applegarth quoted in Jill Treanor, 'Credit Crunch Pinpointed to 9 August 2007 – the Day the World Changed', *The Guardian*, 1 December 2011, http://www.guardian.co.uk/business/2011/dec/01/credit-crunch-pinpointed-august-2007.
36 Lanchester, *Capital*, 6.
37 Lanchester, *Capital*, 16.
38 Alex Callinicos, *Imperialism and Global Political Economy* (Cambridge: Polity, 2009), p. x.
39 Geoffrey Hosking, *Trust: Money, Markets and Society* (Oxford: Oxford University Press, 2012), p. 58.
40 Lanchester, *Capital*, 190.
41 Alex Preston, *This Bleeding City* (London: Faber and Faber, 2010).
42 C. Giles, 'The Economic Forecasters Failing Vision', *Financial Times*, 16 December 2008, pp. 8–9.
43 Graham Turner, *The Credit Crunch: Housing Bubbles, Globalisation and the Worldwide Economic Crisis* (London: Pluto, 2008), p. 14.
44 Lanchester, *Capital*, 45.
45 Charles R. Morris, *The Trillion Dollar Meltdown: Easy Money, High Rollers and the Great Credit Crash* (London: PublicAffairs, 2008), p. xii.
46 Roger Boyes, *Meltdown Iceland: How the Global Financial Crisis Bankrupted an Entire Country* (London: Bloomsbury, 2009), p. ix.
47 Bob Swarup, *Money Mania: Booms, Panics, and Busts from Ancient Rome to the Great Meltdown* (New York: Bloomsbury, 2014), p. 8.
48 Niall Ferguson, *The Ascent of Money* (London: Penguin: 2009), p. 343.
49 Lanchester, *Capital*, 87.
50 Lanchester, *Capital*, 87.
51 Robert Skidelsky, 'On the Threshold – of What?', *Times Literary Supplement*, 19 December 2008, p. 16.
52 Following the one-day crash of the Dow Jones Industrial Average on 20 October 1987, the *Wall Street Journal* reported that Tom Wolfe had been asked to write a new novel addressing this crash. Significantly, the author refused, saying that it would be in poor taste to capitalize on this event (Joanne Lipman, 'Publishers View Wall Street Crash as an Opportunity for Selling – Books', *Wall Street Journal*, 28 October 1987, Eastern Edition, p. 11).
53 Greenspan quoted in Lanchester, *Capital*, 142.
54 Martin Wolf and Gillian Tett in *The Financial Times*, Larry Elliott in *The Guardian* and many columnists in *The Economist* from 2004 to 2007.
55 Warren Buffet quoted in Pym and Kochan, *What Happened?*, 71.
56 Lanchester *Capital*, xiv.
57 Lanchester *Capital*, 16.
58 Lanchester *Capital*, 166.
59 Pym and Kochan, *What Happened?*, 4.
60 John Kenneth Galbraith, *The Great Crash* (London: Penguin, 1976), p. 178.
61 Callinicos, *Imperialism*, x.
62 Pym and Kochan argue that there is much to suggest that Marx would have 'relished capitalism's 21st-century crisis' (Pym and Kochan, *What Happened?*, 5).

63 John Lanchester, 'John Lanchester on Capital – Guardian Book Club', *The Guardian*, 8 March 2013, http://www.theguardian.com/books/2013/mar/08/john-lanchester-capital-book-club.
64 Marieke de Goede, 'Finance and the Excess: The Politics of Visibility in the Credit Crisis', *Zeitschrift für Internationale Beziehungen*, 16 (2009): 295–306, 296.
65 Crosthwaite, Knight and Marsh, *Show Me the Money*, 1.

Chapter 3

1 Manuel Castells, *The Rise of the Network Society* (Oxford: Blackwell, 2000), p. 440.
2 Castells, *Rise of the Network Society* 2000, p. 462.
3 Saskia Sassen, 'Analytic Borderlands: Economy and Culture in the Global City', in Gary Bridge and Sophie Watson (eds), *Companion to the City* (London: Wiley, 2000), p. 234.
4 A. McGrew, 'A Global Society?', in S. Hall, D. Held and T. McGrew, *Modernity and Its Futures* (London: Polity Press in association with Open University, 1992), pp. 61–102, 73.
5 K. Ohmae, 'Managing in a Borderless World', *Harvard Business Review*, 67(3) (1989): 153.
6 Saskia Sassen, *The Global City: London, New York, Tokyo* (Princeton, NJ: Princeton University Press, 2000), p. 267.
7 M. E. Porter, *The Competitive Advantage of Nations* (New York: Free Press, 1990).
8 Sassen, *Global City*, 267.
9 Many of the most iconic skyscrapers have also been built prior to a large-scale economic downturn: the Chrysler Building in New York just before the 1929 Wall Street Crash, and the World Trade Centre in Chicago in the 1970s just prior to the stock market crash.
10 John Lanchester, 'John Lanchester on London in an Age of Inequality', *Radio Open Source*, 20 June 2012, http://radioopensource.org/john-lanchesters-capital-london-in-the-age-of-inequality/.
11 Ben Elton, *Meltdown* (London: Black Swan, 2009).
12 John Lanchester, *Capital* (London: Faber, 2012).
13 As a spatial development to facilitate business and finance clusters, Canary Wharf is one of London's two main financial centres alongside the City. Situated in East London, it contains a combination of retail and banking space. One of the capital's new financial services district from 1995 onwards, Canary Wharf is home to many of the city's tallest buildings. It also has excellent transportation links with City airport, DLR, national rail and underground networks underpinning the development.
14 Sebastian Faulks, *A Week in December* (London: Hutchinson, 2009).
15 John Lanchester, 'Cityphillia', *London Review of Books*, 30(1) 3 January 2008, <http://www.lrb.co.uk/v30/n01/john-lanchester/cityphilia>.

16 Sebastian Faulks, 'Blog: A Week in December', *RHG Digital*, 12 January 2014, http://www.rhgdigital.co.uk/blogs/sebastianfaulks/?page_id=60.
17 John Lanchester, 'Book Launch', *Sheffield Political Economy Research Institute*, 20 February 2013, http://speri.dept.shef.ac.uk/2013/02/12/book-launch-capital-john-lanchester-watch-video.
18 John Lanchester quoted in John Williams, 'A Microcosm of London', *New York Times*, 13 June 2012, http://artsbeat.blogs.nytimes.com/2012/06/13/a-microcosm-of-london-john-lanchester-talks-about-capital/?_r=0.
19 John Lanchester, 'BBC Radio 4: Open Book', *BBC IPlayer*, 12 March 2012, http://www.bbc.co.uk/iplayer/episode/b01cj83r/Open_Book_John_Lanchester_discusses_his_latest_book_Capital.
20 Lanchester, 'Cityphillia'.
21 John Lanchester, 'John Lanchester on Capital: Book Club', *The Guardian*, 8 March 2013, http://www.theguardian.com/books/2013/mar/08/john-lanchester-capital-book-club.
22 Claire Tomalin, 'Capital: Review', *The Guardian*, 4 March 2012, http://www.theguardian.com/books/2012/mar/04/capital-john-lanchester-review.
23 Pepysroad.com is an interactive website designed to augment the publication of the novel. Using the site, readers can role play how their loves would change as a result of living on Pepys Road and how rising house prices would affect their prospects across a lifetime. John Lanchester, *Pepys Road: What Will Your Life Be Like?* March 2012, http://www.pepysrd.com/.
24 Tom Tivnan, 'Capital Story', *We Love This Book*, 12 January 2014, http://www.welovethisbook.com/features/capital-story.
25 John Lanchester in Sophie Elmhirst, 'The Books Interview: John Lanchester', *The New Statesman*, 15 March 2012, http://www.newstatesman.com/books/2012/03/interview-novel-book-london.
26 John Lanchester, 'Cityphillia'.
27 As part of his research for the novel, Faulks 'played Second Life for about an hour' but his experience of the virtual game 'made me want to shoot myself'. Sebastian Faulks, 'Q&A with Author Sebastian Faulks', *Mumsnet*, September 2010, http://www.mumsnet.com/onlinechats/sebastian-faulks.
28 John Lanchester in Boyd Tonkin, 'Inside a City of Dreams: Sebastian Faulks on Money, Morality and Modern London', *The Independent*, 28 August 2009, http://www.independent.co.uk/arts-entertainment/books/features/inside-a-city-of-dreams-sebastian-faulks-on-money-morality-and-modern-london-1777978.html.
29 Sebastian Faulks, 'Seven Days in Seven Lives', *NPR Books*, 18 March 2010, http://www.npr.org/templates/story/story.php?storyId=124782989.
30 In Lanchester's *Capital* (2012), footballer Freddy also regularly achieves immersive satisfaction in the 'playing Championship Manager' (441) and, when he becomes injured playing football in reality, engages more frequently with his sport in a virtual world to attain a similar sense of fulfilment.
31 Sassen, *Global City*, 170.
32 Sassen, *Global City*, 170.
33 David Held and Kevin Young, 'Finance, Failure and Fairness', *LSE Magazine*, 21(1) (2009): 14–15, 14.

Chapter 4

1. Mary Shelley, *Frankenstein* first draft 1818.
2. Kerfoot and Knights, 'Management, Masculinity and Manipulation: From Paternalism to Corporate Strategy Un Financial Services in Britain', *Journal of Management Studies*, 30(4): 659–77; Linda McDowell, *Capital Culture: Gender at Work in the City* (London: Wiley, 1997); 1987; 2009; J. Blomberg, 'Gendering Finance: Masculinities and Hierarchies at the Stockholm Stock Exchange', *Organisation*, 16(2) (2009): 203–25.
3. Karl Figlio, 'The Financial Crisis: A Psychoanalytic View of Illusion, Greed and Reparation in Masculine Phantasy', *New Formations*, (72): 34.
4. Deborah Spar, 'An Economic Crash Women Might Have Helped Avert', *The Washington Post*, 4 January 2009, <http://www.washingtonpost.com/wp-dyn/content/article/2009/01/02/AR2009010202099.html>.
5. Roger Boyes, *Meltdown Iceland: How the Global Financial Crisis Bankrupted an Entire Country* (London: Bloomsbury, 2009), p. ix.
6. Christensen quoted in Graydon Carter, *The Great Hangover: 21 Tales of the New Recession* (London: Vanity Fair, 2010), p. 214.
7. Halldor Guodmundsoon quoted Boyes, *Meltdown Iceland*, 185.
8. Ann-Sofie Nielsen Gremaud, 'The Vikings Are Coming! a Modern Icelandic Self-Image in the Light of the Economic Crisis', *NORDEUROPAforum*, 20 (2010): 205.
9. Boyes, *Meltdown Iceland*, ix.
10. Carter, *Great Hangover*, 219.
11. Anonymous Reykjavik resident quoted in Michael Lewis. 'Frozen Assets: Wall Street on the Tundra', *Vanity Fair*, April 2009, http://www.vanityfair.com/politics/features/2009/04/iceland200904.
12. Dan Smith, 'Iceland's Economic Explosion, Masculinity and the Credit Crunch', *Dan Smith Blog*, 9 March 2009, http://dansmithsblog.com/2009/03/09/icelands-economic-implosion-masculinity-and-the-credit-crunch/.
13. Robert Heston, 'Why Men Are to Blame for the Crunch', *BBC News*, 29 July 2009, http://www.bbc.co.uk/blogs/thereporters/robertpeston/2009/07/why_men_are_to_blame_for_the_c.html.
14. Peston, 'Why Men Are to Blame for the Crunch'.
15. Tim Edwards, *Cultures of Masculinity* (London: Routledge, 2006), p. 2.
16. R. W. Connell, *The Men and the Boys* (Berkeley: University of California Press, 2000); Stuart Corbridge, Ron Martin and Nigel Thrift (eds), *Money, Power and Space* (London: Blackwell, 1994); Charlotte Hooper, *Manly States: Masculinities, International Relations and Gender Politics* (New York: Columbia University Press, 2001).
17. Connell, *Men and the Boys*, 16.
18. Tijo Salverda, 'Behavioural Economics: The End of Manly Economics', *AskMen*, 2009, http://uk.askmen.com/money/investing_300/360_what-is-behavioral-economics.html.
19. Lucy Kellaway, 'Other People's Money', *Financial Times*, 4 March 2011, http://www.ft.com/cms/s/2/6171a6d0-45e3-11e0-acd8-00144feab49a.html#axzz3Dfy8FjLG.

20 Sebastian Faulks, *A Week in December* (London: Hutchinson, 2009); John Lanchester, *Capital* (London: Faber, 2012).
21 Matt Taibbi, 'The Great American Bubble Machine', *Rolling Stone*, 5 April 2010, http://www.rollingstone.com/politics/news/the-great-american-bubble-machine-20100405.
22 Franco Moretti, 'Dialectic of Fear', in *Signs Taken For Wonders* (London: Verso, 1988), pp. 83–108, 105.
23 Judith Halberstam, *Skin Shows: Gothic Horror and the Technology of Monsters* (London: Duke University Press, 1995), pp. 21–2.
24 David McNally, *Monsters of the Market: Zombies, Vampires and Global Capitalism* (London: Haymarket, 2012), p. 9.
25 Karl Marx, 'The Eighteenth Brumaire of Louis Bonaparte (1852)', in Fernbach (ed.), *Surveys from Exile* (London: Harmondsworth, 1974), p. 211.
26 Karl Marx, *Grundrisse*, trans. Martin Nicolaus (London: Harmondsworth, 1973), p. 212.
27 Karl Marx, *Capital: A Critique of Political Economy, Volume 1* (1867), trans. BenFowkes (London: Harmondsworth, 1976), p. 342.
28 Halberstam, *Skin Shows*, 103.
29 Marx, *Capital*.
30 Revathi Krishnaswamy, 'The Economy of Colonial Desire', in Rachel Adams and David Savran (eds), *The Masculinity Studies Reader* (London: Blackwell, 2002), pp. 292–318, 292.
31 Krishnaswamy, 'Economy of Colonial Desire', 293.
32 L. H. M. Ling, 'Cultural Chauvinism and the Liberal International Order: "West versus Rest" in Asia's Financial Crisis', in Geeta Chowdhry and Sheila Nair (eds), *Power, Postcolonialism, and International Relations: Reading Race, Gender, Class* (London: Routledge, 2002), pp. 117–18.
33 Marieke De Goede, *Virtue, Fortune, and Faith: A Genealogy of Finance* (Minneapolis: University of Minnesota Press, 2005), pp. 422–3.
34 Christian Marazzi, *Capital and Language: From the New Economy to the War Economy* (New York: Semiotext[e], 2008), p. 25.
35 A. Herrmann, 'Stockholders in Cyberspace: Weick's Sensemaking Online', *Journal of Business Communication*, 44(1) (2007): 13–35, 29.
36 Gregory Cowles, 'Sins of the Capitalist', *New York Times*, 18 March 2010, http://www.nytimes.com/2010/03/21/books/review/Cowles-t.html.
37 Sebastian Faulks. 'Seven Days in Seven Lives', *NPRBooks*, 2010, http://www.npr.org/templates/story/story.php?storyId=124782989.
38 A. Johnson, *The Gender Knot* (Philadelphia: Temple University Press, 1997), p. 167.
39 Karl Figlio, 'The Financial Crisis: A Psychoanalytic View of Illusion, Greed and Reparation in Masculine Phantasy', *New Formations*, (72): 35.
40 David Knights and Maria Tullberg, 'Managing Masculinity/Mismanaging the Corporation', *Organisation*, 6 June 2011, http://org.sagepub.com/content/earl y/2011/06/01/1350508411408170.full.pdf.
41 A. Clare, *On Men: Masculinity in Crisis* (London: Chatto and Windus, 2000), p. 215.
42 James Paul Gee and Colin Lankshear, 'The New Work Order: Critical Language Awareness and "Fast Capitalist" Texts', *Discourse*, 16 (1995): 5–19, 7.

43 John Benyon, *Masculinities and Culture* (New York: McGraw-Hill International, 2001), p. 89.
44 David Knights and Maria Tullberg, 'Managing Masculinity/Mismanaging the Corporation', *Organisation*, 6 June 2011, http://org.sagepub.com/content/earl y/2011/06/01/1350508411408170.full.pdf.
45 Editorial, 'The Consequences of Bad Economics', *Financial Times*, 9 March 2009, <http://www.ft.com/cms/s/0/cbc4cfd8-0ce4-11de-a555-0000779fd2ac.html>.
46 John Lanchester in Carla Seaquist, 'Books for Our Times: Capital', *Huffington Post*, 19 August 2013, http://www.huffingtonpost.com/carla-seaquist/books-for-our-times-capit_1_b_3777995.html.
47 Alex Callinicos, *Imperialism and Global Political Economy* (Cambridge: Polity, 2009), p. x.
48 Robert Skidelsky, *Keynes: The Return of the Master* (London: Penguin, 2009), p. 169.
49 Michael Lewis, *Boomerang* (London: Penguin, 2011), p. 84.
50 Anonymous Iceland government official quoted in Jenni Murray, 'It's a Man's World: Now Look at the Mess', *The Guardian*, 28 December 2008, http://www.theguardian.com/commentisfree/2008/dec/28/comment-is-free-women.
51 Jacki Zehner quoted in Courtney E. Martin, 'Was the Economic Meltdown a Crisis of Masculinity Run Amuck? It's Time for Women to Step', *Alternet*, June 2009, <http://www.alternet.org/story/140904/was_the_economic_meltdown_a_ crisis_of_masculinity_run_amuck__it's_time_for_women_to_step_in>.
52 Christine Lagarde, France's finance minister, *The International Herald Tribune* (quoted in DealBook, 'What If It Had Been Lehman Sisters?' *New York Times*, 11 May 2010, http://dealbook.nytimes.com/2010/05/11/lagarde-what-if-it-had-been-lehman-sisters/?_php=true&_type=blogs&_r=0In%20the%20future.
53 R. Salam, 'The Death of Macho: The Era of Male Dominance Is Over', *Foreign Policy*, 173 (2009): 65–70.
54 Penny Griffin, 'Gendering Global Finance: Crisis, Masculinity, and Responsibility', *Men and Masculinities*, 16(1) (2013): 9–34, 14.
55 Halla Tomasdóttir, 'A Feminine Response to Iceland's Financial Crash', *Ted Talks*, December 2010, http://www.ted.com/speakers/halla_tomasdottir.

Chapter 5

1 Ruth Sunderland, 'The Real Victims of the Credit Crunch? Women', *The Observer*, 18 January 2009, http://www.guardian.co.uk/lifeandstyle/2009/ jan/18/women-credit-crunch-ruth-sunderland.
2 Ros Altmann quoted in Sunderland, 'Real Victims'.
3 Mirror.co.uk, 'Credit Crunch: 2 Women Sacked for Every Man', *Daily Mirror*, 22 January 2009, http://www.mirror.co.uk/news/uk-news/credit-crunch-2-women-sacked-372410.
4 Carolyn Roberts, 'Beyond Boob Jobs – How Might the Credit Crunch Affect Women?', *The F Word: Contemporary UK Feminism*, 4 November 2008, http://www.thefword.org.uk/features/2008/11/beyond_boob_job.

5   Roberts, 'Beyond Boob Jobs'.
6   Timekeeper, 'Lip Reading: Cosmetics in the Downturn', *The Economist*, 22 January 2009, http://www.economist.com/node/12995765.
7   Seeking material solace in prestige brands post-crunch, female shoppers did turn to cosmetics, pushing L'Oreal sales up 5.3 per cent in 2008 while other industries faced sharp dips. Dr Raj Persaud, 'The Lipstick Effect: How Recessions Reveal Female Mating Strategy', *Huffington Post*, 3 June 2013, http://www.huffingtonpost.co.uk/dr-raj-persaud/lipstick-effect-female-mating-strategy_b_3363955.html.
8   Julie McCaffrey, 'Stressed Out Women Losing Their Libido in the Credit Crunch', 12 January 2012, http://www.mirror.co.uk/news/uk-news/stressed-out-women-losing-their-libido-in-credit-158236; Samantha Booth, 'Women More Likely to Be Victims of a Rise in Crime as a Result of the Crunch – Personal Safety Tips in Press', *Daily Record*, 31 March 2009, http://www.dailyrecord.co.uk/news/uk-world-news/personal-safety-tips-for-women-as-credit-1016442.
9   Alison Flood, 'Big Deals for Credit Crunch Books at Frankfurt', *The Guardian*, 16 October 2008, http://www.theguardian.com/books/2008/oct/16/frankfurt-fair-publishing-deals.
10 Alison Flood, 'A Frankfurt Flattened by the Credit Crunch', *The Guardian*, 20 October 2008, <http://www.theguardian.com/books/booksblog/2008/oct/20/frankfurt-book-fair?>.
11 Meghan Casserly, 'Beach Reads to Make You Think', *Forbes Magazine*, 28 June 2010, http://www.forbes.com/2010/06/28/chick-lit-financial-advice-money-forbes-woman-net-worth-spending.html.
12 Deborah Philips, *Women's Fiction: 1945–2005* (London: Continuum, 2006), p. 116.
13 Susie Mesure, 'End of a Chapter : Chick Lit Takes on The Credit Crunch', *The Independent*, 30 August 2009, http://www.independent.co.uk/arts-entertainment/books/news/end-of-a-chapter-chick-lit-takes-on-the-credit-crunch-1779378.html.
14 Shopaholic is a series of novels written by the UK chick lit author Sophie Kinsella. The books follow protagonist Becky Bloomwood on adventures in shopping and life. As of 2015, there are seven books in the series. The first Shopaholic film was released on 13 February 2009, and the series has also inspired a Shopaholic game.
15 Sophie Kinsella in Decca Aikenhead, 'Sophie Kinsella: "You Can Be Highly Intelligent, but Also Ditzy and Clutzy", *The Guardian*, 12 February 2012, http://www.theguardian.com/books/2012/feb/12/sophie-kinsella-highly-intelligent-ditzy-klutzy.
16 Ruth La Ferla, 'More Gumption, Less Gucci', *The New York Times*, 13 August 2009, http://www.nytimes.com/2009/08/13/fashion/13CHICK.html?pagewanted=all&_r=0.
17 Casserly 'Beach Reads'.
18 Quoted in Casserly, 'Beach Reads'.
19 Craig Pegler, 'Chick Lit's Top Ten Defining Moments of the Noughties', *Chick Lit Club*, http://www.chicklitclub.com/noughtiesdefiningmoments.html.

20 Naidoo quoted in Susie Mesure, 'End of a Chapter: Chick Lit Takes on the Credit Crunch', *The Independent*, 30 August 2009, http://www.independent.co.uk/arts-entertainment/books/news/end-of-a-chapter-chick-lit-takes-on-the-credit-crunch-1779378.html.
21 Stephanie Harzewski (New York: University of Virginia Press, 2011), p. 22.
22 Harzewski, p. 22.
23 Alexandra Lebenthal, *The Recessionistas* (New York: Grand Central Publishing, 2010).
24 Erin Duffy, *Bond Girl* (London: William Morrow, 2012).
25 Ruth La Ferla, 'More Gumpton, Less Gucci', *New York Times*, 13 August 2009, http://www.nytimes.com/2009/08/13/fashion/13chick.html?pagewanted=all&_r=0.
26 Margaret Atwood, *Payback: Debt and the Shadow Side of Wealth* (London: Bloomsbury, 2008), p. 81.
27 Atwood, *Payback*, 9.
28 Atwood, *Payback*, 10.
29 Atwood, *Payback*, 40.
30 Atwood, *Payback*, 42.
31 Atwood, *Payback*, 42.
32 Karen J. Pine, 'The Credit Crunch and YOU: Survey Report', *Sheconomics*, May 2009, http://www.sheconomics.com/downloads/credit_crunch.pdf.
33 Sunderland 2009.
34 Pine, Credit Crunch and YOU.
35 Atwood, 'Real Victims', 42.
36 Ben Elton, *Meltdown* (London: Black Swan, 2009).
37 John Lanchester, *Capital* (London: Faber, 2012).
38 Sebastian Faulks, *A Week in December* (London: Hutchinson, 2009).
39 Rob Shields, *Lifestyle Shopping; The Subject of Consumption* (London: Routledge, 1992), p. 2.
40 Tatiana Boncompagni, *Hedge Fund Wives* (London: Avon, 2009).
41 Mesure, 'End of a Chapter'.
42 Amy Silver, *Confessions of a Reluctant Recessionista* (London: Arrrow, 2009).
43 La Ferla, 'More Gumpton'.
44 Sarah Strohmeyer, *The Penny Pinchers Club* (New York: New American Library, 2009).
45 Jill Kargman, *The Ex-Mrs Hedge Fund* (London: Plume, 2009).
46 Jamie Layton, 'The Ex-Mrs Hedgefund', *BookReporter*, 27 April 2010, http://www.bookreporter.com/reviews/the-ex-mrs-hedgefund.
47 Claire Howorth, 'Park Avenue Princesses Celebrate the Ex-Mrs Hedgefund', *Vanity Fair*, 21 April 2009, http://www.vanityfair.com/online/daily/2009/04/the-exmrs-hedgefund-book-party.
48 Howorth, 'Park Avenue Princesses'.
49 This fictional scheme would appear to be modelled on existing bursaries and funds that aim to encourage more women into the financial sector, including the Ruth Whaley Bursary for Women in Finance and the numerous awards granted by the Financial Women's Association that aim to enhance the role of women in finance internationally.

50 Boncompagni, *Hedge Fund Wives*, 355.
51 Boncompagni, *Hedge Fund Wives*, 356.
52 Sunderland, 'Real Victims'.
53 Sunderland, 'Real Victims'.
54 Gilliam Wilmot, 'Men Have Messed Up: Let Women Sort It Out', *Financial Times*, 26 November 2008, http://www.ft.com/cms/s/0/c7dcb27c-bbc3-11dd-80e9-0000779fd18c.html.
55 Sunderland, 'Real Victims'.
56 Quoted in Angela Monaghan, 'Call for More Women in the Boardroom', *The Telegraph*, 19 October 2008, http://www.telegraph.co.uk/finance/3227466/Call-for-more-women-in-the-boardroom.html.
57 Barbara Casu Lukac, 'The WOMEN-omics special report on the credit crunch', *20-First: Building Gender-Balanced Business*, 2009, http://www.20-first.com/408-0-expert-view-on-the-credit-crunch.html.
58 Lukac, 'The WOMEN-omics'.
59 Cosmo Team, 'Is Chick Lit Out of Touch with Reality?' *Cosmopolitan Magazine*, 4 September 2009, http://www.cosmopolitan.co.uk/_mobile/lovesex/is-chick-lit-out-of-touch-reality-93735?ignoreCache=1.
60 Helen Manders, 'The Penny Pinchers Club', *Curtis Brown*, http://www.curtisbrown.co.uk/sarah-strohmeyer/the-penny-pinchers-club.

Chapter 6

1 Jenny Armstrong, 'Playwrights Make Drama Out of Global Financial Crisis', *The Independent*, 6 September 2009, http://www.independent.co.uk/arts-entertainment/theatre-dance/news/playwrights-make-drama-out-of-global-financial-crisis-1782524.html.
2 Charles Spencer, 'Theatre and the Credit Crunch: Drama Is Thriving in a Crisis', *The Telegraph*, 5 June 2009, http://www.telegraph.co.uk/journalists/charles-spencer/5450480/Theatre-and-the-credit-crunch-drama-is-thriving-in-a-crisis.html.
3 Nica Burns quoted in Chris Wiegand, 'Has the Credit Crunch Curbed Your Theatre-Going?' *The Guardian*, 7 October 2008, http://www.theguardian.com/stage/theatreblog/2008/oct/07/theatre.ticketprices.
4 Spencer, 'Theatre and the Credit Crunch'.
5 Michael Billington, 'The Credit Crunch: Helping to Clear Away West End Rubbish', *The Guardian*, 21 October 2008, http://www.theguardian.com/stage/theatreblog/2008/oct/21/creditcrunch-theatre-westend.
6 Headlong, *American Psycho: The Musical*, 2014, http://headlong.co.uk/work/american-psycho/.
7 National Theatre, *The Power of Yes: Background Pack*, 2009, http://d1wf8hd6ovssje.cloudfront.net/documents/Power_of_Yes_background_pack[1].pdf.
8 National Theatre, *The Power of Yes*.
9 Ruth Sunderland, 'To Understand the Crash, We Need a Bonfire of the Vanities of Our Time', *The Guardian*, 11 October 2009, http://www.theguardian.com/commentisfree/2009/oct/11/ruth-sunderland-david-hare-recession.

10 Andrew Haydon, 'The Power of Yes', *Postcards from the Gods*, 10 October 2009, http://postcardsgods.blogspot.co.uk/2009/10/power-of-yes-national-theatre.html.
11 Christopher Stevens, 'Why the Best Gags are Forged in Hard Times', *Daily Mail*, 2 March 2012, http://www.dailymail.co.uk/news/article-2109023/From-Max-Miller-Thirties-Michael-McIntyre-today–Why-best-gags-forged-hard-times.html.
12 In 2009, there were more than 460 shows on the Fringe that were completely free, an increase of 115 on 2008 (Angie Brown, 'Thank Crunch Its All Free', *BBC News*, 13 August 2009, http://news.bbc.co.uk/1/hi/scotland/edinburgh_and_East/8197789.stm.)
13 Editorial, 'Frank Skinner Lost Millions after Investing in AIG', *The Telegraph*, 21 June 2010, http://www.telegraph.co.uk/finance/personalfinance/investing/7843519/Frank-Skinner-lost-millions-after-investing-in-AIG.html.
14 Steve Bennett, 'Skinner Confirms Credit Crunch Gigs', *Chortle*, 23 January 2009, http://www.chortle.co.uk/news/2009/01/23/8163/skinner_confirms_credit-crunch_gigs.
15 Julian Hall, 'You've Gotta Laugh at the Credit Crunch', *The Independent*, 22 November 2008, http://www.independent.co.uk/arts-entertainment/comedy/features/youve-gotta-laugh-at-the-credit-crunch-1029925.html.
16 Alexandra Topping, 'Bamkers are the New Pantomime Villains: Oh Yes They Are', *The Guardian*, 29 November 2008, http://www.theguardian.com/stage/2008/nov/29/theatre-credit-crunch.
17 John Lanchester, 'Cityphillia', *London Review of Books*, 30(1), 3 January 2008, <http://www.lrb.co.uk/v30/n01/john-lanchester/cityphilia>.
18 In the immediate aftermath, senior staff – including chief auditor David Duncan – were seen destroying paper evidence of business records in an attempt to avoid implication in the ensuing legal case. As a result of the fall of Enron, 20,000 employees lost their jobs and their medical insurance. Enron staff also lost $1.2 billion built in their retirement funds while retired staff lost $2 billion in pension funds. Following a period in which Enron executives cashed $116 million in stock and were paid bonuses of $55 million, the company's employees received an average severance pay of just $4,500 each. Enron and the fate of its employees, executives and associates should have functioned as an early warning of dubious financial practices widespread throughout some business sectors during the pre-crunch period. In reality, the trials, debates and the imprisonment of senior staff did nothing to prevent the ensuing crisis. Although one piece of legislation that was inspired by the Enron scandal–the Sarbanes–Oxley Act–increased penalties for destroying, altering or fabricating records in federal investigations or for attempting to defraud shareholders, it was not used in the following financial and housing crises.
19 Mark Palmer, 'Enron Education Pack', *Royal Court Theatre*, www.royalcourttheatre.com/files/downloads/221/ENRON.
20 Dominic Cavenish, 'Lucy Prebble Interview for Enron', *The Telegraph*, 29 December 2009, http://www.telegraph.co.uk/culture/theatre/theatre-features/6905597/Lucy-Prebble-interview-for-Enron.html.
21 Maren Robinson, 'Enron Study Guide', *Timeline Theatre*, 2009, http://www.timelinetheatre.com/enron/Enron_StudyGuide.pdf.
22 Armstrong, 'Playwrights'.

23 Tiernan Ray, 'Credit Crunch', *BBC World News*, http://www.bbcworldnews.com/pages/ProgrammeFeature.aspx?id=41&FeatureID=952.
24 Rachel Cooke, 'Making Great Drama Out of a Credit Crisis', *The Guardian*, 10 May 2009, http://www.theguardian.com/culture/2009/may/10/freefall-drama-tv-economic-collapse.
25 Cooke, 'Making Great Drama'.
26 Cooke 'Making Great Drama'.
27 Dominic Savage quoted in BBC Press Release, 'Freefall', *BBC*, 10 November 2008, http://www.bbc.co.uk/pressoffice/pressreleases/stories/2008/10_october/24/freefall.shtml.
28 Lisa Osborne, 'Making a Drama Out of Lehman Brothers', *BBC*, 9 September 2009, http://news.bbc.co.uk/1/hi/business/8246153.stm.
29 Gareth McLean, 'Its Crunch Time: Drama or Reality', *The Guardian*, 5 January 2009, http://www.theguardian.com/media/2009/jan/05/televizion-predictions-documentaries-entertainment.
30 Stephen Pile, 'Credit Crunch Television That Waves Goodbye to Greed', *The Telegraph*, 11 October 2008, http://www.telegraph.co.uk/culture/tvandradio/3561991/Credit-crunch-televizion-that-waves-goodbye-to-greed.html.
31 During the fallout from the crunch, the media accused Kirstie and Phil of being directly responsible for the fever for houses and that pushed up property prices in the lead up to the crisis. Jan Moir of *The Telegraph* asked her readers, 'can we blame it all on Kirstie Allsopp?' Allsopp responded quickly to these claims, arguing that she and Phil had 'only ever been responsible. We stick within budgets. We never force anyone to buy anything. To say that a television programme watched by four million people could have such an influence is just silly.' While neither 'property porn' shows such as *Location Location Location* nor their presenters are wholly to blame for the craze for property pre-2007, they were significant symptomatic indicators of wider issues surrounding the super-consumption of credit that caused a property bubble as part of a wider hybrid of high-risk financial speculations during this period. Significantly, they were also an important indicator of a wider move in television programming towards reality documentary during the early twenty-first century (Jan Moir, 'Can We Blame It All on Kirstie Allsopp?', *The Telegraph*, 12 December 2007, http://www.telegraph.co.uk/comment/columnists/janmoir/3644673/Can-we-blame-it-all-on-Kirstie-Allsopp.html.)
32 Nancy Banks-Smith, 'Last Night's TV', *The Guardian*, 17 April 2009, http://www.theguardian.com/culture/2009/apr/17/last-nights-tv.
33 Liz Jones, 'Sorry Kirstie, I Want a Life, Not a Homemade Beeswax Candle', *Daily Mail*, 30 October 2011, http://www.dailymail.co.uk/femail/article-2055154/Kirstie-Allsopp-sorry-I-want-life-homemade-beeswax-candle.html.
34 Stuart Jeffries, 'The New Boring', *The Guardian*, 17 November 2011, http://www.theguardian.com/culture/2011/nov/17/downton-abbey-kirstie-new-boring.
35 Peter Robinson, 'Sorry Adele, but Someone Like You Has Ushered in the New Boring', *The Guardian*, 8 October 2011, http://www.theguardian.com/music/2011/oct/08/adele-new-boring-ed-sheeran.

36 Jeffries, 'The New Boring'.
37 Empire Online, 'Credit Crunch Casting', *Empire Magazine*, October 2009, http://www.empireonline.com/features/credit-crunch-casting/.
38 Roland Grover, 'Hollywood Feels the Credit Crunch', *Business Week*, 3 December 2008, http://www.businessweek.com/stories/2008-12-03/hollywood-feels-the-credit-crunch.
39 Xan Brooks, 'Michael Moore Calls New Film Capitalism: A Love Story', *The Guardian*, 9 July 2009, http://www.theguardian.com/film/2009/jul/09/michael-moore-capitalism-a-love-story.
40 Oliver Stone quoted in Craig Skinner, 'Interview with Oliver Stone', *Hey You Guys*, 7 October 2010, http://www.heyuguys.co.uk/interview-with-oliver-stone-on-wall-street-money-never-sleeps/.
41 Condor quoted in Zoe Strimpel, 'A Credit Crunch Movie That Doesn't Hate Bankers', *City AM*, 10 January 2012, http://www.cityam.com/article/credit-crunch-movie-doesn-t-hate-bankers.
42 Stephen Dalton, 'Credit-Crunch Films Like Margin Call Are Far Too Soft on Wall Street's Robber Barons', *Huffington Post*, 15 January 2012, http://www.huffingtonpost.co.uk/stephen-dalton/margin-call-wall-street_b_1207673.html.
43 Andrew Clark, 'Financial Crisis Puts Wall Street Back Under the Movie Spotlight', *The Guardian*, 17 September 2010, http://www.theguardian.com/business/2010/sep/17/wall-street-film-financial-crisis.
44 Dalton, 'Credit-Crunch Films'.
45 Staff Writer, 'How Wolf of Wall Street Is a Folk Hero to Britain's Bankers', *Georgia News Day*, 22 January 2014, http://www.georgianewsday.com/news/regional/208293-how-wolf-of-wall-street-is-a-folk-hero-to-britain-s-bankers.html.
46 Staff Writer, 'Wolf of Wall Street'.
47 Tim Bowler, 'The Wolf of Wall Street: Why We Like a Villain', *BBC*, 10 January 2014, http://www.bbc.co.uk/news/business-25651792.
48 Bowler, 'Why We Like a Villain'.
49 Cooke, 'Making Great Drama'.
50 Bowler, 'Why We Like a Villain'.
51 Marceline Block, 'Popular Culture Matters Because It Reflects, Expresses, and Validates the Spirit of Our Epoch', *Intellect Publishing*, January 2012, http://www.intellectbooks.co.uk/MediaManager/File/popularculture(jan12)web.pdf.

Conclusion

1 Hugh Pym and Nick Kochan, *What Happened? And Other Questions Everyone Is Asking about the Credit Crunch* (London: Old Street Publishing, 2008), p. 1.
2 Niall Ferguson, *The Ascent of Money* (London: Penguin, 2009), p. 362.
3 John Lanchester, 'Its Finished', *London Review of Books*, 31(10) (28 May 2009): 3–13, 190.

4 Slavoj Žižek, 'Use Your Illusions', *London Review of Books*, 14 November 2008, http://www.lrb.co.uk/2008/11/14/slavoj-zizek/use-your-illusions.
5 David Lascelles and Nick Carn (eds), *The Credit Crunch Diaries* (London: CFI, 2009), p. 170.
6 Alex Callinicos, *Imperialism and Global Political Economy* (Cambridge: Polity, 2009), p. x.
7 Ha Joon-Chang, 'Economics Is Too Important to Leave to the Experts', *The Guardian*, 30 April 2014, http://www.theguardian.com/commentisfree/2014/apr/30/economics-experts-economists.
8 Jim McGuigan, 'Cultural Studies and the Politics of Cool Capitalism', *Cultural Politics*, 2(2) (2006): 137–58, 144.
9 Roger Boyes, *Meltdown Iceland: How the Global Financial Crisis Bankrupted an Entire Country* (London: Bloomsbury, 2009), p. 9.
10 Gary Saul Morson and Caryl Emerson, *Mikhail Bakhtin: Creation of a Prosaics* (Stanford: Stanford University Press, 1990), p. 30.
11 Robert Hans Jauss, Robert Hans, 'History of Art and Pragmatic History in towards an Aesthetic', in Timothy Bahti (trans.), *Towards an Aesthetic of Reception* (Brighton: Harvester, 1982), p. 69.

INDEX

agency 7, 15, 17, 67, 97, 98, 121, 122, 126, 136–7, 155, 163
   consumption as form of 125
AIG 60, 62
Allsopp, Kirstie 153, 154, 155, 184n. 31
Altmann, Ros 116
American Casino (film) 157
Amis, Martin 172n. 9
   Money 24–6
Applegarth, Adam 59
The Apprentice (television series) 152
Armstrong, Jenny 139, 146
Artangel Interaction 152
Ashlock, Jason 120
Atkinson, Daniel
   The Credit Crunch and Other Biscuits 143
Atwood, Margaret 50, 122, 123
Avenue Q 140

Bank of England 53, 60–1
bankruptcy 5, 60, 65, 144, 149, 151
   economic 43
   moral 7, 43
Banks-Smith, Nancy 153
Barclays 60
Batman (film) 157
Bear Sterns 60, 62
Belfont, Jordan 159
Benyon, John 103
Bernanke, Ben 65
Berry, Mary 154

'Big Bang' reforms 22, 45
Billington, Michael 140
binge and purge model 123
Bitner, Richard
   Confessions of a Subprime Lender 50
'Black Monday' 64
Block, Marceline 161
Blow Up! The Credit Crunch Musical 140
BNP Paribas 59
Boncompagni, Tatiana
   Hedge Fund Wives 120, 124, 129–30, 133, 134
Bone, John D. 21, 45
The Bonfire of the Vanities (film) 157
The Book of Mormon 140
borrowers, types of 50
Bowler, Tim 160, 161
Boyles 165
Bradfield, Jon
   Dick Whittington 143
Bradford and Bingley 60
'Broadway Plague' 140
Brown, Gordon 49
Buckingham, David 11
Burns, Nica 140

The Call Centre (television series) 152
Callinicos, Alex 66, 164
Canary Wharf 175n. 13
capitalism 26, 32, 94, 98
   clock time and 33–4

contemporary 97
corporate 108
crisis in 6
deregulated 30
fast 103
finance 89, 160, 165, 172n. 9
flaw of 158
global 77, 95, 164
Gothic monsters of 113
as illusion 145
liberal 66
vampiric 95–9
Capitalism: A Love Story (documentary) 156
Cardella, Avis 119
Carter, Jimmy 50
Cartwright, Justin 52
Other People's Money 54–5, 62, 67
Castells, Manuel 32, 69
Chamlou, Nadereh 136
Chandor, J. C. 158, 159
Chichester Festival Theatre 144
Chicklit.com 120
chick lit novels and women 118–21
cities 69–71
financial architecture of 71–5
town houses of 75–83
virtual 83–7
Clinton, Bill 31, 50
collateralized debt obligations (CDOs) 53, 54, 55, 147, 148
The Comedy Store 143
Condor 158
Connell, R. 93
conspicuous consumption 125
contemporary literature 6
Cooke, Rachel 146
Cosmopolitan magazine 136
credit, crisis of 48–52
credit default swaps (CDS) 54, 60
Crosthwaite, Paul 18, 47, 68

cultural capital 10
cyber-capital 33, 35

Dalton, Stephen 159
Dark Knight Rises (film) 157
debt and Recessionista 122–6
Dee, Jonathan
The Privileges 57–8
De Goede, Marieke 67, 97
DeLillo, Don
Cosmopolis 32–8
deregulation 32, 37, 39, 47, 53, 60, 64
and individualism 16, 22–31, 45, 46, 158
Dergarabedian, Paul 159
derivatives trading 54–6, 65, 144
Derrida, Jacques 10, 11
de-territorialization 69
Devlin, Es 141
Dickens, Charles 94
Bleak House 5
Little Dorritt 5
Nicholas Nickleby 5
DiGaetani, John Louis 1
divorce and Recessionista 127–30
Divorce On-line 127
Dragons Den (television series) 152
Dryden, John
The Day That Lehman Died (radio drama) 150–2
Duffy, Erin
Bond Girl 121–2
Duncan, David 183n. 18

Edinburgh Festival Fringe (2009) 142–3
Eliot, George 4–5
Silas Marner 5
Ellis, Brett Easton
American Psycho 28–30

INDEX

Elton, Ben
  Meltdown 51, 52, 62, 72–3, 124, 131, 133
Emerson, Caryl 166
Enron 183n.18
entrepreneurialism and Recessionista 131–5
Epstein 2
European Central Bank 59
expansion Vikings 90–5

Fannie Mae and Freddie Mac 50, 60
Faulks, Sebastian 176n.27
  A Week in December 8, 51–2, 55–6, 73–5, 76–7, 78, 83–6, 94, 98, 100–2, 104–6, 110–11, 113, 124, 131
Ferguson, Charles 156
Ferguson, Niall 9, 163
Figlio, Karl 102
films, during financial crunch period 155–61
financial confessional writings
  Cityboy 7
  Diary of a Very Bad Year 7
  How I Caused the Credit Crunch 7
financialization 1–2, 7, 21, 23, 24, 36, 37, 46, 70–1, 72, 80–2, 86, 87, 89–91, 93, 94, 99, 103, 107, 109, 113, 114, 137, 160–3, 167
  economic domination of 98
  financial performance 139
  crunch film and 155–61
  crunch TV and 146–55
  staging of crunch and 139–46
Financial Times, The 95, 135, 144
Fortune Magazine 144
Fowler, Alastair 10
Franzen, Jonathan 57

Frontline: The Warning (film) 157
Fukuyama, Francis 31–2, 66
  'The End of History' 31
The F Word (feminist blog) 116

Galbraith, John Kenneth
  The Great Crash 1929 66
Gee 103
genre
  in contemporary context 12
  cultural capital and 10
  evolutionary quality of 11–12
  in historical context 11
  as inferior texts 11
  in literary studies 10
  meaning of 9
  as spectral contract 11
genreflecting 9, 170n.26
Ghekko, Gordon 157–8
'Ghekoisation', of society 45
Giddens, Anthony 24
Gilligan, Melanie
  Crisis in the Credit System 151–2
Gissing, George
  New Grub Street 4
  The Whirlpool 5
Glass-Steagall Act 53
globalization 1, 2, 12, 14, 16, 17, 21, 22, 30–4, 37–9, 41, 42, 44–7, 52, 58, 61, 63, 66–70, 72–3, 77, 78, 86, 91, 93–7, 99, 102, 105, 110, 111, 116, 149, 150, 156, 162–4, 166
Goldman Sachs 95
Great British Bake Off (television series) 154
Greenfield, Lauren 156
Greenspan, Alan 51, 64, 65
The Guardian 118
Guber, Peter 155
Guodmundsoon, Halldor 91

Halberstam, Judith 95, 96
Haldane, Andy 3
Hare, David
 The Power of Yes 141–2, 145
Harper's Bazaar 117
Haslett, Adam
 Union Atlantic 40–4
Haydon, Andrew 142
HBOS 60
Headlong
 American Psycho (musical version) 140–1
Heston, Robert 92
homo economicus 111–15
Hooper 97
Hull 103
hypermasculine capitalism 97
Hytner, Nicholas 141

Iceland 90–3, 111
Independent, The (newspaper) 9
Inside Job (film) 156
institutionalized risk practices 57–8
The International Herald Tribune 112

Jameson, Frederic 14
Jauss, Robert Hans 166
Jeffries, Stuart 154
Jones, Liz 154

Kaminsky, Stuart M. 9
Kellaway, Lucy 94
Keynes, John Maynard 54, 66, 142
Kindleberge, Charles P.
 Manias, Panics and Crashes 64
King's Head Theatre 143
Kinsella, Sophie 119, 180n. 14
Kirstie's Fill Your House For Free (television series) 154

Kirstie's Handmade Britain (television series) 154
Kirstie Allsopp's Homemade Homes 153–4
Klein, Naomi 14
Knight, Peter 68
Kochan, Nick 47, 163, 174n. 62
Krippner, G. R. 1
Krishnaswamy, Revathi 97

Lagarde, Christine 112
Lancaster 65, 72
Lanchester, John 15, 17, 32, 65–6, 74, 96, 107
 Capital 48–9, 67, 73, 78–82, 94, 98, 104, 105, 108–10, 113, 124, 131, 176n. 30
language, role in masculine reification of economic and financial discourses 100
Lanksheer 103
Lauder, Leonard 117
Layton, Jamie
 Ex-Mrs Hedgefund 128–9
Lebenthal, Alexandra
 The Recessionitas 121
Lehman Brothers 60, 62, 149–51
leverage 53, 56
Lewis, Michael 111
liberalization 2, 25, 32, 42, 47, 58, 66, 80, 98
Ling, L. H. M. 97
lipstick effect and Recessionista 116–17
Lloyds TSB 60
Location, Location, Location (television series) 153–4
London Interbank Offered Rate (LIBOR) 59
Lukac, Barbara Casu 136
Luyendijk, Joris 160
Lyttelton Theatre 141

McLaughlin, Kevin 4
McNally, David
Monsters of the Market 95
Mahan, Jeffrey H. 9
Marazzi, Christian 100
Margin Call (film) 158–9
margin call, concept of 158
Marsh, Nicky 6, 68, 172n. 9
Marx, Karl 1, 24
 Das Kapital 66, 96
 The Eighteenth Brumaire 96
 The Grundrisse 96
Mary Queen of Charity Shops (television series) 152
Mary Queen of Shops (television series) 152
masculine economy 89–90, 103–7
 expansion Vikings and 90–5
 financial, and risks 99–102
 homo economicus and 111–15
 morality of financial sector and 107–11
 vampire capitalists and 95–9
Mesure, Susie 125
Moir, Jan 184n. 31
'Moneygeddon' 3
Money Never Sleeps (film) 157–8, 159
money-without-morals culture 45
Moore, Michael 156
moral economy 6, 44
moral imperialism 97
morality, of financial sector 107–11
Moretti, Franco 95
Morrison, Blake 37, 63
Morson, Gary Saul 166

Naidoo, Keshini 120
narrative fiction 7
National Council for Research on Women 89
National Theatre 141

The Nations Favourite Airline (television series) 152
neoliberalism 2, 21, 45, 103, 105
New Boring 155
New Century Financial 65
'Nightmare on Wall Street' 156
'9–8–7' effect 58–63
ninja loans 50
Noël Coward Theatre
Northern Rock 59, 60

Osborne, Lisa 149

Pepysroad.com 176n. 23
Philips, Deborah 118
Pile, Stephen 153
Pine, Karen
 Sheconomics 123
Plunder: The Crime of Our Time (film) 157
Prebble, Lucy
 Enron 144–5
Preston, Alex 7
 This Bleeding City 61–2
Price, Chuck 55
'property-porn' programmes 153
Pym, Hugh 47, 163, 174n. 62

The Queen of Versailles (documentary) 156

Rand, Ayn 142
Reagan, Ronald 23
Recessionista 115–16, 118–22
 debt and 122–6
 divorce and 127–30
 entrepreneurialism and 131–5
 lipstick effect and 116–17
 women on board and 135–7
Relocation, Relocation (television series) 153–4
'Reykavikisation of world economy' 59

INDEX

Rickett, Joel 118
risk culture 52–8
Roberts, Carolyn 116
Robinson, Peter 154
Rolling Stone Magazine 95
Rosenberg, Betty 170n. 26
Royal Court Theatre 144

Samuels, Michael
   The Last Days of Lehman Brothers (television film) 149–50
Sanghera, Sathnam 7
Sarbanes–Oxley Act 183n. 18
Sassen, Saskia 69
Savage, Dominic
   Freefall (television film) 146–9
Scorsese, Martin 159
securitization 41, 49, 51, 53–4, 68
Segura, Jonathan 119
'sex and shopping novels' 118–19
Sheik, Duncan 141
Shelley, Mary 89
Shields, Rob 124
Shopaholic series novels 180n. 14
Showalter, Elaine 3
Silver, Amy
   Confessions of a Reluctant Recessionista 125, 127–8, 131–3
Silverstein, Michael 120
Skidelsky, William 43
Skinner, Frank
   Credit Crunch Cabaret 143
Smith, Dan 92
Society of London Theatre 140
Soros, George 65
Spar, Deborah 89
special investment vehicles (SIVs) 53–4
Spencer, Charles 140
Spencer, Phil 153, 184n. 31
Spencer Ogden 159
stage plays, during financial crunch period 139–46
Stam, Robert 10, 11

stand-up comedy 142–3
state intervention 60
Steinbeck
   The Grapes of Wrath 161
Stevens, Christopher 142
Stoker, Bram
   Dracula 96
Stone, Oliver 157
Strohmeyer, Sarah
   The Penny Pinchers' Club 126
subprime mortgages 50–1, 54, 65
Sunderland, Ruth 115, 135, 142
Swales, John 12
Swarup, Bob 64
Sykes, Plum
   Bergdorf Blondes 119
   The Debutante Divorcee 119

Talbot, Charlie 140
Taylor, D. J. 30
The Telegraph 140
television series, during financial crunch period 146–55
Tett, Gillian 160
Thackeray, William Makepeace
   The Newcomes 5
Thatcher, Margaret 22, 23
thrift tv genre 155
Thwaites, Tony 12
time, as money 31–8
Too Big to Fail (film) 157
town houses 75–83
tranching 53
transnational business masculinity 93
Trollope 94
   The Way We Live Now 4, 161
Turner, Graham 49

Under Offer: Estates Agents on the Job (television series) 152
US Bureau of Economic Research 38
US Federal Reserve 59, 64

US Financial Crisis Inquiry
  Commission 47
US Publishers Weekly 119

vampire capitalists 95–9
Vanity Fair 129
Varsava, Jerry A. 33
verbatim theatre 141
virtual cities 83–7
Vogue (US) 117, 129

Wall Street (film) 157, 159
Wall Street and Main Street,
  relationship between 38–45
Warner, Craig 149
*We All Fall Down: The American
  Mortgage Crisis* (film) 156

Weiss, Barbara 5
Whimster, Sam 22
Willett, Sabin
  Present Value 39–40, 44
Williams, Rowan 165
Wilmot, Gillian 135
Wolfe, Tom 94, 172n. 11,
  174n. 52
  Bonfire of the Vanities 26–8,
    57
The Wolf of Wall Street
  (film) 159–60
women on board and
  Recessionista 135–7

Zehner, Jacki 112
Žižek, Slavoj 13, 164

www.ingramcontent.com/pod-product-compliance
Lightning Source LLC
Chambersburg PA
CBHW050139240426
43673CB00043B/1730